POWER
PLAY

This book is dedicated to all the victims of the violence arising from the Troubles

POWER PLAY

THE RISE OF MODERN SINN FÉIN

DEAGLÁN DE BRÉADÚN

MERRION
PRESS

First published in 2015 by
Merrion Press
8 Chapel Lane
Sallins
Co. Kildare

© 2015 Deaglán de Bréadún

British Library Cataloguing in Publication Data
An entry can be found on request

978-1- 78537-031-1 (paper)
978-1- 78537-033-5 (PDF)
978-1-78537-043-4 (Epub)
978-1-78537-044-1 (Mobi)

Library of Congress Cataloguing in Publication Data
An entry can be found on request

CONTENTS

ACKNOWLEDGEMENTS

This project began in early 2014 when literary agent Peter O'Connell approached me to write a book on modern-day Sinn Féin. It was another year before I got down to writing it. Journalistic discretion means that not everyone who helped out can or would wish to be named here but they all know who they are and that my appreciation is genuine. As always, Maria and all the family were unfailingly supportive and encouraging.

Others who gave assistance in different ways include Arthur Beesley, Stephen Collins, Kieran Fagan, Ursula Halligan, Gerry Moriarty, Conor O'Clery, Fergus O'Farrell, Mark Simpson and Irene Stevenson. None of them is responsible for faults in this book.

Some of the interviews were transcribed by Mary Shanahan who was extremely prompt, accurate and professional. On-the-record interviews with Sinn Féin members were facilitated by Ciarán Quinn, Shaun Tracey and Seán Mac Brádaigh. Thanks are also due to the National Library of Ireland and RTÉ for help in locating archive material.

I wish to stress that no unwarranted slight or insinuation against the character, integrity or reputation of any person or organisation is intended in these pages. Readers who wish to contact me in relation to the content should email ddebre1@aol.com or write c/o the publishers.

LIST OF PLATES

1. Sinn Féin 2013 ardfheis in Castlebar (l/r): Trevor Ó Clochartaigh, Pearse Doherty, Gerry Adams, Mary Lou McDonald, Martin McGuinness and Sandra McLellan. (pic: Brenda Fitzsimons, *Irish Times*)

2. Gerry Adams (left), Ruairí Ó Brádaigh (seated) and Martin McGuinness, at the Sinn Féin Wolfe Tone Commemoration at Bodenstown, June 1986. (pic: Peter Thursfield, *Irish Times*)

3. Partners for peace (l/r): Gerry Adams, Taoiseach Albert Reynolds and SDLP leader John Hume shortly after the IRA ceasefire of August 1994. (pic: Matt Kavanagh, *Irish Times*)

4. The Chuckle Brothers: Northern Ireland First Minister Ian Paisley and Deputy First Minister Martin McGuinness at a press conference in Dublin, February 2008. (pic: Dara Mac Dónaill, *Irish Times*)

5. Mary Lou McDonald with Gerry Adams at the general election count centre in the RDS in May 2007, when she failed to win a Dáil seat in Dublin Central. (pic: Dara Mac Dónaill, *Irish Times*)

6. Mary Lou McDonald TD addresses the Sinn Féin Ard Fheis in Derry, March 2015, with Senator Trevor Ó Clochartaigh in the background. (pic: Dara Mac Dónaill, *Irish Times*)

7. Sinn Féin TDs Caoimhghín Ó Caoláin and Martin Ferris at Leinster House, October 2009. (pic: Eric Luke, *Irish Times*)

8. Sinn Féin's 14 TDs assemble at Dáil Éireann after the February 2011 general election. (pic: Cyril Byrne, *Irish Times*)

9. Sinn Féin's new generation: Senator Kathryn Reilly from Cavan, July 2013. (pic: Dara Mac Dónaill, *Irish Times*)

10. Lynn Boylan celebrates her election to the European Parliament after topping the poll in Dublin, May 2014. (pic: Dara Mac Dónaill, *Irish Times*)

11. Sinn Féin MEPs meet party leaders at Leinster House, June 2014 (l/r): LiadhNíRiada, Matt Carthy, Mary Lou McDonald TD, Martina Anderson, Gerry Adams TD and Lynn Boylan. (pic: Brenda Fitzsimons, *Irish Times*)

12. Sinn Féin Lord Mayor of Dublin, Críona Ní Dhálaigh lays a wreath for the 40th anniversary of the August 1975 killing of three members of the Miami Showband by loyalists. (pic: Eric Luke, *Irish Times*)

13. Theoretician and activist Eoin Ó Broin addresses the 2012 Sinn Féin ardfheis in Killarney. (pic: Alan Betson, *Irish Times*)

14. Windsor Castle chat (l/r): Prime Minister David Cameron, Taoiseach Enda Kenny and Deputy First Minister Martin McGuinness at the banquet hosted by Queen Elizabeth and Prince Philip for the state visit by President Michael D. Higgins, April 2014. (pic: Alan Betson, *Irish Times*)

15. Martin McGuinness and Gerry Adams carry the coffin of veteran republican Joe Cahill in Belfast, July 2004. (pic: Dara Mac Dónaill, *Irish Times*)

16. Pearse Doherty arrives at Leinster House after his November 2010 by-election victory in Donegal South-West. (pic: Eric Luke, *Irish Times*)

17. Sinn Féin abortion rebel and Meath West TD Peadar Tóibín. (pic: Dara Mac Dónaill, *Irish Times*)

1. WE NEED TO TALK ABOUT SINN FÉIN...

'Something is happening here, but you don't know what it is, do you, Mister Jones?' (Bob Dylan)

THERE ARE MANY PEOPLE, including members of other political organisations, who don't want to give Sinn Féin a mention, at least not in any way that might allow the party a competitive advantage. Some of them are adherents of Leon Trotsky, but even they would have to acknowledge the truth of their master's dictum: 'You may not be interested in war, but war is interested in you.'

Except, of course, that Sinn Féin is no longer at war. Or rather, it is no longer the propaganda voice of the 'armed struggle' carried out by the Provisional IRA. That campaign is over, according to the Independent Monitoring Commission (IMC), established by the British and Irish Governments as part of the peace process. When I asked the Commissioner of the Garda Síochána ('Guardians of the Peace'), the Republic of Ireland's police force, Nóirín O'Sullivan, on 24 April 2015, if the IMC assessment was still valid, she replied: 'Absolutely. The report of the International Monitoring Commission, that still stands. They reported that the paramilitary structures of the IRA had been dismantled.' Speaking in Dublin to the Association of European Journalists, Commissioner O'Sullivan added that individuals, 'who would have previously had paramilitary connections', were currently involved in criminal activity, especially along the border between the two parts of the island. The Commissioner was echoing the words of the IMC. It stated, in its 19th report, issued in September 2008: 'Has PIRA abandoned its terrorist structures, preparations and capability? We believe that it has.' Following two Belfast murders in the summer of 2015 the Commissioner was asked to review the situation for the Government (see also Epilogue).

While the IRA, or individual members, may still allegedly strike out on occasion, the 'Long War', as the Provisionals called it, is officially over. As a result, Sinn Féin has gone from being the Provos' brass band, to becoming a key player in mainstream politics, north and south. Since 1999, with a gap of a few years, Sinn Féin ministers have been part of the power-sharing administration in Northern Ireland. For the last eight years, as the second-largest party in the Stormont Assembly, Sinn Féin has held the post of Deputy First Minister, in the person of former IRA leader Martin McGuinness.

South of the border it is, at time of writing, the second-largest party in opposition, with 14 out of 166 members in Dáil Éireann, and three Senators from a total of 60 in the Upper House. This significant but still-modest representation is expected to increase considerably in the next general election, due to be held by 9 April 2016 at the latest. At least, this is what opinion polls have been suggesting for some time. In the last general election, held on 25 February 2011, the party secured 9.9 per cent of first preference votes, under the Irish system of proportional representation. But as it became clear in succeeding months that the new Fine Gael-Labour coalition was implementing similar austerity policies to its Fianna Fáil-led predecessor, elements of public opinion began to move towards the 'Shinners'. The average for nine polls conducted by four different companies in the first four months of 2015, for example, was 21.5 per cent.(May to mid-September average is 19.1 per cent.)

This compares with 25 per cent over the same period for the main government party, Fine Gael; 18.3 per cent for the chief opposition party, Fianna Fáil; eight per cent for minority coalition partner, Labour; and 26 per cent for 'Others' – which includes independents and smaller parties. Indeed one poll, conducted by the Millward Brown company and published in the *Sunday Independent* in mid-February 2015, had Sinn Féin as the most popular party at 26 per cent, one point ahead of Fine Gael. An Ipsos MRBI poll in the *Irish Times* in late March had the two parties level, at 24 per cent. The average percentages for May-July were: Fine Gael at 26.25; Fianna Fáil at 20.25; Sinn Féin at 19.5; Labour at 7.75; Others at 26.25.

The biggest casualty has been the Labour Party, which scored 19.5 per cent in February 2011 after a feisty election campaign, based on pledges to resist the bail-out terms imposed by the 'Troika' of the European Union, International Monetary Fund and European Central Bank (ECB), following the collapse of the Irish banking system in 2008.

The Labour Party leader at the time, Eamon Gilmore, famously said, in relation to the strictures of the ECB on Ireland, that voters had a choice between 'Frankfurt's way or Labour's way'. Labour even deployed the slogan 'Gilmore for Taoiseach' during the election, but ended up as the 'mudguard' of the next government – it was to be Frankfurt's way after all. Two polls at the end of 2014 had Labour at a startling five per cent although the position of the party improved over the following four months.

Poll ratings are not always reflected at the ballot-box. You need the organisational structure 'on the ground', and people who respond to pollsters don't always bother to cast their votes, or may not even be registered to vote. Fianna Fáil got 25.3 per cent support in the 2014 local elections although its average opinion poll ratings had not improved to that extent on the 17.45 per cent that the party received at the ballot-box in 2011. Sinn Féin's performance in the 'locals', in contrast, was below what the opinion surveys had indicated.The party nevertheless did well in the same day's European Parliament elections, where grassroots organisation was somewhat less important.[1]

Sinn Féin is subject to an unrelenting stream – richly deserved, according to the party's critics – of negative publicity and unfavourable media coverage, which is mainly related to the behaviour of some IRA members in the past, and how it was dealt with by the movement. But this didn't seem to inflict any long-term damage: Sinn Féin kept bouncing back. Commenting on the phenomenon in the *Sunday Business Post* of 26 April 2015, Pat Leahy called Sinn Féin the undeniable 'coming force in Irish politics', as shown by the previous two years of polling research. In the same edition of that newspaper, Richard Colwell of the Red C polling company commented upon Sinn Féin's ability to 'swat away losses on the back of any controversy just a month later'. He referred to the 4 per cent loss endured by the party 'on the back of a significant controversy surrounding its handling of alleged sex abusers within its ranks'. That was in the Red C poll published on 28 March but, just a month later, that support returned, leaving Sinn Féin with 22 per cent of the first preference vote. (However, a Red C poll in the 13 September *Sunday Business Post* had Sinn Féin at 16 per cent.)

Just as Labour did before the last general election, Sinn Féin takes an anti-austerity stance on the issues of the day. This has paid off in terms of support, and looks likely to win extra seats for the party at the next election. Unless there is a very dramatic change in public opinion, a one-party government next time can be ruled out. The Dáil is being reduced in size from 166 to 158 TDs, making the minimum number of Dáil seats required for a majority 79, since the Ceann Comhairle (Speaker) of the House traditionally supports the Government in the event of a stalemate. Fianna Fáil and Sinn Féin would be an unprecedented alliance, as would Fianna Fáil and Fine Gael, although they all trace their historical roots back to the original Sinn Féin, founded in 1905. Some observers see Fianna Fáil-Fine Gael as the more likely combination, though this would cause problems among the grassroots membership of Fianna Fáil in particular.

In current discourse, Sinn Féin are, in many ways, the pariahs of Irish politics. That is partly due to genuine revulsion at deeds carried out by the IRA during the Troubles, such as the horrific 1972 abduction of widowed mother of ten Jean McConville from Belfast, whose body was found on a beach in County Louth in 2003. Despite these continuing controversies, the party retains a high standing in the polls, and there appears to be a disconnect between what Sinn Féin's critics are saying and the mindset of a sizeable proportion of the electorate. This may be due to a perception that, apart from the occasional foray by dissident republicans, the Troubles in Northern Ireland are a thing of the past. It is hard to avoid the conclusion that Sinn Féin supporters share the view expressed by party president Gerry Adams on the McConville case: 'That's what happens in wars.'[2]

Critics of the party tend to forget that Sinn Fein's IRA associates were part of a very long tradition of republican violence. The *Irish Left Review* carried a piece by Fergus O'Farrell who pointed out that some of the leaders of the War of Independence 1916-22 were responsible for actions which aroused a similar moral disgust:

> More civilians were killed during Easter week than British soldiers or Irish rebels [...] On Bloody Sunday [*21 November 1920*], the IRA [*including future taoiseach Seán Lemass, D. de B.*] carried out an operation against what they believed to be a British spy ring in the city – they killed 14 men that morning. As careful historical research has made clear, not all of these men were spies, let alone combatants [...] When the innovative Minister for Finance Michael Collins rolled out the 'Republican Loan' to raise money for the establishment of an independent Irish state, the British sent a forensic accountant, Alan Bell, to Dublin to investigate the money trail. Concerned that Bell would scupper the revenue-raising scheme, Collins dispatched members of The Squad to deal with the inquisitive accountant. Bell

was escorted off a city-centre tram and executed in the street in broad daylight.

O'Farrell goes on to point out that Fine Gael pays tribute to Collins every year at the place where he was assassinated and that Fianna Fáil and Labour have, as their respective icons, Éamon de Valera and James Connolly, both of them part of the 'tiny, unrepresentative armed group', whose actions resulted in the deaths of so many civilians in Easter 1916.[3]

The author of the present book subscribes to the sentiments of the 19th-century nationalist leader Daniel O'Connell, who said that freedom should be 'attained not by the effusion of human blood but by the constitutional combination of good and wise men'.[4] The only reservations I would have are in cases where the territory of the state is invaded by some foreign power and, of course, O'Connell's failure to include women among the 'good and wise'! Unfortunately, however, a vast quantity of blood has been spilled in pursuit of a 32-county independent Ireland. What makes Sinn Féin interesting these days is that it decided, as part of the Good Friday Agreement of 1998, to end its support for violence in favour of peaceful, democratic, consensual methods. Since I had reported in detail on those negotiations, it seemed worthwhile exploring the political aftermath, and the success or otherwise of what could be described as the biggest shift in the strategy and ideology of Irish republicanism for very many years. At time of writing, the Sinn Féin project seems to be meeting with some success, but this could, of course, change. As someone once said – possibly Mark Twain or perhaps Samuel Goldwyn – 'Predictions are hard to make, especially about the future'. It is unclear, at present, whether the entire Sinn Féin venture will succeed or run into the sand, but there are valuable lessons to be learnt either way.

Sinn Féin's rise has coincided with the emergence of Syriza in Greece and Podemos in Spain as major electoral forces. The pronouncements of all three against austerity are very similar and, with Syriza in power in Greece and Podemos knocking on the door in Spain, the prospect of Sinn Féin in government as part of an anti-austerity coalition cannot be ruled out. This may be an appalling vista to elements in the other parties, parts of the media and the middle and upperclasses, but the trade union movement has been taking a keen interest.

Giving an address at Glasnevin Cemetery on 31 January 2015, in memory of 'Big Jim' Larkin, leader of the 1913 Lockout in Dublin, the President of SIPTU (Services, Industrial, Professional and Technical Union), Jack O'Connor made what could turn out to be a significant intervention. Predicting that the year ahead would 'turn a new chapter in the history of Ireland and of Europe', O'Connor, who leads some 200,000 members, said that the trade union movement would be seeking to retrieve the ground lost during the economic crisis. Among the 'difficult compromises' which had been made, he included 'the call on Labour to step into hell in the current coalition to head off the threat of a single-party Fine Gael government, or worse'. But now, 'in the light of improving economic conditions', he was recommending a new strategy. The SIPTU chief welcomed Syriza's 'dramatic' election victory in Greece the previous Sunday, 'which signals the beginning of the end of the nightmare of the one-sided austerity experiment'. He continued:

> Dramatic possibilities are now opening up here in Ireland as we approach the centenary of the 1916 Rising. At this extraordinary juncture, history is presenting a 'once in a century' opportunity to reassert the egalitarian ideals of the 1916 Proclamation, which were suffocated in the counter-revolution which followed the foundation of the State. It is incumbent upon all of us Social Democrats, Left Republicans and Independent Socialists, who are inspired by the egalitarian ideals of Jim Larkin and James Connolly, to set aside sectarian divisions and develop a political project aimed at

winning the next general election on a common platform – let's call it 'Charter 2016'.

Pointing out that this would be 'the first left-of-centre government in the history of the State', the SIPTU chief continued by calling upon parties and individuals on the Left to not simply 'do well in the election', but to display 'a level of intellectual engagement around policy formation, free of the restrictions of sectarian party political interests'. The point was to secure a Dáil majority for the Left, which needed to set these differences aside and 'seize the moment'.

There was no mention of Sinn Féin in the speech, and the only reference to the Labour Party was in the context of the previous general election. But an alliance of 'Social Democrats, Left Republicans and Independent Socialists' could only mean those two parties along with others from the 'broad left' among the Independent TDs, as well as their followers and co-thinkers.[5] The speech was welcomed in a statement later that day by Senator David Cullinane, Sinn Féin's spokesman on trade union issues, who said that his party was 'committed to forming broad alliances with parties and independents to maximise the potential for an Irish Government that is anti-austerity'.[6]

Next day, Justine McCarthy reported in the Irish edition of the *Sunday Times* that Sinn Féin had been in talks for more than two months with trade unions, left-wing groups and independent TDs to agree a platform for the general election, with the talks gaining impetus from Syriza's election victory in Greece the previous weekend. Union officials and co-ordinators of the Right2Water campaign against the water charges, Brendan Ogle of the Unite trade union and Dave Gibney from Mandate,were named as two of the 'key promoters' of the talks. TD Richard Boyd Barrett, a member of the Socialist Workers' Party, a Trotskyist group, was quoted as backing the talks. He added, though, that 'Sinn Féin have to decide whether they're building a specifically Left project or whether they just want to be in government.'

Another Dáil deputy, from a different wing of the Trotskyist left, Joe Higgins of the Socialist Party (SP), said that his organisation was not involved in the talks, and wouldn't be prepared to make an election pact with Sinn Féin which was not a party of the left and was 'taking an anti-austerity position in the South while implementing austerity in the North'. [7] The SP also has a different approach on the national question and its position was set out in greater detail in its newspaper, *The Socialist*:

> Jack O'Connor, leader of the South's biggest union SIPTU, has been openly courting Sinn Féin. SIPTU are affiliated to the Irish Labour Party, and its support has collapsed as it has been implementing massive austerity as part of the Southern coalition government. North and South the union leaders, rather than organising a real concerted struggle against the austerity being implemented by both governments, would rather back the likes of Sinn Féin in order to get a few crumbs from the table.[8]

Writing in *An Phoblacht* (The Republic), Sinn Féin's chairman Declan Kearney, a key party strategist, said that the basis for going into government in the South should be the advancement of 'republican objectives', and not simply entering coalition for its own sake. He added that 'formal political discussion should commence on how to forge consensus between Sinn Féin, progressive independents, the trade union movement, grassroots communities, and the non-sectarian Left'. These talks should focus 'on the ideas and strategies which will ensure the future election of a Left coalition in the South dedicated to establishing a new national Republic'.[9]

Meanwhile, in the *Sunday Business Post*, Pat Leahy reported that 'Sinn Féin is moving to formally rule out coalition as a minority partner with either Fianna Fáil or Fine Gael after the next election'. He said that a motion was expected to go before the party's ardfheis (national conference) in early March, with backing from the ardchomhairle (national executive committee), mandating the leadership to this effect.[10] About two weeks after O'Connor's Glasnevin speech, Sinn Féin sent out a press notice that Adams and Deputy Leader Mary Lou McDonald would be 'available for media comment on key challenges facing people prior to the general election'. It was what we media folk call a 'doorstep', ahead of a Sinn Féin meeting at the Teachers' Club in Dublin's Parnell Square. Perhaps because it was held in the evening there were only two journalists present, myself and a colleague from one of the daily papers.

I asked Adams what kind of line-up Sinn Féin would be prepared to accept, in the event of a coalition being on the table, and assuming there could be agreement on a common programme before taking office. Replying that a Sinn Féin majority government would be the party's first preference, he continued:

> First of all, I see this very clearly in two phases, and the first phase is to get the biggest possible mandate for Sinn Féin. That will, of course, influence the other parties; that will perhaps, in some way, determine how the other parties get on as well. The second phase is to negotiate a programme for government. And clearly, given our politics, there's an incompatibility between our position[and], say, for example, [that of] Fine Gael. Also, one of the big benefits of Labour being in government, for other political parties, is that you learn not to do what they have done, which is [for] a minority party to append itself to a senior partner, a conservative party. So we will not do that. And, actually, even though I understand the legitimacy of the question, I actually don't think there's much point, given that the people haven't voted. We have to be humble; it's the people's day, they will decide who will form the government. So,

mandate first, programme for government second. And
we'll decide on the basis of that.

He welcomed Jack O'Connor's remarks, especially where the SIPTU
leader said the type of government he was proposing wouldn't be
able to do everything at once, and would have to set priorities. He
continued as follows: 'If we were able to, in one sentence, say our
preference, it has to be an anti-austerity government, which may be
wider than the Left. Who knows who's going to come out of, you
know, the [*general election*]... Shane Ross is certainly anti-austerity.
Who knows, among the Independents, who might come out of all
of that. But again I'm making the mistake of speculating about all of
that.'

Formerly a member of Fine Gael, Shane Ross was elected to the
Dáil in 2011 as a non-party Independent TD, and took the lead in
forming an alliance with other Independents, some of them on the
Left, with a view to working out a deal with the next government,
possibly in return for cabinet seats. In an issue published the day
after Adams spoke to me, the *Phoenix*, a magazine which takes a
close interest in the internal life of the republican movement,
outlined a possible scenario whereby Sinn Féin could be the largest
element in an anti-austerity group in coalition with Fianna Fáil:

> Behind the scenes, Sinn Féin activists, including the
> leadership, are planning a coalition proposal that could
> get round the problem of being a minority party in
> government. The strategy – based on the acceptance that
> Fianna Fáil would have more seats than Sinn Féin – is
> to create a post-election alliance of Sinn Féin with Left
> Independents and even Labour. On a rough calculation
> that sees Fianna Fáil with 35 seats; Sinn Féin 30; Left
> Independents 10 and Labour perhaps 10, such a
> coalition would have a majority of 80-plus seats out of
> 158 in the next Dáil. But it would also see such an

alliance having more than Fianna Fáil. This would allow Sinn Féin[…] to argue that the Left Alliance was the largest part of such a coalition with a mandate for a left programme in government.[11]

In the *Sunday Times*, Justine McCarthy reported that union leaders Brendan Ogle and Dave Gibney had met at Leinster House with a Sinn Féin group, headed by deputy leader Mary Lou McDonald, to discuss a left-wing, pre-election alliance:

> The meeting opened on a confrontational note. The previous Sunday, addressing a party meeting in Mullingar, Sinn Féin president Gerry Adams had welcomed a call by the SIPTU president Jack O'Connor, for the Irish left to unite on 'a common platform'. There is a sharp divergence of both style and strategy between SIPTU, which has about 200,000 members and is officially affiliated to the Labour Party, and other unions such as Mandate and Unite, which are commonly branded 'militant'. In his Mullingar speech, Adams said that elements of the trade union movement must end their 'unrequited support' for Labour. Ogle and Gibney regard Labour as toxic and having scant hope of being in the next government. To them, SIPTU is backing a loser. SIPTU and Labour are joined at the hip, they warned Sinn Féin[…]The most immediate bone of contention between SIPTU and the Right2Water unions is water charges. SIPTU, which counts water utility workers among its members, believes there is a need for water charges and an administrative structure. The others are campaigning for the abolition of charges and for water to be funded by progressive taxation.[12]

The following day, the Right2Water unions announced a two-day conference for the start of May. This was later changed to 'an international May Day event', followed by a policy conference nearly two weeks later, on 13 June. Both occasions would be by invitation only, due to space restrictions. The May-Day event would feature speakers from the European Water Movement, as well as from 'progressive grassroots movements' such as Podemos and Syriza. The policy conference would 'discuss a set of core principles which will underpin a "Platform for Renewal"in advance of the next General Election. These core principles will be the minimum standards a progressive government will be expected to deliver in the next Dáil'.[13] Adams issued a statement welcoming the initiative: 'It mirrors my own suggestion of a Citizens' Charter, encapsulating the fundamental principles that could take us towards a citizen-centred, rights-based society.' In his Glasnevin speech, O'Connor had suggested something similar, with the title of 'Charter 2016'. The terms set out by Adams had a flavour of Syriza and Podemos about them: 'Such a charter could be endorsed by various progressive political parties and independents, community groups and trade unions in advance of the next election. This would not compromise any political group, and does not imply any electoral pact. I believe that a Citizens' Charter could form the basis for a new departure in Irish politics.'

The Labour Party's annual conference took place in Killarney on the last weekend in February, and a number of Labour ministers, as well as Jack O'Connor, were on the panel for the *Saturday with Claire Byrne* show on RTÉ Radio 1. When asked about the SIPTU leader's proposal, Environment Minister Alan Kelly said: 'Sinn Féin aren't a left-wing party. They're a populist movement with a Northern command.' Expressing security concerns, he said he didn't believe, as deputy party leader, that Labour would be negotiating a partnership in government with Sinn Féin: 'How can you do that credibly when the first thing on the agenda of whoever is doing so would be the fact that the Department of Justice, Defence and probably Foreign Affairs would be vetoed away from them?'

The SIPTU leader responded: 'In my engagement, since I became president of our union in 2003, with the leaders of Sinn Féin, I believe them to be very good and well-intended people. I believe that Sinn Féin has many socialists in it. I believe that we could work with them.' But O'Connor said he did not foresee any break in the formal link between his union and the Labour Party. (In the May 2014 local and European elections, for example, Labour candidates received a total of €20,040 from the union as well as paying an annual affiliation fee of €2,500.[14]) At a news conference a few days later, when I asked Mary Lou McDonald for her response to Minister Kelly's claim that Sinn Féin was run by a 'Northern command', she replied: 'We don't operate to a command structure. We are thoughtful, free-thinking individuals who, each in our own way and in our own time, has chosen freely and voluntarily to be part of this great political party and this great political project […] There are no sheep, and there is nobody who takes commandments from on high.'

In the March edition of *An Phoblacht*, columnist and aspiring Sinn Féin TD, Councillor Eoin Ó Broin, noted O'Connor's call for Left unity and the separate initiative of the Right2Water unions in hosting a conference to shape a common political platform. He asked:

> Can we really build that ever-elusive Left unity? Divisions between the anti-austerity unions and those supportive of the Government run deep. Will SIPTU be invited to attend the May Day 'Platform for Renewal' dialogue? […] And is it possible to have an anti-austerity government without the involvement of the Labour Party and the socially-liberal constituency they represent? […] It is time for the Irish Left to build common ground. We have a very rare chance to build a real alternative to the status quo, to be part of a new politics, a new political economy, a new Republic. Let's not waste that chance.

Delegates at the Sinn Féin ardfheis, held in Derry between 6 and 7 March, unanimously backed a motion that the party would not enter into a coalition government led by either Fine Gael or Fianna Fáil. It was jointly proposed by branches ranging from Donegal to Cork and Roscommon to Dublin. Ó Broin told delegates:

> We can start to build an Ireland of equals, a united Ireland, a better, fairer Ireland. But this can only happen if Sinn Féin makes a clear and unambiguous statement that we will not under any circumstances support a government led by Fianna Fáil or Fine Gael... If Sinn Féin can lead a government that invests in a fair recovery, in secure and well-paid jobs, in universal public services, in strong and vibrant communities, in a real republic that is committed to ending poverty and inequality – then and only then should our party be willing to take up residence in Government Buildings.[15]

It could well be that a coalition is negotiated in which Sinn Féin would numerically be the largest party. That would fulfil the terms of Motion 52 at the ardfheis. But the alternative scenario, cited earlier in this chapter, whereby Sinn Féin might not be the biggest party overall but would be the largest element in an anti-austerity majority, would arguably still be a permissible option. Much would of course depend on who held the office of taoiseach (prime minister). In the past, there had been talk of a 'rotating taoiseach' between Labour and its coalition partner. Motion 52 committed Sinn Féin 'to maximise the potential for an anti-austerity government in the 26 Counties'. A profile of Adams in the *Phoenix* had reported north-south tensions within Sinn Féin on the coalition issue. The article, published on 13 December 2013, stated:

> Adams and his closest comrades are more susceptible to coalition government with, say, F[ianna]F[ail] than

those southern Sinn Féin activists who have little obvious IRA baggage […] The party organisation is still dominated by northern members whose position on party policy can differ from the southerners and certainly will, when the question of coalition in the Republic comes to the fore. The fear among some southern Sinn Féin activists is that the price Sinn Féin leaders would pay in any coalition negotiations for a Sinn Féin-led hands-on government approach to the North would be concessions on the economy and taxation.

The manner in which Sinn Féin surpassed Fianna Fáil on many occasions in the opinion polls and in the number of seats won in the May 2014 European elections was, of course, galling for a party which had been the sole or majority holder of government office for a total of sixty-one years since 1932. Small wonder, then, that Micheál Martin's position as Fianna Fáil leader was being questioned.

Never slow to highlight Sinn Féin's deficiencies as he saw them, Martin launched a multi-pronged assault on the rival party in mid-April 2015. He hit out at Sinn Féin on RTÉ's *Late Late Show*, then in the course of a massive double-page interview with the *Sunday Business Post* and, later the same day, in his annual leader's speech at the Fianna Fáil commemoration in Arbour Hill – the Dublin cemetery where the 1916 leaders are buried – and finally in a radio debate with Adams.He told *Late Late Show* presenter Ryan Tubridy that Fianna Fáil would not be going into coalition with Sinn Féin 'in any shape or form'. Martin added that Sinn Féin was 'a cult-like group in many respects, and you don't get diversity of opinion'. He also ruled out government with Fine Gael because that party 'have gone too right-wing for us'. In his *Sunday Business Post* interview, he said Sinn Féin was seeking to 'undermine the very institutions of the state'.[16]

The Fianna Fáil leader's speech to the party faithful at Arbour Hill was exactly 3,000 words long, but almost half of these were devoted to a critique of Sinn Féin (there was no mention of Fine Gael or Labour). He claimed that Sinn Féin was making 'a deeply sinister attempt to misuse the respect which the Irish people have for 1916'. Martin said it was a 'false claim that they have some connection to 1916 and to the volunteers who fought then'. This was part of a Provo agenda to 'claim legitimacy for the sectarian campaign of murder and intimidation which they carried out for 30 years'. He continued: 'This goes to the heart of why Sinn Féin remains unfit for participation in a democratic republican government.' The Provos had killed 'servants of this republic' (members of the Irish security forces) and Sinn Féin was selling T-shirts with the slogan 'IRA – Undefeated Army'.[17]

The Fianna Fáil leader won plaudits from *Sunday Independent* columnist Eoghan Harris, who wrote: 'Martin's polemic against the Provos came from deep in his personal moral core. It called to mind Jonathan Swift's *saeva indignatio*, the savage indignation of which W.B. Yeats wrote so movingly.'[18] Given the tone and length of Martin's Arbour Hill condemnation, it was inevitable that Adams would feel it necessary to respond in a formal way and in some detail. Normally, the media are informed by email, or at least by text message, in advance of Sinn Féin events that are open to them. But this one was clearly arranged in some haste for the following Wednesday. I was talking to some Sinn Féin staff and politicians in Leinster House when they mentioned 'Gerry's keynote speech' which would be given in a place with the not-very-republican title of Royal College of Physicians of Ireland, a handsome building close to Leinster House.

When I worked as a reporter in Northern Ireland, the Republicans habitually arrived late for press and other public events, and the journalists consoled themselves for the long wait with the wry observation: 'We're on Sinn Féin time.' This is not the case any more, in my experience, and the hall was full at 7pm, when the meeting was due to start. Members of the Sinn Féin parliamentary party were there in strength and sitting at the front. All the leading figures from the Dublin area appeared to be present, including some holding prison records for IRA activities. Adams began his speech with the usual digs at Fianna Fáil's record in government, where Martin was a cabinet minister for 14 years, and then got to the nub of the matter:

> Micheál Martin also raises the hoary old myth of there being a good Old IRA in 1916 and in the Tan War, and a bad IRA in the 1970s, the 1980s and the nineties. Of course, he ignores the reality that Volunteers in 1916 were responsible for killing women and children here in the streets of Dublin and that, through the Tan War, the IRA was responsible for abducting, for executing and secretly burying suspected informers. But he tries to sanitise one phase of war and demonise and criminalise another one. So let there be no doubt about it, war is terrible. All war. War is desperate. And those of us who have lived through the recent conflict are the ones who have worked to ensure that the conflict is ended for good, and that we never – none of us, ever – go back there again. And that's why Sinn Féin is and was pivotal to the peace process. So those of us – and people died in this city also –but those of us who have come from communities that were ravaged by conflict, those of us whose neighbours were killed, those of us who buried our friends and our family members, who carry injuries to this day, those of us in this state and in the Northern State and in Britain and elsewhere who endured the prisons: we don't need lectures from Micheál Martin or anyone else about conflict. We have been there [*prolonged applause, whistling and cheering*]. Let me say this: Republicans did not go to war: the war came to us. So there is an obligation on political leaders to work to resolve conflict, to build reconciliation, not to fight a false war, not to refight a false and scammy-type

rhetorical approach at looking at the past in a totally skewed way. Micheál Martin needs to wake up and realise that the war is over. It's now time to build the peace [*applause*]. But there has to be a dividend, an economic and social dividend in the peace for everyone, not just in the North but here in this state also. So his selective lookbacks on Irish history convince no one [*pause*]. We at least are consistent. We are as proud of Bobby Sands and Mairéad Farrell as we are of the Volunteers of 1916, and those who fought the Black and Tans [*applause*].

The meeting ended after the speech, which lasted twenty minutes. Outside in the corridor, a glass case held mementos of Napoleon Bonaparte, who also knew a thing or two about conflict, albeit on a wider scale. Sinn Féin people said they had been anxious to rebut Martin's attack on them, but without alienating the Fianna Fáil grassroots. Indeed, Adams said in his speech that he had spoken to long time Fianna Fáil activists, who were 'disappointed' and 'disillusioned' because the leadership had 'strayed from its original republican origins'. A Sinn Féin TD told me that Fianna Fáilers in his constituency were unhappy with their party leader's remarks, as they were hoping to get Sinn Féin transfers in the next election.

All's fair in love and war and, arguably, Martin needed to have a few swipes at Sinn Féin, not only to express strongly-held convictions, but to shore up his leadership and stop 'Adams and Co' from nibbling away at Fianna Fáil's support. Martin's position in the party had been under some pressure, due to poor poll showings. His Arbour Hill oration came a week ahead of the annual Fianna Fáil ardfheis (national conference) and a month before a by-election in the Carlow-Kilkenny constituency, where it was considered critical for Martin's future that Fianna Fáil should take the seat – as it did by a comfortable margin.

There is polling evidence that, between them, Sinn Féin, Fianna

Fáil and Labour could end up with a majority in the Dáil. However, as Martin pointed out on the *Late Late Show*, Sinn Féin's performance in the 2014 local elections was significantly lower than the opinion surveys suggested, whereas Fianna Fáil did better than the polls had indicated beforehand. In any case, given Martin's constant denunciations of Sinn Féin and what he calls 'the Provisional movement', it would be quite a turnaround if he somehow ended up in government with them. In the past, however, the Progressive Democrats and the Labour Party slated Fianna Fáil without mercy, but then decided that their best course of action was to join them at the cabinet table.

At a press conference during the Fianna Fáil ardfheis in the Royal Dublin Society (foreign observers must wonder at the number of places in this Republic with the word 'royal' in their titles) on the last weekend of April 2015, I asked Martin what his approach would be in the next Dáil, given that he had ruled out coalition with Fine Gael and Sinn Féin. He replied:

We're going to fight the election first, Deaglán, and we're going to fight the election on the issues, which I think is a legitimate position to have. And I have said this to a number of journalists who have been interviewing me in recent times. The debate moves very quickly on to a post-election scenario, as if it's already happened. It hasn't happened: we haven't had the general election. We have to fight the election on the issues and that's what we're doing, in terms of the policy issues … and we're going out there to maximise our vote and our seats so that we can influence, in whatever way that may turn out, the implementation of those policies.

One of Martin's colleagues later told me that Fianna Fáil had worked out, in fairly precise terms, that Fine Gael stood to lose 22 out of its 69 Dáil seats, and Labour would go down by 16 seats from 34 to 18.

(Most observers would find the Labour prediction rather optimistic.) The priority was to ensure that as many of these lost seats as possible went to Fianna Fáil. The attacks on Sinn Féin were motivated by the perception that a good deal of Sinn Féin's support was 'soft', and could be swayed in Fianna Fáil's direction. Speaking on condition of anonymity, this member of the parliamentary party said there was a strong possibility the next election would result in a minority government which would not last long and that the Dáil would be dissolved again fairly quickly. He ruled out coalition with Fine Gael, but felt that an agreement between Fianna Fáil and an anti-austerity grouping led by Sinn Féin was a real possibility, despite what his party leader was saying. Other parties in the past had denounced their opponents and then gone into government with them: that's the way the game was played.

Another prominent party figure from a rural area said the attacks on Sinn Féin had been a good idea, but that it was nevertheless likely there would be a Fianna Fáil-Sinn Féin coalition in the end, although he pointed out that any coalition proposal would be subject to approval by a special Fianna Fáil ardfheis. Meanwhile, a prominent Fianna Fáil stalwart based in a Dublin constituency said the party should remain in opposition, as a tie-up with Fine Gael would mean that about one-third of the membership would drop out, and another third would start looking to Sinn Féin. He said that, apart from some office-hungry TDs, there was little appetite for coalition with Sinn Féin either.

The prospect of a coalition involving Fine Gael and Sinn Féin would appear, on the surface at least, to be even more remote. The idea was floated in the past by a senior Fine Gael advisor at the time, Frank Flannery, but this was before the change of mood, symbolised by Syriza, came about in European politics. In the aftermath of the 2007 general election, when no party had a clear majority, Sinn Féin publicly urged Enda Kenny to contact the party for discussions. Cavan-Monaghan TD Caoimghín Ó Caoláin told interviewer Róisín Duffy on RTÉ radio's *This Week* programme, on 10 June 2007, that

Sinn Féin was 'very open-minded' as to who should become taoiseach, because the real issue was the programme for government.

That would be quite a turn-up for the books and might well cause problems with some of the unions, but past experience shows that anything can happen when political power is at stake.[19]

When the election does take place, one of Sinn Féin's greatest challenges will be to win transfers from voters whose first loyalty is to other parties. The Irish system of proportional representation means that the electorate can vote for candidates in order of preference. When the first choice from the ballot paper is either elected with a surplus of votes over the quota or else eliminated, the vote may be transferred to the second choice. If the second choice is elected or eliminated, the vote may be transferred to the third choice, and so on. Given the continuous attacks on Sinn Féin in the Dáil and the media on issues ranging from the abduction of Jean McConville to the manner in which the republican movement is said to have dealt with allegations of sexual abuse by IRA members, Sinn Féin may well find it difficult to get transfers in the general election. However, the party looks set to be a much stronger presence in the next Dáil. There is no evidence at this stage to suggest it will be a bigger party than Fine Gael, but some of the poll evidence suggests that it could give Fianna Fáil a run for its money. Whether it will have a prospect of entering government on satisfactory terms is very much up in the air. It seems safe to say that, once the results are in, Sinn Féin will have moved further from the margins, and closer to the mainstream, in Irish political life.

2. HELLO MARY LOU – GOODBYE GERRY?

SHE IS OFTEN SPOKEN of as the future leader of Sinn Féin. And if or more likely when – the party enters a coalition government in Dublin, it is inconceivable that she would not be a cabinet minister. Mary Lou McDonald is rarely out of the news, and this chapter explores the background to her political career and the journey she has made from Rathgar and Fianna Fáil to Leinster House and Sinn Féin.

With the general election drawing close at the time of writing, McDonald is a high-profile player in Republic of Ireland politics. If the dice fell the right way and Sinn Féin could lay claim to the job of tánaiste (deputy prime minister) or even – heaven forbid, their critics say – taoiseach(prime minister), it is not entirely fanciful to suggest that she could be in the running. This is partly due to her own abilities and performance as deputy leader of the party, but it is also down to the fact that Gerry Adams is such a highly-controversial figure. The scenario prior to the formation of the first inter-party government in 1948 has been evoked in this context.[1] On that occasion, the leader of the biggest party in the preliminary negotiations was totally unacceptable to others at the table. Richard Mulcahy was head of Fine Gael, but his role in the ruthless Civil War executions of anti-Treaty republicans ruled him out as taoiseach. The main opponents of such a move were Clann na Poblachta

(Family/Children of the Republic). Many of its activists were former IRA members, and party leader Seán MacBride had been IRA chief of staff in the 1930s. The issue was resolved when Fine Gael proposed John A. Costello, a prominent Dublin barrister and professional colleague of MacBride's, to head up the new government, although Mulcahy retained the title of party leader. There is, of course, a considerable difference between the political outlook held by Richard Mulcahy and the worldview of Gerry Adams. Yet the theory goes that, just as the Fine Gael leader had to take a step back, so would Adams need to temper any ambitions he might have. Mulcahy got the job of Minister for Education as a consolation prize in 1948 and some have suggested that, given his interest in the Irish language, the portfolio of Arts, Heritage and the Gaeltacht might be suitable for Adams. It is, of course, a highly-speculative scenario. Alternatively, Adams might emulate MacBride by taking over Foreign Affairs, a post in which he would revel, though it would cause flutterings and maybe panic attacks in some of the chancelleries of Europe.

Sinn Féin is admittedly very loyal to Adams, and would have great difficulty in accepting that he was somehow ineligible for the office of taoiseach or tánaiste. Who knows, though, what might happen in what were called the 'smoke-filled rooms' – before the tobacco-in-the-workplace ban, that is. Of course, there is no guarantee at time of writing that the party will be 'in the mix' when the next government, or indeed its successor, is being formed. Quite apart from government positions, there has been endless speculation about McDonald as the most likely contender to take over from Adams as Sinn Féin leader. It is virtually *de rigueur* for any media profile of the deputy leader to dwell at some length on the prospect of her taking the top job in the party.

The 'Backroom' column in the *Sunday Business Post* put it in the following colourful terms: 'Just as Micheál Martin is a human reminder to potential Fianna Fáil voters of the [Brian]Cowen years, so too Gerry Adams is a human reminder to potential Sinn Féin voters of the dark days of the IRA. Maybe it's time the party thought of replacing the 'Big Bad Wolf' at its head with Mary Lou. It could make the difference between Sinn Féin getting into the next government and, dare we say it, *leading* the next government [emphasis added].[2] At any large Sinn Féin gathering, the 2015 ardfheis in Derry or the Easter Rising commemorative parade in Dublin in April 2015, for example, it is very obvious that, while the party has drawn an impressive level of support from young working-class males, it badly needs to broaden its appeal. McDonald's presence in the leadership – despite one observer noting that 'her south county lilt is overlaid with a hint of a Dub drawl – is made into a greater asset by virtue of her being a woman from a middle-class background.[3]

Journalist Harry McGee has written that, given the symbolism of the 1916 Centenary, Adams will undoubtedly lead Sinn Féin into the next election, which is due to take place by April 2016 at the latest. Assessing Mary Lou's prospects after that, McGee wrote: 'There are few politicians who impress TDs from rival parties more than McDonald. She is a great communicator, authoritative and focused, though at times too obdurate. She can sometimes be caught out on detail. McDonald is deputy leader, a woman, who is also well-got with the party's key leaders in Northern Ireland. That makes her the front-runner.'[4]

When asked, in an interview for this book, if she saw herself going for the leadership within the next five years, McDonald replied: 'I wouldn't put a precise time-frame on any of this, but I have said externally and internally that, as and when the vacancy arises, I am interested. I mean, unless I radically change my mind in the intervening period'. She went on to stress, however, that she had no wish to see Adams stepping down:

No, I am not in any hurry. I think Gerry has proven his worth again and again and again and, despite what his detractors say, the facts are that the party has been built, our support has been built, strongly, north and south, under his stewardship. He would be the first to tell you that he didn't do it on his own; it is a collective leadership. You have Martin McGuinness in the mix, you know, a whole range of different characters.

When asked if she would be putting Adams under any pressure to go, she replied: 'Oh God no, absolutely not.'[5] Her answer was similar to the one she gave Alex Kane in the *Belfast Telegraph*, when he asked her if she wanted the job: 'Not in the short term, but I wouldn't rule it out in the longer term. It's not something I'm concerned with now, but at some stage, if there were a vacancy, I would certainly consider it.'[6]

Other names mentioned for the leadership include: Donegal TD Pearse Doherty, who is the party's finance spokesman; former MP for Newry and Armagh and one-time republican prisoner, Conor Murphy; and the North's Education Minister, John O'Dowd. However, observers believe that McDonald is the chosen one, and that the succession will take place at a time that is deemed appropriate. In or out of government, and whether or not she succeeds Adams as Sinn Féin leader, there is little doubt that McDonald will continue to be a significant figure in Irish politics for years to come.

So who is she, and what is her background? How did someone considered to have been born with the metaphorical silver spoon in her mouth and a well-lit pathway into the professional classes end up as deputy leader to a band of self-proclaimed revolutionaries? Born on May Day 1969 in Dublin's Holles Street hospital, McDonald grew up in the leafy suburb of Rathgar. The family home was at Eaton Brae, a quiet enclave off Orwell Road, and close to the impressive property that houses the Russian – formerly Soviet – Embassy. A family friend says that, despite the location, her circumstances were by no means luxurious.

In an interview for a very interesting book in 2008, about

politicians whose first name is Mary, she told former MEP for Fine Gael Mary Banotti that she was originally meant to be called Avril, as she was due to arrive in April. Though christened Mary Louise, this was quickly shortened to Mary Lou: 'When I was a child I would very rarely be called Mary Louise unless I got into trouble. When the voice was raised and I got my full title I knew that I had crossed some line.'[7] The classic Ricky Nelson pop-song *Hello Mary Lou (Goodbye Heart)* became one of her pet hates, though her canvassers in the Dáil constituency of Dublin Central consider it an asset. She herself wrote after the 2011 general election: 'The song filled the Cabra air and echoed throughout the north inner city. A group of women jived to it on Sheriff Street, proof-positive according to one activist that the song was a vote-getter. I sincerely doubt it.'[8]

Most profiles of Mary Lou describe her father Patrick McDonald as a surveyor, but when interviewed for this book, she pointed out that 'building contractor' was the correct description. Like so many people from the building trade, he joined Fianna Fáil. Her mother, Joan, was also a member of that party 'for a short while', she recalls: 'When we were growing up, she'd be the kind of person who'd be writing letters to prisoners of conscience. She'd be into Amnesty International and she was very involved in the Burma Action Group. As much as she would have a view on domestic politics, my mother would always have had a broader political sense of things.' The biggest role in shaping the young Mary Lou's outlook, however, was apparently played by her maternal grandmother, Molly, whom she describes in the Banotti interview as 'very political in her thinking, very nationalist, very old-style republican.' Interviewed for the present book, McDonald said: 'She died some years ago and I miss her. She was a big influence on me.'[9]

Despite the dreams and desires of socialists and Marxists over many generations, the historic dividing-line in the politics of the Republic of Ireland was not class, but what side your forebears had taken in the Civil War. That awful conflict erupted over the terms of the Anglo-Irish Treaty of 1921, and ultimately gave birth to Fianna

Fáil and Fine Gael, as well as hardening the stance of Sinn Féin on the militant fringe. A brother of Molly's (and grand-uncle to Mary Lou), James O'Connor from Bansha, County Tipperary, took part in the War of Independence and later sided with those who opposed the Treaty and the Irish Free State that arose out of it. On 13 December 1922, as civil war raged, the young railway worker was one of a group of anti-Treaty IRA activists arrested in County Kildare, close to the Free State army camp at the Curragh. The episode is recalled in a book on how the war was fought in County Kildare. In a fascinating chapter poetically entitled, 'Seven of Mine, said Ireland', author James Durney tells us that two months before their arrest the Rathbride Column, as they were called, had sent a runaway engine down the main Kildare line.[10]

The *Irish Times*, on 23 December 1922, quoting an unofficial briefing by the Free State authorities, reported that the IRA members had attempted to dislocate the Great Southern and Western Railway line using two spare engines to set up an obstruction at Cherryville. This was a major security threat because, as Durney points out: 'The Cherryville junction was vitally important as it had railway links to west and south.' The unit was also said to have ambushed Free State troops at the Curragh Siding, on 25 November. There were accusations as well that looting was carried out on shops and other business premises in the locality, although these claims were strongly rejected by surviving relatives and supporters.

Whether as a result of surveillance or inside information, the anti-Treaty unit was traced to a dugout or tunnel underneath the stables of a farmhouse at Moore's Bridge, about 2.5 kilometres (1.5 miles) from the Curragh camp. The intelligence officer of the group, thirty-one-year-old Thomas Behan was shot dead, during or after his arrest. While it is alleged that he was shot out of hand, the official record states that he was trying to escape from his place of detention.

Having been found guilty by a military court of possessing arms and ammunition, seven members of the group were executed on the morning of 19 December 1922. Three of them were aged between

HELLO MARY LOU – GOODBYE GERRY?

eighteen and nineteen years. Each of them was shot by firing squad, one after the other. They are said to have shaken hands with their executioners, and to have sung *The Soldiers' Song*, which has a chorus that begins: 'Soldiers are we, whose lives are pledged to Ireland.' This was a clarion-call of the Volunteers in the General Post Office at Easter 1916, and later, in the Irish-language version *Amhrán na bhFiann*, became Ireland's national anthem.

Two members of the column were spared: Pat Moore (whose brother, Bryan, was shot as commanding officer of the unit) and Jimmy White (whose brother, Stephen, was executed with the other six). Durney comments that 'it was probably a step too far to execute two sets of brothers at the one time'. The column had been arrested at the family farmhouse of Bryan Moore and his sister, Annie, who was also taken into custody. Annie's fiancé, Patrick Nolan, was among those executed. In a state of inconsolable grief, she was taken to the female wing of Mountjoy jail in Dublin. In a last letter to his parents, Nolan wrote: 'Dearest Mother, there are a few pounds in my suitcase, you can have them, or anything else in the house belonging to me.' James O'Connor wrote to his mother: 'I am going to Eternal Glory tomorrow morning with six other true-hearted Irishmen'. It was the largest group to be executed during the Civil War, in which there were seventy-seven official executions. The seven are known as the Grey Abbey Martyrs, and their deaths are still commemorated by republicans today.

Mary Lou has rural connections, with her mother – O'Connor's niece – coming from the Glen of Aherlow, and the family retains strong Tipperary links. These connections are important in Ireland; her father was born in Dublin, but with roots in County Mayo.[11] Mary Lou's parents separated when she was only nine years old. Such occurrences were relatively rare in the Ireland of that time, a state where divorce was banned until 1995. In the Banotti interview, she said: 'That was a big disruption in our family life but it was something we got through.' The children remained with their mother. All of them did well in their careers. Mary Lou told me: 'We worked hard, that is the ethos of our house. If you wanted to get ahead, you got cracking and there was an expectation that you'd do well at school and work hard. We were just, I suppose, lucky as well.'[12] There were four children in the family, two boys and two girls: 'I've an older brother called Bernard, then there's myself and the set of twins, Patrick and Joanne.'[13] A scientist by profession, Joanne has been associated with Éirigí [Rise Up!], a left-republican group that is critical of the Good Friday Agreement and seeks to build a mass radical movement but does not advocate a renewed campaign of violence. Mary Lou says they get on very well: 'I only have one sister. I love my sister and we're on great terms. She's got two lovely children, I've got two children. We're very close, we're a very, very close family.'[14] Mary Lou had just turned twelve when IRA prisoner of the British and abstentionist MP for Fermanagh-South Tyrone, Bobby Sands, died on hunger strike. She was later quoted as saying that this was a 'road to Damascus' moment.[15] She clearly recalls the 'sheer brutality' of the ten hunger strikers being allowed to die: 'And that was beamed into your front room.'[16] She attended a Catholic girls school on nearby Churchtown Road: Notre Dame des Missions, founded in 1953 by the order of nuns which bears that name. In a table of private schools, published in the *Irish Independent* on 17 September 2014, Notre Dame was listed as charging €4,300 per annum, with day-fees at other private schools in the Dublin area generally ranging from €3,600 to €12,000-plus.[17] The points she got in her Leaving Certificate at Notre Dame were insufficient for her purposes, so she repeated the exam the following year at Rathmines Senior College. She then started a four-year course in English Literature at Trinity College Dublin (TCD), no longer seen as a unionist enclave since the Catholic Church lifted its ban in 1970 on members attending the college.[18] In tandem with her social background, McDonald's schooling contributed to the self-confidence that is one of her hallmarks as a politician. As she told Banotti: 'I had a great education and a great sense of myself.'[19] She has warm memories of her teachers at Trinity, among them being the eloquent and feisty Independent Senator David Norris. 'It wasn't so much that he taught – he performed! And it was absolutely brilliant,' she told me. The prominent Kerry-born poet and academic Brendan Kennelly also gets full marks from Deputy McDonald: 'Brilliant in tutorials, a really good teacher, very affable and very connected with the students.'[20] Despite the impact the hunger strikes had on her when she was younger and her parents' interest in political issues, she kept aloof from such involvement at TCD. This seems strange in light of her later activity, since for many people it is their only period of activism. How was she able to keep clear of the political arena? 'Well, actually, with relative ease, because I liked my books, I liked my friends and I always worked when I was in college. So I always kept myself very well out of it.'[21] Her mind was on the glories of literature in the Saxon tongue: 'I liked all the Anglo-Irish [writers]. I particularly liked Beckett's theatre. I know it's very dark: I got a kick out of that. I liked the Metaphysical Poets and American literature. I went through a phase of Sylvia Plath; I think every college student does.'[22] She had a break abroad before the end of the four-year degree course: 'I took a year out when I was studying in Trinity and I went to live in Almeria, in Andalucia, in the south of Spain. It was after third year: a gap year. I taught there – the typical kind of thing.' She still heads off to Spain for a holiday when she gets a chance. After the Easter break in 2012, Labour's Pat Rabbitte responded to her latest criticism of the Government in the Dáil with the memorable quip: 'Such tanned indignation!'[23]

After graduation from Trinity she spent a year at the University of Limerick (UL), where she took a Master's degree: 'That was in European Integration Studies: law, economics, politics. I think I was the only person in the class that didn't have a degree in Economics or European Studies.'[24] When asked what motivated the shift from English Literature to European Studies, she says she had an interest in the European Union and its institutions: 'I go on instinct on lots of things. I didn't have a masterplan where I carefully plotted-out every step of a career-path... That's self-evident!'[25] After UL, she worked as a researcher in a Dublin-based think tank, the Institute of International and European Affairs. The IIEA was founded in 1990 by former general secretary of the Labour Party, Brendan Halligan.'I went on to Dublin City University (DCU) where I started my PhD. It was in Industrial Relations/Human Resource Management.' This was meant to be a follow-up to her MA thesis at UL which was concerned with the 1993 re-organisation of the state airline, Aer Lingus. 'I was in the IIEA, went into DCU, was working away, did some teaching, working away on my research, and then I went to the Irish Productivity Centre, to work as a consultant.'[26] Romance enters the story too: during the heady days of 1990, when the nation was buoyed with hope because of the Irish soccer team's performance in the World Cup, Mary Lou met her future husband, Martin Lanigan, in Peter's Pub in downtown Dublin. They married in 1996 in a Catholic wedding at University Church, and they had their reception in the historic Tailors' Hall, which featured in the events leading to the 1798 rebellion. Martin works in the emergency section of a utility company. They have two children, Iseult, born in 2003, and Gearóid, named after her husband's father, who arrived in 2006.

Mary Lou's first involvement in politics came in the mid-1990s when she joined the Irish National Congress (INC), a campaign group which promotes the aims and ideals of Irish republicanism on a non-party basis. The INC was originally set up in 1989, under the chairmanship of leading artist Robert Ballagh, to prepare for the 75th anniversary of the 1916 Rising two years later. In the anti-republican, revisionist climate of the time, official celebrations were going to be quite modest and far different in scale from what would later be planned for the centenary in 2016.

McDonald and Finian McGrath, who was subsequently elected to the Dáil as an Independent, both served in the position of leas-chathaoirleach (vice-chair) of the organisation in the mid-90s. McDonald chaired the organisation for a year from March 2000.[27] McGrath told me:

> The idea was, we were trying to do a copy of the ANC [*African National Congress*] in South Africa, because Mandela was on the way into power at the time and we just had this idea of having a broad republican nationalist front that would include every [*individual or organisation*]– including Sinn Féin, including independents like myself – that had a national vision for the country.

McGrath says that they worked closely as joint vice-chairs of the INC: 'She was a fantastic speaker, a woman of great belief. She had a great vision for our country at the time and was also very proactive in developing and supporting the early stages of the peace process, when a lot of people were hostile to it.'[28] The INC newsletter of April 2000 which announced her appointment as chair by the national executive also declared the organisation's intention to hold 'an anti-sectarian protest' in Dublin on 28 May.[29] This was in opposition to a proposed march by the Dublin and Wicklow lodge of the Orange Order and the unveiling of a plaque at 59 Dawson Street, in the city centre, where the first meeting of the Grand Orange Lodge of Ireland was held on 9 April 1798.

The Order sees itself as an unapologetic defender of Protestant civil and religious liberties, but its critics, with equal forthrightness, claim that its activities are damaging to community relations. There were major tensions and disturbances in Northern Ireland on an annual basis over a proposed Orange Order march through a nationalist area on the Garvaghy Road in Portadown. The INC was very involved in this issue, and McDonald herself visited the scene. The parade in Dublin was called-off and the counter-demonstrators were accused of intimidation. In a letter published in the *Irish Times* on 10 May, McDonald rejected this allegation and the notion that the Order had been 'demonised' by herself and other critics.

On 28 May, Dublin's Lord Mayor, Councillor Mary Freehill of the

Labour Party, unveiled the Dawson Street plaque. No one from the Orange Order was present but the *Irish Times* reported that the crowd of about 150 included a 'bevy' of protesters from the INC: 'These carried placards with messages such as "Dublin says No to sectarianism", as well as a mock Orange banner comparing the Order to the Ku Klux Klan. A spokeswoman, Ms Mary Lou McDonald, said the Congress was not opposed to the unveiling of the plaque. The protesters were there to register their "strenuous objections" to the way the Lord Mayor had engaged with the Orange Order. She accused Cllr Freehill of failing to recognise the scale of the sectarian problem in Ireland and of 'ingratiating' herself with an organisation "which continues to foster division and fear".[30] The Lord Mayor was quoted as saying that, 'the Order represents a significant strand in the politics and culture of those claiming a British-Irish identity. It is part of our shared history and should be recognised as such'.

In a letter published on 27 June in the *Irish Times*, McDonald said one of the reasons for the INC demonstration was 'to remind elected representatives of their responsibility to defend the right of Irish citizens to live free from sectarian harassment, as expressed in the Good Friday Agreement'. Responding in the letters page on 3 July, Julitta Clancy of the Meath Peace Group said she was 'delighted to learn that the INC now seems to be accepting the Agreement which it strongly opposed in 1998'. Replying, McDonald said that, 'contrary to Ms Clancy's assertion, the Irish National Congress did not oppose the Good Friday Agreement'. She reiterated in an interview for this book that the INC did not oppose the Agreement, although there were 'mixed views' about it among the membership. 'The Articles 2 and 3 issue was very, very "angsty" for the Irish National Congress,' she said, adding that she did not share those concerns. 'At the time that issue of Articles 2 and 3 was huge for nationalist Ireland, I suppose most markedly for people in the South.'

Separate referendums were held on the two sides of the border in the aftermath of the successful conclusion of multi-party talks at Stormont's Castle Buildings on Good Friday, 10 April 1998. The electorate in the Republic were asked to vote on a new version of Articles 2 and 3 which accepted that the North could not become part of a united Ireland without the consent of a majority in each jurisdiction. A front-page report in the *Sunday Business Post* on 15 March 1998 said the Irish Government was proposing to change Articles 2 and 3 without any meaningful *quid pro quo* from the British, and that 'the Irish National Congress is to launch a petition next week among the North's 675,000 nationalists to protest at the Government's planned action which the INC holds is a devastating destruction of the definition of the nation'. No such petition was launched in the end and plans for an intensive INC campaign to defend Articles 2 and 3 evaporated when Sinn Féin assented to the Good Friday pact. The organisation's newsletter for January 1999 states that the INC adopted 'a critical but not hostile approach' to the Agreement and subsequent referendums.

While it may be technically correct to say that the INC, as an organisation, did not oppose the Good Friday/Belfast Agreement outright, it was clearly very unenthusiastic about elements of the deal, especially – but not exclusively – the changes in Articles 2 and 3. The newsletter states: 'During the referenda campaign on the Belfast Agreement and constitutional changes, the INC launched a media campaign criticising the proposed wording as well as the indecent haste and lack of debate surrounding the amendments. To counteract the unanimously one-sided media coverage the INC also produced a *Critique of the Belfast Agreement* pointing out some of its shortcomings.' The INC chair from 1989 to 1998, Robert Ballagh, declared his intention to vote No in the referendum held in the Republic. This was because the Irish territorial claim was being removed but the British one still remained. Secondly, he believed the Agreement was 'flawed' and did not guarantee peace.[31]

Initially, Gerry Adams indicated that Sinn Féin might well vote for the Agreement in the North and against it in the southern referendum, because of the proposed changes in Articles 2 and 3. Sinn Féin TD for Cavan-Monaghan, Caoimghín Ó Caoláin initially also expressed opposition to 'any dilution or diminution of Articles 2 and 3'. But in the end, 331 out of the 350 Sinn Féin delegates at a special conference in Dublin on 10 May 1998 voted to accept the Agreement and, by implication, to vote Yes in both referendums.

McDonald told this writer that she was persuaded to join the INC by a Fianna Fáil activist, Nora Comiskey, a son of whom was a lifelong friend of Mary Lou's husband. Nora Comiskey also persuaded her to join Fianna Fáil. Asked why she chose that party, she told me: 'Probably a mixture of things, my family in the main, although it is not true to say all of them would have been Fianna Fáil. You know how this shakes down in terms of families that fell on one or other side of the Civil War politics. And then I had a very close friend who remains a close friend of mine, who is a lifelong Fianna Fáiler and a lifelong republican, Nora Comiskey'. McDonald joined a cumann (branch) of the party in the Dublin West constituency which encompassed Castleknock, where she lived at the time. Several long-time members from different wings of Fianna Fáil have insisted to me that she was 'shafted' by supporters of local TD and future, highly-respected finance minister Brian Lenihan Jr, who later died of cancer at the age of fifty-two. She equally-strongly rejects this version of events: 'That's not true. I don't think that's fair. I read these accounts that, "She left because she didn't get a nomination for a seat". I tell you – no such thing, and in no shape, manner or form was I shafted by the Lenihans or by anybody else.' A long-time Fianna Fáil activist told me that 'Lenihan ran her out of it', and that this was bitterly resented in the McDonald camp. But Mary Lou is categoricaly insistent that, far from having her ambitions frustrated and blocked by the local party establishment, she felt instead that there was a lack of a serious social policy dimension in Fianna Fáil's version of republicanism:

> What happened was this. I arrived in: they were lovely people, Nora in particular. Everything was going along, happy days. I went to one meeting, I went to another

meeting. There was a discussion, and I raised the idea of – I don't think I even used the word 'equality', I think I used the word 'equity'– and there was a kind of a puzzled intake of breath in the room.[32]

She addressed the party's ardfheis, which was held at the Royal Dublin Society premises in November 1998. The issue was policing in Northern Ireland, and the *Irish Times* reported:

Ms Mary Lou McDonald, Dublin West, speaking on the reform of the RUC [*Royal Ulster Constabulary, predecessor of the current Police Service of Northern Ireland*], said the RUC was composed exclusively of people from one tradition and they were utterly incapable of carrying out fair policing. There had been victims who had died at the hands of the RUC. There needed to be root-and-branch change to the policing system.[33]

McDonald had the feeling that her interest in the North, especially the Orange Order dispute with nationalist residents in Portadown over its demand to march along the Garvaghy Road, was not widely shared in the party. This contributed to her decision to leave Fianna Fáil after about a year:

I had been active then on the parading issue in Garvaghy Road and all of that, and there was kind of a very mixed response to that within the party, and a level of disengagement. So it all amounted to me saying, you know, this is just the wrong place for me. It wasn't to cast an aspersion on anybody else: it was the wrong place for me to be. That was the sense, so I was sort of a misfit in that whole scenario.[34]

Along with suggestions that her progress was obstructed in Fianna

Fáil, there is an apparently contradictory claim that she turned down a nomination to run for a 'safe' council seat in the June 1999 local elections. She flatly denies this also: 'Listen, I was neither shafted nor was I offered a seat. It didn't arise.' Asked how her move to Sinn Féin came about in the end, she says:

I suppose, first of all I knew some of the lads through the Irish National Congress, although that wasn't the crucial thing... I remember going to a meeting in the Mansion House. Gerry [Adams] spoke at it, I can't remember if Martin [McGuinness] spoke at it, I don't think he did. But certainly Gerry spoke at it, and I just said to myself: 'These people actually have their act together. And they know what they are doing'... Maybe it was a bit of a leap of faith on my part because I would have known certain individuals within Sinn Féin, but I wouldn't have grown up in a place where Sinn Féin was organised and kind of a known quantity and all of that stuff... But it was just the politics of it sort of appealed to me: that blend of support for the peace process, Irish unity, all of that matters a great deal to me. But then, joined, inextricably bound up with that: social justice and social equality... For my politics, I wanted both of those things, I didn't want a little bit of one or a little bit of the other, I wanted both of those things, so that's where the Sinn Féin appeal was for me, and it was the right decision... The party was smaller at that stage, it was a more closed circle in a sense. So you arrived along as a kind of a new person in it; right enough, people take the measure of you and suss you out, which is all fair enough, but notwithstanding all of that I think I knew pretty quickly that I was in the right spot.

She believes the party is more open to new recruits nowadays: 'I think for people joining now, perhaps particularly women, they come into a very different atmosphere and a very different environment.' (There was a time when joining Sinn Féin might have led to some Garda surveillance because the IRA campaign was in full swing but McDonald says she did not experience any of that.)[35]

She told Alex Kane in 2013: 'When I got politically involved, when I became active, I was looking for somewhere you could actually make a difference, and Sinn Féin provide that space. There's a kind of stereotypical thing about what a 'Shinner' should look like and that doesn't tally with the reality.' Kane commented: 'She was a perfect catch for Sinn Féin, exactly the sort of person they needed: the sort of person who would normally have pursued a career in Fianna Fáil. She was young, bright, articulate and attractive.'[36] A general election was called in the Republic in 2002, and McDonald was chosen as the Sinn Féin candidate in Dublin West. This was her first time to run for public office and she secured 2,404 votes, equivalent to 8.02 per cent of first preferences. Coming seventh in a field of nine, she was eliminated on the third count. Brian Lenihan Jr topped the poll for Fianna Fáil, with Trotskyist candidate Joe Higgins of the Socialist Party (who got almost half of Mary Lou's transfers under the Irish system of proportional representation), and Labour's Joan Burton, taking the other two seats.[37]

Her internal rise in Sinn Féin has been a rapid one. In 2001, she became a member of the ardchomhairle (executive council); four years later she succeeded Mitchel McLaughlin – currently the speaker of the Northern Ireland Assembly – as chair of the party. And in 2009 she took over from Pat Doherty – currently abstentionist MP for West Tyrone – as vice-president. McDonald attracted controversy when she took part in a commemoration ceremony at the statue of former IRA leader Seán Russell in Dublin's Fairview Park on 17 August 2003. A photograph in the Sinn Féin newspaper *An Phoblacht* for 21 August 2003 shows McDonald, at this stage a declared candidate in the following June's elections to the European Parliament, smiling benignly at Belfast republican Brian

Keenan, who gave the main oration.

Born in Fairview, Russell took part in the 1916 Rising and sided with the anti-Treaty IRA through the Civil War and beyond. In 1926, he was part of a mission to buy arms in the Soviet Union. In 1938 he was appointed chief of staff of the IRA. Regarding itself as the true government of Ireland, the organisation declared war on Britain in January 1939 and began a campaign of bomb attacks on British targets, especially electricity supply-points. An apolitical militarist, Russell did not care who provided arms to the republican movement and took very literally republican father-figureWolfe Tone's dictum that 'England's difficulty is Ireland's opportunity'. He travelled to the US to drum up support, got arrested, skipped bail, secured passage on a steamer heading for Italy and, in May 1940, ended up in Berlin. After three months' training in explosives, he headed back to Ireland on a German U-boat in the company of Spanish Civil War veteran Frank Ryan, who had just been released from one of Franco's prisons into German hands. However, Russell became ill and died at sea on 14 August 1940, with the result that the mission was aborted. Reporting on Keenan's speech in Fairview, *An Phoblacht* said:

> Brian reviewed the strange history of Seán Russell from his birth in Fairview in 1893 to his death at the end [sic] of the Second World War. He talked about the part Russell had played during the '20s and the '30s in the ideological disputes surrounding the Republican Congress and the formation of Saor Éire, and his role, as IRA Chief of Staff, in the disastrous campaign in England during the Second World War [...] 'I don't know,' Brian acknowledged, 'what was in the depth of Seán Russell's thinking down the years, but I am sure he was never far from Pearse's own position, who said, 'as a patriot, preferring death to slavery, I know no other way'.[38]

Keenan, who died of cancer five years later, was himself the mastermind of an IRA bombing campaign that unsettled London in the mid-1970s. He was jailed for eighteen years in 1980 for his involvement in the deaths of eight people, including author and broadcaster Ross McWhirter, who had offered a £50,000 reward for information leading to the arrest of IRA bombers, and oncologist Gordon Hamilton-Fairley, one of several people killed by car bombs.[39] Earlier, Keenan had travelled extensively to establish contacts in East Germany, Lebanon and Syria, and negotiate arms deals for the IRA, most notably with Libya's Colonel Gaddafi in 1972. But following his release on parole in 1993, Keenan used his influence to persuade the IRA leadership to embrace the peace process. At his funeral, members of the Balcombe Street Siege group – the IRA unit that Keenan organised in England in the mid-1970s – carried his coffin.

Two weeks after the Fairview ceremony, columnist Kevin Myers castigated McDonald in the *Irish Times* for her participation in a ceremony to honour a 'filthy wretch', whose collaboration with the Nazis took place after Hitler had publicly pledged to exterminate the Jews of Europe. Noting that McDonald was a candidate in the European elections, Myers wondered what she would say to her parliamentary colleagues if 'by some extraordinary freak' she won the seat: 'At the EU bar, would she break into a jolly rendition of *Horst Wessel* [the Nazi Party anthem], a beer tankard in her hand?'[40] The issue surfaced again, inevitably, in the run-up to the European elections. The weekend before the 11 June polling day, Fianna Fáil candidate Eoin Ryan said Keenan was a senior IRA figure who had served a prison sentence in England for explosives offences. He added:

> The people of Dublin and Ireland should know the kind of company Mary Lou McDonald keeps. And what of the person McDonald and Keenan gathered together to 'pay respect' to – Seán Russell, a self-proclaimed ally of Hitler, Nazi Germany and former leader of the IRA.

A Sinn Féin spokesman responded: 'I think Eoin Ryan should look at his own party's history before starting to throw around accusations... considering Eamon de Valera signed a book of condolences on the death of Adolf Hitler.'[41] Myers returned to the subject twice more in his 'Irishman's Diary' column, most notably on 1 February 2005, the year after the election, when he wrote: 'Not merely has Mary Lou McDonald increased in size since her election to the European Parliament, but she is the only MEP who has publicly honoured a Nazi quisling... When Big Mac gave the keynote [sic] oration for Russell, she was truly speaking the language of Sinn Féin-IRA and its weird, demented ethos... Big Mac is just junk.'

McDonald told this writer she had no regrets over her participation in the Russell ceremony:

> No, I mean, for God's sake, if you could criticise anything, you would criticise factions within the IRA at different stages that had such a militarist view on things that they didn't see broader politics.I don't think for one minute that Russell was an arch-Nazi or a Nazi supporter. The facts actually, if viewed rationally don't support that case, but that's what Myers is trying to do. But at that time if I recall, Kevin Myers had taken a good number of side-swipes and hard runs at me. That is his prerogative but – pretty nasty stuff!

Asked if it hurt to be attacked in that way, she replied:

> Not hurt I was more taken aback by it, because I suppose I hadn't been through, like others, the school of hard knocks. Bear this in mind: one day I was going about minding my own business, then, when I ran in that European election in 2004, literally within a matter of months, anywhere you would go people knew your name and recognised you.That's quite a transition for a person, in a very quick period of time. And then you get

the criticism and you have to take it, but it throws you a little bit off balance. Nowadays, it wouldn't have that effect on me at all, but that's just experience and the value of growing older.

(The Russell statue was vandalised in December 2004 by an unnamed group who said in a statement he was a Nazi collaborator; it was later repaired.)

Regarding the response to her European candidacy, she told Banotti (a grand-niece of rebel leader and founder of the Free State, Michael Collins): 'The only thing that irked me, as a woman, was the suggestion, sometimes said up-front and sometimes just implied, that I was maybe cute but not that bright. They were saying that this woman was being run because she was being groomed as the new face of Sinn Féin and she was respectable. And never a thought that maybe this is a capable person, someone who has the confidence of those she works with to go out and do this job. This irritated me, but I suppose it was par for the course.'

It would have been interesting to see the reaction of former neighbours in the leafy suburbs to her election campaign, but the party wasn't having any of that. Alison O'Connor wrote in the *Sunday Business Post*: 'A request to see McDonald, who grew up in the south Dublin suburb of Rathgar, canvassing in her heartland of middle-class Dublin was ignored. Instead, an initial offer came to accompany her on a canvass of an inner-city flats complex, and eventually an old local authority estate in Crumlin.'[42]

Journalist Michael O'Regan wrote with foresight, six months in advance of the June 2004 European contest: 'Dublin could provide Sinn Féin with its first Euro MEP in Ms Mary Lou McDonald, who polled 2,404 first preference votes in Dublin West in the 2002 general election. The party has since grown in strength in the capital, with Ms McDonald's profile increasing. Political observers notice that she was given a very high profile by the party during the Northern elections, posing for photographs and television cameras with the leader, Mr Gerry Adams.'[43] It was an indication of the effort being put into the campaign and the reception it was getting that the pseudonymous Drapier column in the *Irish Times* reported hearing that a rally in the middle-class suburb of Dundrum in south Dublin on 30 March, where Adams and McDonald were speaking, drew 'a huge overflow attendance with the crowd in the hall spilled outside'.[44]

Meanwhile, Sinn Féin's apparent reluctance at the time to dispense with the legacy of the 'Long War' in the North was becoming a political weapon in the hands of the party's opponents. Progressive Democrat TD for Dun Laoghaire, Fiona O'Malley highlighted the sale of paramilitary souvenirs in Sinn Féin shops. She said the sale of T-shirts bearing the logo 'IRA – UndefeatedArmy' and lapel pins with the slogan 'Sniper at Work' were helping to fund Sinn Féin election candidates. (This issue has been raised in more recent times by Fianna Fáil leader, Micheál Martin.)When asked at the time if she approved of the 'Sniper at Work' badges, McDonald turned the question around and replied: 'Look, what I don't approve of is the endless gimmickry that the PDs are indulging in.' Asked if she would wear an 'IRA – UndefeatedArmy' T-shirt, she deftly responded that she did not wear T-shirts at press conferences.[45]

An *Irish Times*/TNS mrbi opinion poll published on 21 March surprised many when it showed McDonald ahead of outgoing Green Party MEP Patricia McKenna in a battle for the last seat in Dublin. The election team of Fianna Fáil's Eoin Ryan were watching McDonald like hawks. When they discovered that she had described herself as a 'peace negotiator' and 'full-time public representative' on the ballot-paper, they complained to the Returning Officer's staff. Ryan said:

> I am not aware of any position to which Ms McDonald has been elected by the public. Her claim to be 'a peace negotiator' requires clarification. What peace has she negotiated and with whom? If she can describe herself as a peace negotiator, then so is every member of Oireachtas Éireann. The Sinn Féin candidate's claim to have been elected by the people to any office is utterly bogus.[46]

However, the Returning Officer said there were no formal rules as to what titles could be used by candidates, other than people claiming to represent parties which did not exist. Mark Hennessy observed in the *Irish Times* on 2 June 2004 that Sinn Féin's policy on the European Union had developed from outright opposition to 'critical engagement'. Noting that the party's best hope for success in the election was Bairbre de Brún in the North, he added: 'One seat in the Republic would be a tremendous result.'

The European and local government elections took place on 11 June, and McDonald won the fourth and final seat in the Dublin Euro-constituency to become the party's first MEP in the 26 counties. Fianna Fáil, Fine Gael and Labour all held their Dublin seats but McDonald beat the Green Party's Patricia McKenna into fifth place, with 60,395 first preferences compared to the latter's 40,445. McDonald's share of the vote at 14.32 per cent was more than double the 6.64 per cent that Seán Crowe scored for Sinn Féin in the same constituency at the previous European election in 1999.[47] It was the small hours of the morning when her election was announced, and Frank McNally captured the atmosphere of the occasion in his report:

> Mary Lou McDonald was carried shoulder-high from the RDS count-centre early yesterday. Outside, right on cue, a ghetto-blaster struck up the old Country and Western favourite: *Hello Mary Lou (Goodbye Heart)*. But, the habitual noisy part of the Sinn Féin celebrations over, the new MEP then called her campaign workers into the sort of huddle favoured by football teams. It was a larger huddle than any football team's, because Sinn Féin have a lot of workers, and McDonald happily acknowledged her debt to them. Among other things, she assured the huddle that this was not Mary Lou McDonald's seat – it belonged to Sinn Féin. Even at 3.30 am, the message was unblurred and the campaign zeal unrelenting.[48]

Transfers are of major importance in the Irish electoral process. It has always been a major challenge for Sinn Féin candidates to attract second or other preferences in the system of Proportional Representation. But McDonald broke through the barrier on that occasion. And as well as winning two seats in the Strasbourg parliament, Sinn Féin doubled its representation on the local authorities. The following month, it was announced that the new Sinn Féin MEPs would be part of the United European Left/Nordic Green Alliance (GUE/NGL). Sinn Féin had hosted a Belfast visit by the group the previous March. A high proportion of its members were communists or former communists. However, Bairbre de Brún said this would not affect Sinn Féin support in the US: 'I think people in America will take a commonsense approach.' At time of writing GUE/NGL also includes the Greek ruling party, Syriza, Spain's Podemos and an Independent MEP for the Midlands-North-West constituency in Ireland, Luke 'Ming' Flanagan.[49]

There is no such thing as government and opposition in the European Parliament, so committee membership is vitally important. McDonald was appointed to the committee on Employment and Social Affairs, as well as becoming a substitute member of the committee on Civil Liberties, Justice and Home Affairs. After the election campaign, the new MEP was back in the eye of the storm when she was among those who carried the coffin of Joe Cahill, one of the founders of the Provisional IRA, who died on 23 July 2004. A letter-writer in the *Irish Times* said: 'Pictures of Mary-Lou McDonald carrying the coffin of that monster Joe Cahill shocked me to the bone.' The letter concluded: 'I want my vote back!' The episode surfaced again in a *Sunday Independent* article by Emer O'Kelly on 24 October 2004, under the headline: 'We should start to see Mary Lou as the enemy'. Italy's Rocco Buttiglione had been nominated as the EU's Justice Commissioner but his conservative Catholic views on homosexuality and the role of women in society aroused opposition among MEPs. O'Kelly wrote:

One of those questioning (and indeed damning him) was that well-known defender of civil liberties, Ms Mary Lou McDonald, Sinn Féin MEP...She is a representative of the political wing of a subversive private army dedicated to the overthrow of the Irish State...When Joe Cahill, described as a 'veteran republican' died a few months ago, just weeks after Ms McDonald was elected to Europe, she helped carry his coffin to the grave. Cahill's republicanism, veteran or otherwise, included a string of murders *ar son na h-Éireann* [Trans: on behalf of Ireland].

The Minister for Justice in the Fianna Fáil-Progressive Democrats government at the time, Michael McDowell, appeared on Today FM's *Sunday Supplement* show with McDonald on 17 October 2004. When he said the IRA Army Council made all the key decisions for the republican movement and that senior figures in Sinn Féin were members of that body, McDonald challenged him to name them. McDowell replied: 'If you really did want me to name them, you would then accuse me of trying to wreck the peace process.' McDonald said: 'I have no balaclava. Sinn Féin is a democratic party and we are part of the political mainstream. Sinn Féin is no safe haven for criminality.'[50]

Sinn Féin was caught up in a whole range of controversies throughout 2005. Possibly the most damaging, because of the horrific circumstances, was the murder of thirty-three-year-old father of two, Robert McCartney, from the mainly-nationalist Short Strand area, who was attacked outside a Belfast pub on the night of 30 January 2005. Republicans were blamed for the killing, and the dead man's sisters launched an international campaign to achieve justice. The incident was condemned by Sinn Féin and there was a bizarre statement by the IRA that it was willing to shoot McCartney's killers. Prior to the party's ardfheis in March of that year, McDonald said: 'Sinn Féin couldn't have been more crystal clear in our condemnation of that murder and calls for people to come forward with information.'[51]

On 9 May 2005, McDonald and de Brún found themselves isolated at the European Parliament, when a motion condemned the McCartney murder and also criticised Sinn Féin for alleged failure to cooperate in the investigation. MEPs backed the resolution by 555-4, and there were 48 abstentions. Unionist MEPs joined with colleagues from an Irish nationalist background in supporting the proposal. McDonald and de Brún backed a separate motion that was less critical of the party and the IRA, but which supported the McCartney family's efforts to bring those responsible to trial.[52]

The next Irish general election was very much on the party's mind, and McDonald was being groomed for the Dublin Central constituency although another Sinn Féin candidate nearly took the seat on the previous occasion. In the previous general election in 2002, Councillor Nicky Kehoe, a former republican prisoner, only missed out by 57 votes. Normally, a candidate with such strong local support would be expected to run again, but it was clearly a Sinn Féin priority to get McDonald into the Dáil. Kehoe supporters were reported to be unhappy with the leadership decision.

An unsigned profile of McDonald published in *Phoenix* magazine on 12 August 2005 stated: 'Cllr Nicky Kehoe had looked to be a shoo-in for Dublin Central following a near-miss in 2002 and a huge vote in the locals (3,609 first preference votes in Cabra-Glasnevin)... McDonald had at one stage been suggested as a candidate for Dublin West, her former base when she was a member of Fianna Fáil, but it now looks as if she will be proposed for Dublin Central.'

Sinn Féin opted to run her in that constituency and the party's hopes were high that she would win a Dáil seat, as part of a significant increase in Sinn Féin representation at Leinster House. Niamh Connolly wrote in the *Sunday Business Post*: 'There is serious tension with supporters of local election poll topper Nicky Kehoe, after McDonald was chosen to run in Dublin Central ahead of him.'[53] Accompanying McDonald as she carried out an election canvass, journalist Tom Humphries observed: 'There is a strange dissonance between the knee-jerk media response to Sinn Féin's engagement in southern politics and the response Mary Lou gets on the doorsteps.'[54] A further *Phoenix* profile, published on 18 May 2007, six days before the general election, said:

> Can Mary Lou win a seat in the Taoiseach's constituency?... Last October a poll commissioned by the *Irish Mail on Sunday* seriously unnerved Dublin Sinn Féin activists, showing her on just 6 per cent, behind the Green Party's Patricia McKenna (7 per cent), Labour's Joe Costello TD (11 per cent) and Fine Gael's Cllr Paschal Donohoe (12 per cent). Other polls indicated that this was not a rogue poll and it appeared that while doughnutting with Adams at meetings in Downing Street, Stormont and elsewhere was good for the image, it was no substitute for hard graft in Ballybough and Summerhill... Since October it has been a six-and-a-half day week in Dublin Central for McDonald...

The general election took place on 24 May and, as the votes were being counted, it became clear that Sinn Féin candidates were doing quite poorly. There was a strong expectation, for example, that McDonald herself would succeed, but that was to underestimate the Taoiseach of the day and master of the electoral arts, Bertie Ahern, whose transfers in Dublin Central were critical in getting party colleague Cyprian Brady over the line, although the latter had only received 939 first preferences. McDonald got almost 1,800 fewer first preference votes than Nicky Kehoe had secured in 2002 on a slightly lower overall turnout. It was a serious blow in personal terms, and she told Banotti later: 'When the fateful day arrives and the result is disappointing, it is gutting, it is very difficult personally.' She went on a family holiday to Spain to get over it, but said in the same interview that, whether winning in 2004 or losing in 2007, 'I found it an incredibly long process afterwards to try and get my head back together again'.

McDonald's next electoral outing was in the European elections of 2009. A by-election was scheduled for the same date in Dublin Central to fill the vacancy left by the untimely death from cancer of the radical Independent TD Tony Gregory. Sinn Féin opted to run McDonald again for Europe, despite the fact that the Dublin Euro-constituency could now only elect three MEPs instead of the previous four. As its Dáil candidate the party ran Christy Burke, a long-time member of Dublin City Council and former republican prisoner.

Having won the last of four seats in the Dublin Euro-constituency in 2004, it was always going to be a challenge for her to get re-elected five years later, when the number of MEPs was reduced. McDonald did not retain her seat, and Burke likewise failed to get elected to the Dáil. But the local elections were held the same day and Burke kept his Council seat, then quit Sinn Féin three days later. In a piece on 3 December 2010, *Phoenix* magazine commented: 'What galls many party members is that she could have won a Dáil seat in the last election if the right decisions were taken... McDonald failed to win a seat that Kehoe would have won in Dublin Central and Sinn Féin's Joanna Spain lost in [*Dublin*] Mid-West where McDonald would also have won had she been a candidate.'

But she ran again for the Dáil in Dublin Central, in the 2011 general election. Fianna Fáil were at a low ebb, and Ahern wasn't running this time. When the votes were counted, McDonald was the last of four TDs to be elected. Christy Burke, running as an Independent, didn't help – he got 1,315 first preferences.[55] In 2012 on the TV3 political talk show, *Tonight with Vincent Browne*, Deputy McDonald was chosen by a panel of assessors as 'Opposition Politician of the Year'. Mary Lou's career was back on track. But although the speculation continued, there was no sign of Gerry Adams moving aside for the republican from Rathgar.

3. THE ARMALITE AND THE BALLOT-BOX

THOUGH SINN FÉIN WAS founded in 1905, the party today has little enough in common with the organisation established by the journalist and propagandist for Irish nationalism, Arthur Griffith, who later headed the delegation which agreed to the Anglo-Irish Treaty of 1921.

The one major thread of continuity with the original Sinn Féin has been the policy of abstentionism from Westminster. In his book published in 1904 and entitled, *The Resurrection of Hungary*, Griffith argued that Irish MPs should emulate their Hungarian counterparts who had adopted 'a manly policy of passive resistance and non-recognition of Austria's right to rule'.[1]

The Hungarians had achieved political and economic autonomy under a dual monarchy, whereby they stayed at home in Budapest instead of going to Vienna. Griffith argued that the Irish could do the same by adopting a similar policy and remaining in Dublin instead of going to Westminster.

The passive resistance element of his approach did not pass on to his successors in Sinn Féin but the abstentionist policy still survives. At time of writing, Sinn Féin candidates elected as MPs do not take their seats in the House of Commons.

In view of the major changes in Sinn Féin and IRA policies and tactics over the last thirty-odd years, there has been some speculation about a change of tack in this respect as well. This arose again in advance of the British general election of 7 May 2015 and there were media suggestions that Sinn Féin could wield significant influence by setting aside its stay-at-home approach.

Writing in the *Sunday Business Post*, columnist Tom McGurk recalled how the unionist bloc exacted a price from Prime Minister John Major in the 1990s for keeping his Conservative Party government in power:

> Were Sinn Féin to adopt a new policy of 'qualified abstentionism' – in other words, a tactical approach where it would only go to Westminster and vote when the party considers the matter of serious significance – what could the republican objection be?... Nor do I believe that anyone could credibly argue that such a policy of 'qualified abstentionism' undermines any determining principle of Irish Republicanism... The political reality in the real world, as Sinn Féin has discovered since the party abandoned abstentionism on both sides of the border, is that historic principles can become political cul de sacs.[2]

In a column for the Belfast-based *Irish News*, Tom Collins pointed out that unionists and the moderate nationalists of the Social Democratic and Labour Party (SDLP) would make use of any leverage they might have if they held the balance of power at Westminster. He continued:

> One party unable to trade its support – explicit or tacit – for political advantage is Sinn Féin. They have been refused entry to the Commons by the British insistence that they swear an oath to the Crown, and by their own

unwillingness to see the oath for what it is – a meaningless irrelevance... It's time Sinn Féin called Westminster's bluff and turned up. Some left-wing MPs have slurred their words, others have crossed their fingers behind their backs, some – it is claimed – have resorted to gibberish. Gaelic is acceptable, apparently; that opens up a whole host of possibilities.[3]

In the same paper two weeks later, columnist Tom Kelly wrote: 'Sinn Féin has... said it wants to see regime change at Westminster and hopes for a Labour administration. That being the case, who would be surprised that even if they fight the upcoming election on an abstentionist ticket, that they wouldn't rack up at the Palace of Westminster to vote, if Labour needed the numbers? Some may say "never" but "never" has never been a shibboleth for Sinn Féin under the leadership of Gerry Adams.'[4]

In an interview with Stephen Walker on BBC Northern Ireland's *The View*, one of Sinn Féin's five MPs, Francie Molloy from the Mid-Ulster constituency, categorically denied that any such move was planned. Interestingly, the interview was conducted at the Palace of Westminster and, when asked if the policy would be reviewed in the event of a hung parliament, Molloy said: 'No, definitely not... It's not up for the ardfheis. It's not up for review. It's not up for a decision at this point in time.'

The use of the phrase 'at this point in time' was remarked upon later in the same programme by Peter Kellner, of the polling and market research company YouGov, who commented that 'it allows you to say "times have changed".'[5]

In his biography of former Sinn Féin president Ruairí Ó Brádaigh, American academic Robert W. White writes that, during an ardchomhairle (national executive) meeting in the early 1980s, Molloy had suggested that Owen Carron should take his seat at Westminster. Carron had won the Fermanagh-South Tyrone by-election of August 1981, which was caused by the death of hunger striker Bobby Sands.[6] In response to a query from myself, Francie Molloy, who is currently Sinn Féin MP for Mid-Ulster, said he made the suggestion 'when Owen was an Anti H-Block Armagh MP'. Carron later got elected to the Northern Ireland Assembly as a Sinn Féin candidate and, when he sought to retain his Westminster seat, without success, in the 1983 UK general election, he ran on behalf of Sinn Féin. Molloy told me he had previously proposed that Sinn Féin end its policy of abstention towards Dáil Eireann at Leinster House. This body was seen as usurping the true Irish parliament, the First Dáil, established in 1919, and the Second Dáil, which was elected in May 1921.

On Saturday 10 January 1970, two historic events took place in Dublin. One was a major anti-apartheid protest against the presence of the all-white South African rugby team at the stadium on Dublin's Lansdowne Road.[7] The present writer was one of about 10,000 people who took part in the march and, walking past a nearby hotel on the way home, someone pointed out that a Sinn Féin ardfheis (annual conference) was being held there. I did not realise it at the time, but it was an occasion that would have wide and fateful ramifications for both parts of the island.

The ardfheis continued the next day, with a debate on a motion to drop abstentionism. This continued until 5.30pm, when a vote was taken. A two-thirds majority was required under the party constitution but support for the motion fell short, at 153 votes out of 257.[8] However, when asked to back a motion of allegiance to the anti-abstentionist leadership of the movement, thereby implicitly endorsing the new policy, about one-third of delegates walked out and announced the setting-up of what became known as Provisional Sinn Féin.[9] A secret convention of the Irish Republican Army (IRA) had already been held the previous month in Boyle, County Roscommon, where a motion to drop abstentionism was approved 28-12, and the minority split away to set up an alternative IRA headed by the 'Provisional Army Council' – the 1916 Proclamation was issued by the 'Provisional Government'. A statement issued by this new body urged republicans not to be 'diverted into the parliamentary blind alleys' of Westminster, Leinster House and Stormont'.

The statement outlined the background to the split from the Provisionals' point of view: 'The adoption of the compromising policy referred to is the logical outcome of an obsession in recent years with parliamentary politics, with consequent undermining of the basic military role of the Irish Republican Army. The failure to provide the maximum defence possible of our people in Belfast and other parts of the six counties against the forces of British imperialism last August is ample evidence of this neglect.'[10]

In between the two meetings, leading pro-abstentionist Ruairí Ó Brádaigh visited seventy-seven-year-old Tom Maguire at his home in County Mayo. Maguire had been a member of the First and Second Dáil Éireann, regarded as the only legitimate assemblies in Irish republican ideology. In December 1938, Maguire was one of a group of seven people elected to the Second Dáil (which was never formally dissolved) who signed over what they regarded as the authority of government to the IRA Army Council. That body henceforth considered itself the only legitimate government of Ireland. In a statement issued on 31 December 1969, Maguire said:

An IRA convention, held in December 1969, by a majority of the delegates attending, passed a resolution removing all embargoes on political participation in parliament from the Constitution and Rules of the IRA. The effect of the resolution is the abandonment of what is popularly termed the 'Abstentionist Policy'. The 'Abstentionist Policy' means that the Republican candidates contesting parliamentary elections in Leinster House, Stormont or Westminster give pre-election pledges not to take seats in any of those parliaments. The Republican candidates seek election to the 32-county Parliament of the Irish Republic, the Republican Dáil or Dáil Éireann, to give it its official title. The declared objective is to elect sufficient representatives to enable the 32-County Dáil Éireann to be reassembled... Accordingly, I, as the sole surviving member of the Executive of Dáil Éireann, and the sole surviving signatory of the 1938 Proclamation, hereby declare that the resolution is illegal and that the alleged Executive and Army Council are illegal, and have no right to claim the allegiance of either soldiers or citizens of the Irish Republic... I hereby further declare that the Provisional Executive and the Provisional Army Council are the lawful Executive and Army Council respectively of the IRA and that the governmental authority delegated in the Proclamation of 1938 now resides in the Provisional Army Council and its lawful successors.[11]

The statement from Maguire probably helped to prevent the anti-abstentionists from securing the vital two-thirds majority. The two competing wings of the republican movement came to be known as the Official IRA/Official Sinn Féin and the Provisional IRA/Provisional Sinn Féin. Republicans wear an Easter lily badge every year to commemorate the 1916 Rising. When the 'Officials' produced one which used adhesive instead of the traditional pin, their branch of the movement quickly became known at street level as the 'Stickies' while the Provisionals were called simply the 'Provos'.

The Officials were led by Cathal Goulding and Tomás MacGiolla, the Provisional leaders included Ó Brádaigh, Dáithí O'Connell and Seán Mac Stiofáin. Although abstentionism was the formal reason for the split, there were other issues involved. The Goulding-MacGiolla leadership was seen as having let down the nationalist community in Belfast by failing to put preparations in place for the onslaught by loyalist mobs the previous August. Some nationalists in Belfast reportedly equated the letters IRA with 'I Ran Away'.[12]

The Ó Brádaigh-O'Connell-Mac Stiofáin faction, on the other hand, was depicted as consisting of conservative Catholics and right-wingers. Years later, reflecting on the split, Gerry Adams wrote that

'For many of the dissidents the issue was not abstentionism itself but what it had come to represent: a leadership which had led the IRA into ignominy in August [1969].'[13]

But apparently this was not the case south of the border.[14] The Officials were variously portrayed as reformists or crypto-communists who had abandoned the 'national struggle'. The Provos felt vindicated when, on 29 May 1972, the Official IRA called an indefinite ceasefire while reserving the 'right to defend any area under aggressive attack by the British military or by sectarian forces from either side'.[15]

The Provisional movement was at first dominated by southern-based individuals, but the balance of power began to shift after the extended ceasefire that took place from February to September 1975, although it continued to exist, in theory, until the following January. As part of the truce, seven 'incident centres' were set up in nationalist areas of Belfast, Derry and elsewhere. These were staffed by republicans, with a direct phone line to the Northern Ireland Office of the British Government to resolve any issue which jeopardised the ceasefire. Republican leader Máire Drumm said they were a 'power-base for Sinn Féin'. Afterwards, Ó Brádaigh said that republicans were told by the British Government that it 'wished to devise structures of disengagement from Ireland'. For his part, Secretary of State Merlyn Rees insisted this meant that, if paramilitary violence came to an end, then the British would reduce security to a 'peacetime level'.[16]

There was a fairly widespread feeling at the time, and not just in republican circles, that the British commitment to the North had become quite fragile.[17] But instead of leading to British withdrawal, the ceasefire contributed greatly to the dislodgement of Ó Brádaigh and fellow-southerners of his generation from leadership of the movement. Richard English makes the point, in his 2003 book on the IRA, that the members of the organisation had been given to understand that the British were edging towards the exit-door and, when it turned out that this wasn't the case, the southern-based leadership lost a good deal of credibility.[18]

On 30 January 1975, ten days before the truce began, there was a development which would have massive implications within a few years for the republican movement and the entire island. A committee headed by Britain's Lord Gardiner issued a report which called for an end to 'special category status' whereby persons who were imprisoned for offences arising from the Troubles were effectively treated as political prisoners, and did not have to wear prison uniforms or carry out prison work. The Report said: 'The introduction of special category status for convicted prisoners was a serious mistake... The earliest practicable opportunity should be taken to bring special category status to an end.' The British Government accepted the recommendation, which came into effect from 1 March 1976. The first prisoner to arrive under the new dispensation, Kieran Nugent, refused to wear a prison uniform. Declaring that 'they'll have to nail it to my back', he wrapped himself in a blanket instead. His example was followed by hundreds of other republicans, and ultimately led to the hunger strike of 1981 in which Bobby Sands and nine other prisoners died after refusing food as a protest against the ending of political status.[19]

There have been subtle differences between republicans on either side of the border. At the time of the Anglo-Irish Treaty of 1921 most IRA members in the North went with Michael Collins, whose personal attitude to partition was more militant than other pro-Treaty leaders and perhaps even some on the anti-Treaty side, who were focused on the issue of sovereignty and the oath of allegiance involving the British monarch, which was part of the Treaty.[20]

In later years in the South, Provo leaders like O'Connell and Ó Brádaigh were solidly in the Civil War tradition of outright opposition to the institutions that arose from the Treaty, and their attitude to Leinster House was more negative than the stance of their Northern counterparts. Ó Brádaigh had been one of four Sinn Féin candidates elected to the Dáil on an abstentionist ticket in the 1957 general election. He ran – unsuccessfully – as an abstentionist independent republican candidate in the Fermanagh-South Tyrone constituency during the Westminster election of 1966. Seán Ó Brádaigh, a brother of Ruairí's, was later quoted as saying that moves to abandon the abstentionist policy probably began in the Maze/Long Kesh prison camp, and that there was a foolish view of the southern state among northern republicans.[21]

Gerry Adams was imprisoned from July 1973 to March 1977 but, over a period of about 18 months, from August 1975, articles began to appear on a regular basis in Sinn Féin's northern paper at the time, *Republican News*, under the pen-name 'Brownie' and most, if not all, of the columns are attributed to him. They covered a fairly wide range of topics. One of the more interesting contributions appeared on 11 October 1975 under the heading 'Active abstentionism'. In an imaginary conversation, Adams addresses the traditional aim to re-establish the Second Dáil and a republican government for all of Ireland: 'But sez the man in the street, "Where the hell is this government?"... Do Republicans really believe that the ordinary people will give their allegiance to a Parliament which really doesn't exist?' The remedy he advocated was 'active abstentionism' in parallel with 'active republicanism', i.e., more political activity to go with the more robust and traditional republican methods of 'struggle'.[22]

Competing strands in the republican tradition hold an annual commemoration at different points in the year by the graveside of 1798 leader Wolfe Tone in Bodenstown, County Kildare. It is a big occasion in ceremonial and ideological terms, and Sinn Féin in particular likes to use it to set out the agenda for the coming twelve months and beyond.

Evidence of a new southern strategy emerged in a Bodenstown oration by veteran republican Jimmy Drumm (husband of Máire, who had been shot dead by loyalist paramilitaries the previous October) at the Sinn Féin commemoration in June 1977. In a speech written by Adams and Danny Morrison, Drumm said that the burden of fighting a successful 'war of liberation' could no longer be left 'exclusively on the backs of the oppressed in the Six Counties'.

He stressed that the 'isolation of socialist republicans around the armed struggle is dangerous'. There was an obvious necessity to create links 'with the mass of the Irish people' by taking 'a stand on economic issues and on the everyday struggles of people'. In this way, republicans could forge ties with the 'workers of Ireland and radical trade unionists' to generate an 'irrepressible mass movement [that] will ensure mass support for the continuing armed struggle'.[23]

Although Drumm was clearly suggesting greater involvement in social issues and the trade union movement, he did not go into the issue of elections. In fact, at that time, republicans stood aloof from the electoral process. Civil rights activist and former Westminster MP Bernadette Devlin McAliskey ran as an Independent in the European Parliament election of 1979, in which she came seventh, with a respectable 33,969 votes, despite a call by Sinn Féin for a boycott of the process.

After another spell of detention from February to September 1978, Adams became vice-president of Sinn Féin. In an oration at Bodenstown in June 1979 he advised 'constructive and thoughtful self-criticism' for the movement. He continued: 'We also require links with those oppressed by economic and social pressures. Today's circumstances and our objectives dictate the need for building an agitational struggle in the 26 Counties, an economic resistance movement, lining up republicans with other sections of the working class.'[24]

While a new political agenda to supplement the activities of the IRA was obviously in the works, there was a distinct lack of detail. It sounded like old-style left republicanism, consisting of street agitation, and tie-ups with the more militant end of the trade union movement but no clear focus.

On the paramilitary side, major changes were taking place arising from the perception that the 1975 truce was a total disaster. In their history of the Provos, Patrick Bishop and Eamonn Mallie recount how the IRA Army Council gave its approval in autumn 1976 for the establishment of a semi-autonomous Northern Command headed by Martin McGuinness. According to the authors he became chief of staff the following year, giving way to Adams after the latter was released from prison, but resuming the top IRA post when his fellow-northerner was re-arrested in 1979. In light of the subsequent cordial relationship between McGuinness and Queen Elizabeth, this would mean that he was chief of staff when the IRA killed her cousin, Lord Mountbatten, with three others in a bomb explosion on board the Shadow V leisure craft at Mullaghmore, County Sligo, on 27 August 1979.[25] The IRA's organisational changes were adopted in the context of a new, 'long war' strategy based on the belief that the British will to retain control of Northern Ireland would be worn down by a campaign of violent attrition in the classic guerrilla tradition.

Abstentionism did not apply to elections for local councils south of the border, and a call to extend this approach to councils in the North was made at the Sinn Féin ardfheis in November 1980. The idea was rejected but on the grounds of tactics and timing rather than principle.[26]

The abstentionist policy was gradually losing ground, but still looked like it would be remaining in place for a good while to come. Ironically, the clearest-ever example of republicans taking a stand on a basic principle incidentally served to speed-up the process. The episode in question was, of course, the 1981 hunger strike in the H-Blocks at the Maze/Long Kesh prison in which ten republicans, with an average age of twenty-five, died to assert the principle that they were freedom-fighters and not criminals.

The leader of the hunger strike, Bobby Sands, began his fast on 1 March 1981, five years to the day since the ending of 'special category' status. The arrangement was that others should begin to refuse food at staggered intervals in order to maximise the publicity and propaganda outcome. Four days later, on 5 March, nationalist MP for Fermanagh-South Tyrone, Frank Maguire, died of a heart attack at the age of fifty-one years. Three weeks later , by which time three other prisoners had joined the hunger strike, Sinn Féin announced that Sands would contest the resulting by-election, scheduled for 9 April.

Others in the nationalist/republican camp stood aside, and Sands went forward under the label of 'Anti-H-Block/Armagh Political Prisoner' (female republicans were held in Armagh). The initiative succeeded beyond the wildest dreams of the republicans. Sands made world headlines when he won by 1,446 votes over unionist candidate Harry West. British Prime Minister Margaret Thatcher had left for a visit to India, and was at a meeting in New Delhi with her counterpart Indira Gandhi, who is reported to have sarcastically commented that it must be delightful to see the people expressing their views by non-violent means.[27] Meanwhile, protesters on behalf of the hunger strikers acquired a new slogan: 'Bobby Sands – MP!'

Sands died on 5 May 1981, and British law was changed to prevent other prisoners from standing. The subsequent by-election was won by Sands's election agent Owen Carron who was a member of Sinn Féin, but stood as an 'Anti-H-Block Proxy Political Prisoner'. It was later claimed by Richard O'Rawe, H-Block prisoner and public relations officer for the hunger strikers, that an offer to settle the dispute from the British was rejected in order to ensure Carron's electoral success. This claim has, however, been sharply rejected by the Sinn Féin leadership.[28] According to an internal British memo, Sands himself refused to comply with a personal message from Pope John Paul II instructing him to call off his fast.[29] His funeral in Belfast was attended by an estimated 100,000 people, and the mood among nationalists throughout the island was compared to the reaction provoked by the executions of the 1916 leaders.

There was a general election in the South on 11 June in which two H-Block prisoners, Kieran Doherty and Paddy Agnew, were elected to the Dáil. Neither took his seat, and Doherty died on hunger strike on 2 August, aged twenty-five years. Along with other anti-H-Block candidates, they contributed, at the time, to the removal from office of Charles Haughey and Fianna Fáil. A fateful year culminated in a highly dramatic and effective intervention at the Sinn Féin ardfheis in November 1981. The party's director of publicity, who had been a spokesman for Bobby Sands and chief organiser of his by-election campaign, Danny Morrison, highlighted the role that elections could play in addition to the use of the assault rifle which had become symbolic of the IRA campaign: 'Who here really believes we can win the war through the ballot-box? But will anyone here object if, with a ballot-paper in one hand and the Armalite in the other, we take power in Ireland?'[30]

In an unprecedented development, Sinn Féin took part in elections to the proposed new Northern Ireland Assembly in October 1982, and won five of the 18 seats with 10.1 per cent of the valid poll. The successful candidates included Adams and McGuinness, but Sinn Féin refused to take their seats. In March 1983, a Sinn Féin candidate won a district council by-election in Omagh – the first of its kind contested by the party for almost fifty years. But the biggest success of all was in the UK general election of 9 June 1983, when Gerry Adams became the new abstentionist MP for West Belfast, beating the SDLP's Joe Hendron and sitting MP Gerry Fitt (Independent). The tide was with Adams, who replaced Ó Brádaigh as president of Sinn Féin the following November. The latter had stepped down from the position in protest at the dropping of the Éire Nua (New Ireland) policy, which envisaged a regional parliament for a nine-county Ulster, in a federal united Ireland. This was seen by critics as a vehicle for continued unionist domination. The new MP and Sinn Féin chief had a narrow escape on 14 March 1984, when he was shot several times in a loyalist paramilitary attack, along with three other Sinn Féin members, while they were driving back from a court appearance. There was some disappointment for Sinn Féin when Danny Morrison finished almost 60,000 votes behind John Hume in the June 1984 European Parliament elections, but the SDLP leader was unbeatable among nationalist voters.

Margaret Thatcher came close to death in a bomb explosion that killed five people at the hotel she was staying in for the Tory conference at Brighton in October 1984. Morrison said in the

Observer: 'If that bomb had killed the British Cabinet, examine then what would have happened. There would have been a rethink within British political circles, and it probably would have led to a British withdrawal in a much shorter period. It would have been unique in British constitutional history, apart maybe from Guy Fawkes.'[31]

District council elections were held across the North in May 1985, and first-timers Sinn Féin won 59 seats compared to 102 for the SDLP. The growing political involvement of Sinn Féin while the IRA campaign still continued at a very violent level was causing serious concern among members of the political establishment in Dublin and London, who found the prospect of the republicans overtaking the moderate SDLP distinctly unappetising. It was one of the factors that led to the Anglo-Irish Agreement of 1985, which greatly upset unionists as it gave the Irish Government a say in the administration of Northern Ireland.

The problem for republicans considering change, however, was that dropping the policy of abstentionism would require amending the constitutions of both the IRA and Sinn Féin, in that order, and these could only be brought about by a two-thirds majority. Formally they were separate and distinct organisations, but without advance approval from the IRA no change in Sinn Féin policy would be possible. If there was IRA consent to the change in advance then the Sinn Féin ardfheis motion was virtually certain to go through.

An IRA statement was issued on 14 October 1986, and was carried in full on the front page of *An Phoblacht* two days later. It revealed that, 'IRA delegates from all over Ireland secretly met in a General Army Convention for the first time in 16 years... Several sections of the Constitution of Óglaigh na hÉireann were amended and, by more than the required two-thirds majority, the delegates passed two particular resolutions. The first removed the ban on Volunteers discussing or advocating the taking of parliamentary seats. The second removed the ban on supporting successful republican candidates who take their seats in Leinster House.'[32]

As he had done back in 1969, Ó Brádaigh called to see Tom

Maguire, now aged ninety-four, who issued another statement: 'I do not recognise the legitimacy of any Army Council... which lends support to any person or organisation styling itself as Sinn Féin and prepared to enter the partition parliament of Leinster House.'[33] The lines were drawn for an impassioned debate at the Sinn Féin ardfheis, at the Mansion House in Dublin on 2 November, when Motion 162 from the Ardchomhairle called for an end to abstention from Leinster House. Belfast veteran Joe Cahill, who had been sentenced to death in the 1940s after an IRA unit shot and killed Constable Patrick Murphy, a father of nine children, said in support of the motion: 'The dedication and commitment which brought me to the foot of the scaffold in 1942 is the same in my heart today as it was then, and will be until the day I draw my last breath.'[34]

With equal passion on the other side of the argument, Ó Brádaigh pleaded: 'In God's name, don't let it come about that... those in Leinster House who have done everything, the firing squad, the prison cells, the internment camps, the hunger strike, the lot, and weren't able to break this movement, that they can come out and say "at last we have them toeing the line"... Never, that's what I say to you, never.'[35] A key intervention was made in the debate by Martin McGuinness, seen as the very personification of the republican struggle at the time. He said:

> I can give a commitment on behalf of the leadership that we have absolutely no intention of going to Westminster or Stormont... I reject the notion that entering Leinster House would mean an end to Sinn Féin's unapologetic support for the right of Irish people to oppose in arms the British forces of occupation... Our position is clear and it will never, never, never change. The war against British rule must continue until freedom is achieved. But we are not at war with the government of the 26 Counties — the reality of this fact must be recognised by us all. And, in accepting this reality, we must also

accept that after sixty-five years of republican struggle, republican agitation, republican sacrifice and republican rhetoric, we have failed to convince a majority in the 26 counties that the republican movement has any relevance to them. By ignoring reality we remain alone and isolated on the high altar of abstentionism, divorced from the people of the 26 counties and easily dealt with by those who wish to defeat us... If you allow yourself to be led out of this hall today, the only place you're going – is home. You will be walking away from the struggle. Don't go my friends. We will lead you to the republic.[36]

After five hours of debate, the motion was approved by 429 votes to 161. Opponents of the move had made preparations in advance to set up an alternative political party. When the result of the vote was given, Ó Brádaigh, O'Connell and about 100 supporters left for the West County Hotel on the outskirts of Dublin, where a new organisation was announced: calling itself Republican Sinn Féin. There were about 130 people in attendance, and the *Sunday Times* called it the 'Night of the Golden Oldies'. In due course, a new paramilitary body with a very similar outlook came on the scene. Known as the Continuity IRA, their level of activity never compared with that of the Provos.[37] There was also a left-wing breakaway called the League of Communist Republicans (LCR), which was founded by a number of prisoners in the Maze/Long Kesh. It had echoes of the political approach adopted by the 1934 Republican Congress. The LCR remained active for about five years. In broad terms, though, as Martyn Frampton points out in his study of Sinn Féin's political strategy, Adams and McGuinness had retained a very high level of unity compared with previous breakaways and the departure of the traditionalists and the far left meant that the party leadership had considerable flexibility for future initiatives.[38]

Meanwhile, the Provisional IRA welcomed the ardfheis decision. Reflecting the different attitude of most of the northern and younger members of the movement on the issue of republican legitimacy, the statement said: 'To suggest that the IRA is not legitimate because of the decision it has taken on abstentionism is ridiculous. The IRA predates the Second Dáil and the First Dáil. Its constitution is a military constitution, and our legitimacy stems from organised popular resistance to British rule in Ireland, a tradition which was reinforced in 1916, by the Fenians, by the Young Irelanders, by the United Irishmen.'[39]

The example of the Scottish nationalists in recent times strongly suggests that participation in Westminster does not hinder – and may even help to facilitate – the drive for independence. Analysing the traditional Irish republican mindset, Agnès Maillot describes how abstentionism and armed resistance started out as strategies for achieving the twin aims of full independence and reunification of the national territory. With the passage of time, these strategies developed into basic principles.[40] Sinn Féin has set aside support for armed resistance, and dropped abstentionism towards Leinster House and a reformed Stormont. It will be interesting to watch its approach to participation within the House of Commons in the coming years if the slender majority of the Tories starts to disappear, and/or there is some movement on the stipulation that MPs must take an oath to the British monarch. Fianna Fáil leader Eamon de Valera showed how an obstacle of that nature can be dealt with if circumstances so required.[41]

In securing Sinn Féin consent to enter the 'Free State' Dáil, Adams and McGuinness succeeded where De Valera had failed, though the latter facilitated their achievement by getting rid of the Treaty's oath of allegiance involving the British monarch. There was, however, a long road to travel before this fundamental change of policy began to pay dividends for Sinn Féin in terms of parliamentary representation. It took another twenty-five years before the party had sufficient numbers in the Dáil to be seen as a serious threat to the political establishment.

4. FROM REBEL TO RULER - MARTIN McGUINNESS

EVERYONE INVOLVED IN THE Northern Ireland peace process has come a long way, but few have travelled farther than Martin McGuinness. He has gone from being a leader of the Irish Republican Army to the post of Deputy First Minister in a power-sharing administration – which is in crisis as we go to press – and developing a special rapport with Britain's Queen Elizabeth.

His name first drew public attention in late 1969. It was just over a year since the epoch-making incident where demonstrators for civil rights were beaten off the streets of Derry (also known as Londonderry), by the Royal Ulster Constabulary (RUC). Television footage of the attack aroused huge anger among nationalists throughout the island, and a conflict began that would take thirty years to resolve – although there are many issues still to be tackled.

Twelve months later, on 25 October 1969, a crowd of about 200 protesting nationalists were being moved along Derry's Strand Road by British troops. RUC Head Constable E. Campbell testified later that four or five youths were shouting abusive remarks. Among them was Martin McGuinness from Elmwood Street. Soldiers were ordered over the crowd-control barrier, and he was arrested. The nineteen-year-old was brought before Resident Magistrate John Sheerer the following Monday. R.H.C. O'Doherty, acting for McGuinness, told the court that, 'In the heat of the moment [*the*] defendant made some abusive remarks across the barrier. He apologised to the soldiers for anything he had said.' The defendant was fined £50 for disorderly behaviour and the *Irish Times* report added: 'The Resident Magistrate accepted the defendant's plea that he was not part of a riotous crowd but said his conduct was a type of disorderly behaviour which could not be condoned. He was bound over for two years.'[1]

Within two years, Martin McGuinness had gone from being a quiet apprentice butcher to a key paramilitary leader, causing havoc for the British and unionist authorities. The name surfaces again in the *Irish Times* of 10 April 1972, in a front-page report on a public meeting called by the Provisional IRA in the Brandywell, part of what was then a self-declared autonomous nationalist area known as 'Free Derry'. Henry Kelly wrote: 'Mr Martin McGuinness, understood to be leader of the Provisionals in Derry, said: "We are fighting on. We are not stopping until we get a united Ireland."[2] Later in the month, the paper published a profile by Nell McCafferty of 'the boy who rules Free Derry' and who, at that stage, had something like rock-star status with elements of the international media.[3] But the following January, McGuinness was in front of a court in Dublin which jailed him for six months on a charge of IRA membership. A year later, also in the Republic of Ireland jurisdiction, he was sentenced to a further twelve months on the same charge as well as for refusing to give an account of his movements.

In a Hollywood script about the Provos, Gerry Adams would be Butch Cassidy, with Martin McGuinness in the part of the Sundance Kid. The relationship between the characters played by Paul Newman and Robert Redford was epitomised in the Kid's remark at one stage: 'You just keep thinkin', Butch. That's what you're good at.' At the same time, it would be a grave error to underestimate the

Derryman's capacity as a strategist or, indeed, to downplay Adams's role at the cutting edge of the IRA campaign. McGuinness's paramilitary past became a hot issue when he ran in the Irish presidential election in 2011 – this is covered in Chapter Six. Previously, in a draft submission on 1 May 2001 to the Saville Inquiry into the events of Bloody Sunday in Derry in 1972 when British paratroopers killed thirteen people at a civil rights march (another victim died four-and-a-half months later), he confirmed that he was the IRA's second-in-command in the city at the time. At a press conference in Belfast on 2 May 2001 he acknowledged his membership in person. While he has given little else away about his guerrilla years, he is generally believed to have been a key figure in the prosecution of the Provo campaign from the early 1970s to the mid-1990s. When he was being convicted of IRA membership by the Special Criminal Court in 1973, McGuinness said, in an unsworn statement, that he had been an officer in the Derry Brigade for over two years.

Could this be the same Martin McGuinness, advocate of peace and cross-community power-sharing, that I am just about to interview at Stormont Castle for this book? The location is awash with symbolism. It used to be the official residence of the first Prime Minister of Northern Ireland, Sir James Craig (1871-1940). The man who declared that, 'We are a Protestant Parliament and a Protestant State' (admittedly in response to similar Catholic boasts about the other State on the island), must be turning in his grave.[4]

In more recent times, it was used as an office by the Secretary of State for Northern Ireland, but now Stormont Castle is home to the Northern Ireland Executive, which leads the power-sharing administration, and the Office of the First Minister and Deputy First Minister. A previous IRA leader who later took up what he called a 'slightly constitutional' position was there before McGuinness. I refer to the historic visit by Seán Lemass, then head of government in Dublin, who met the Northern Ireland Prime Minister Terence O'Neill, at Stormont Castle on 14 January 1965. Lemass fought in the General Post Office, headquarters of the Easter Rising in 1916. He took part in the operation ordered by Michael Collins on Dublin's 'Bloody Sunday' in November 1920 when fourteen suspected British agents were shot dead and was also a member of the anti-Treaty IRA in the Civil War that erupted after the Anglo-Irish Treaty of 1921. In recent years, Lemass has been lionised in Irish public opinion for his subsequent role in government.

A short distance away, Parliament Buildings stand astride Stormont Hill. Opened in 1932, their architecture and location always seem like a massive gesture of defiance against those who wished to see those six northern counties as part of an independent State. That feeling is accentuated by the larger-than-life statue of Edward Carson as you approach the place. Even republicans would have to agree it is an imposing piece of work, with the subject in combative oratorical pose. The Dublin-born barrister who brought down playwright Oscar Wilde also blocked plans for a thirty-two-county Home Rule administration in Ireland.

As I make my way up a steep incline through a shower of rain, old TV footage comes to mind of the last Prime Minister of Northern Ireland, Brian Faulkner, addressing a unionist crowd from a balcony in 1972 after the Stormont parliament was abolished and replaced with direct rule from London.

But I am not going to Parliament Buildings today. At the Carson statue I turn right, remembering that I have to go to Stormont Castle, where the power-sharing ministers meet, and not the similarly-named Stormont House, where British Secretary of State Theresa Villiers has her office.

McGuinness is there to greet me: the nineteen-year-old who yelled at British squaddies in October '69 has become a soft-spoken man in his mid-sixties. The teenager who was bound to the peace is now a self-proclaimed peacemaker.

The walls of his bright, spacious office are adorned with photographs of the Deputy First Minister, sometimes accompanied by First Minister Peter Robinson of the Democratic Unionist Party

(DUP), who has stepped aside as we go to press. There are pictures with President Obama and with his predecessor, George W. Bush. One I wasn't expecting features Vladimir Putin, who was attending the summit of G8 countries at Enniskillen in June 2013. The manner in which he was greeted gave the Russian president a crash-course in Irish politics. McGuinness recalls: 'I said, "Welcome to Ireland" and Peter said, "Welcome to Northern Ireland".' The most telling photo of the lot shows McGuinness with the Reverend Ian Paisley when the latter stepped down as First Minister on 5 June 2008. The Derryman is presenting his power-sharing partner with two framed poems. One contains the celebrated lines on the confluence of hope and history by Nobel laureate Seamus Heaney (1939-2013) which became the anthem of the peace process. The other is a poem by McGuinness himself.[5] I knew the pair had worked well together but had not fully realised the genuine affection that existed, certainly on the Deputy's side as he talks about 'Ian'. I expected him to refer to his former colleague as 'Dr Paisley', rather than by his first name. He tells me with obvious delight:

> When Ian stood down as First Minister in 2008, I asked Seamus Heaney would he hand-write the 'Hope and History' poem. He wrote it on the most beautiful parchment paper you've ever seen, and we got it framed. And I also wrote a poem about Native American Indians and disappearing sea-trout on the west coast of Ireland. I won't explain the connection! But I presented him with the two. That's my one there, that's Seamus's. So about two months later, Ian was looking to talk to me about something... They had given Ian a small office and sitting-room on the first floor up at Parliament Buildings... and, up on the wall, were the two poems side-by-side.

Now, today isn't just any old day for this interview. Exactly eight years before, on 26 March 2007, I was in Parliament Buildings with other reporters when, without any forewarning, a great drama unfolded. Paisley, the firebrand cleric – 'whose middle name was never', as I wrote at the time – finally came on board in the peace process. Sitting at the same table as Gerry Adams, he proclaimed his intention to lead the DUP into a power-sharing administration with Sinn Féin. That was also the first day McGuinness had a conversation of any kind with Paisley, a fact I had gleaned in my advance research for the interview. The Deputy First Minister is pleasantly surprised to be reminded of the anniversary. 'How come I never remembered that?' he mused, to which I replied: 'You're not doing a Google search on yourself.'

Paisley became First Minister and McGuinness took the Deputy's post on a day full of high emotion six weeks later, when the attendance included British Prime Minister Tony Blair, Taoiseach Bertie Ahern, former taoiseach Albert Reynolds, Senator Edward Kennedy – a major backer of the peace process – and his sister, former US ambassador to Ireland, Jean Kennedy Smith. McGuinness himself had the idea of inviting a group of special needs adults called *The Sky's the Limit* to mime opera and ballads for the occasion, and this was eagerly agreed by Paisley.

Such was the high good humour of Paisley and McGuinness on the day that they were promptly dubbed 'The Chuckle Brothers'. I have been told by well-informed sources that, as soon as they started in their new jobs – and on Paisley's initiative – the pair requested NI Secretary of State Peter Hain to vacate Stormont Castle, so that they could take it over. McGuinness jocosely suggested the letter should be addressed to 'The Occupier' but this was not taken up, although Paisley was amused when his new partner in office pointed out to him: 'Your first act as First Minister is to write a "Brits Out" letter.' Mr Hain and his officials were gone within four days.[6]

Pressing him on the issue, I say that obviously the public relationship with Paisley was very amicable, but was it really as good as that behind the scenes? He replies:

It was remarkable. From the first minute we sat down and Ian Paisley said those immortal words to me: 'Martin, we can rule ourselves. We don't need these people coming over from England telling us what to do'. And for me that was common ground that both of us could stand on. Throughout that year that he was First Minister, even though he was elderly, we had a very civilised and cordial working relationship with each other. Not alone that, we actually became friends. It was a friendship that endured even after he left. Once Ian made the decision to come into government – as with most of the things that he did in the past – then he threw himself heart and soul into it, such as his opposition to the Good Friday Agreement and all of his past history. I think there was some criticism of what I said when he died, when I described him as a friend. But there was no greater friend of the peace process, once he decided to come into the process in a wholehearted, inclusive way – both Eileen and Ian Paisley – and I think she was as important as Ian was in all of that. And then he asked me to come to the house some months before he died and I spent almost two hours with Eileen and him. He was looking forward to opening up a library in East Belfast. He had 50,000 books and he wanted me to attend the opening of it in the spring of this year. But unfortunately he died before that. I think it was on a Friday, and I went to the house on the Saturday and spent an hour with the family. We had a very close relationship and it is a very close relationship that has continued on with Eileen. And indeed the rest of the family.

The later Robinson-McGuinness partnership was not so obviously jovial and some wag called them 'The Brothers Grimm'. I ask McGuinness if it has been a purely business and political relationship, or are they on friendly terms personally?

> Well we have disagreements about different matters, and there's nothing unusual about that in a coalition government. Ideologically, we are different parties, different people, but we are always civilised. We have never personally fallen out. There is not a day that I am here that I don't meet with Peter Robinson. It's not like what we had with Seamus Mallon and David Trimble where they didn't speak to each other for weeks on end. I was part of that administration way back from December 1999 until October 2002, where personal relationships were very bad.[7] That's never happened with Peter and myself . . . When Ian had to stand down as leader of the DUP and First Minister, there were people in the DUP telling me the reason that had to happen was because there were [other] people within the DUP who didn't like the friendly relationship between Ian Paisley and myself. And that then suggested to me that the public relationship, if you like, with Peter, would be different, but privately he and I have a working relationship, we're civilised and cordial to each other, there's never been a day when we don't speak.

Clearly relations had improved somewhat since 8 May 2001 when, under parliamentary privilege at Stormont, Robinson quoted what he said was a security document sent to his house which named McGuinness and others, including Gerry Adams, as members of the IRA Army Council. The week prior to the interview I had been in Parliament Buildings, taking the political temperature. In truth, I was in two minds about going there because so little happened that was considered newsworthy outside the North. But no sooner had I set foot in the place than all hell broke loose. Although there had not been the slightest hint of it at the party's ardfheis, which took place the previous weekend in Derry, suddenly Sinn Féin called a halt to the implementation of the Stormont House Agreement that covered a whole range of issues and was concluded among the main Northern parties and the British and Irish governments, just before Christmas.

The row was over changes to the welfare system. Sinn Féin claimed their partners in government had pulled a fast one when finalising the figures. The DUP stoutly insisted that this was not the case and that the other party was playing politics.

Inevitably it is a question I raise with the Deputy First Minister. He says it is a very complex matter but that discussions are taking place with the DUP and he is hopeful of a successful outcome. When I point out that Sinn Féin's critics are suggesting it is all a deliberate distraction from other issues of the day, he shows a flash of anger: 'I regard that as an insult, that's to suggest that we in Sinn Féin don't care about children with disabilities, adults with severe disabilities, the long-term sick, or families with children.'

The former IRA commander invokes India's legendary pacifist leader, when he says the issue goes 'right to the heart of what Gandhi once said: any government is judged on the basis of how they support the most vulnerable, marginalised, disabled, within society'. (What Gandhi actually said was that, 'A nation's greatness is measured by how it treats its weakest members' – but Martin McGuinness does not regard himself as part of any British nation.)

Donning my fiscally-responsible hat, I ask him where will the extra money be found to finance the welfare measures Sinn Féin is seeking? He replies:

> We never suggested that the British were going to give extra money for supporting people who were going to be detrimentally affected by welfare [changes]. What we have always said is that, if we have to deal with this, then we will have to find it within our own resources. We totally disagree with the decisions that the British Government have taken, but they have made it

abundantly clear that they are not going to provide any extra money for welfare. And that essentially means we have a duty and a responsibility to try and find the money to support those people on welfare, from within our own resources.

It soon becomes very clear that the Deputy First Minister is no great fan of David Cameron or the government he is leading at the time of our interview. He feels the Tory-led administration in London is out of tune with the peace process:

> As far as I can see, this British government is intent on crucifying this Executive. They don't get it. They don't get the connection between a society that has emerged from conflict, that needed benefits, economically, from the fruits of peace. And that's been very dismaying, for me anyway. And of course all of this started shortly after Ian Paisley and I took power in 2007. It's been a steady agenda of austerity from this Tory administration and I have raised this at every meeting with David Cameron, both here and, more importantly, in Downing Street.

The present writer thought he had seen the Deputy First Minister quoted as saying he would like to see Labour winning the general election due on 7 May 2015, but McGuinness said this was not correct: 'No, what I am quoted as saying is that it's my view that this Executive will be in an even worse position if the Tories are re-elected in the aftermath of the next election in a few weeks' time.'

I express surprise at his view of Cameron as being somewhat insensitive to the needs of the peace process and a society emerging from conflict, given the way the prime minister apologised for Bloody Sunday. McGuinness replies: 'Up until the autumn of last year I had met with the President of United States more often than I had met with David Cameron.'

I assume, wrongly, that he has different presidents in mind, but in fact he is referring only to President Obama. He believes Labour has a better understanding of the situation: 'I have had conversations with the Labour Party. The Labour Party have a stake in what happened here. They were very much part of the good history of the peace process.' (Subsequent to our interview, McGuinness was part of a Sinn Féin delegation that met Mr Cameron in Westminster, on 21 July 2015, to discuss the stand-off over welfare issues.)

McGuinness is eight years in the job now and it's a good seventy-five miles, or 120 kilometres, from Stormont to Derry, but he doesn't stay over in Belfast: 'I go home every night. I believe there is no bed like your own bed. I have been urged over the years to get an apartment in Belfast and I have resisted. Even if I am in Dublin at midnight, I'll still go home. You can be away too often from your own family and I am very family-orientated.'

So what's a typical day, then, for a Deputy First Minister (Sinn Féin prefers to call him 'Joint First Minister' and he has used that term himself also, although it's not a term Paisley or Robinson have been keen on)? 'Today wasn't typical,' he says, 'I was up at five o'clock. But I am normally up at six o'clock and in Belfast for nine o'clock. It takes two hours to get here in the morning from Derry and then I have a full schedule of events all day. Some days you'll get home about half-seven/eight o'clock. Other times...last Friday night I was here till midnight with Peter.' But most nights he gets home 'around nine o'clock'.

He was Minister for Education from 1999 until the Northern Ireland Assembly was suspended in 2002. In the following year's elections, the DUP and Sinn Féin became the two largest parties, ahead of the Ulster Unionist Party and the moderate nationalist Social Democratic and Labour Party (SDLP) and many observers thought there would never be power-sharing again. McGuinness recalls a meeting with the British Prime Minister of the day to discuss the situation:

Tony Blair was at his wit's end. There were just four of us in the room – Tony and [Downing Street chief of staff] Jonathan Powell, Gerry Adams and myself – and Tony started to speak about how his strategy would be about trying to get the Ulster Unionists back into lead position within unionism. About seven minutes in, I stopped him and I said: 'Tony, hold on a minute. It's not going to happen. The DUP are going to be the lead party within unionism for the foreseeable future. What we have to do is get the DUP into government with Sinn Féin.' And Tony said: 'Well, Martin, Ian Paisley will never share power with you.' And I said: 'Well, I don't believe that. I believe if we work together we can make it happen.' And of course it took a couple of years, but it did happen, in 2007. I had an advantage on Tony because I was obviously speaking to people who were close to the DUP, and I had a sense that it was do-able. I thought it was a strategy that was well worth pursuing and, thankfully, Tony did pursue it, and it came off.

Reporters are always curious about other people's contacts, and the concept of a former IRA leader having a better grasp of DUP strategy than the British PM is an intriguing one. I ask him: 'Would they be inside the DUP?' He replies: 'No, people who were close to the DUP and I knew were solidly representing the thought processes that were going on within the higher echelons of the DUP.'[8]

Unless the Assembly is dissolved earlier because of inter-party differences, the next elections to that body are on 5 May 2016 and I ask McGuinness if he thinks Sinn Féin could end up then as the biggest party in the North? 'I am never presumptuous about what the electorate will do. When you look at the last European election and the local government elections, Sinn Féin emerged as the largest party. The last Westminster election, we were the largest party, so I think it is achievable that Sinn Féin will become the largest party in the North at the next Assembly elections. And as always, if that turns out to be the case, we will use that mandate wisely.'

Sinn Féin had the highest number of votes in the 2014 local elections and 2010 Westminster elections in the North but the DUP won more seats. McGuinness pooh-poohs the suggestion that, if Sinn Féin became the largest party in the Assembly, this could set off a wave of panic among unionists: 'If Sinn Féin were to emerge as the largest party, some unionists mightn't like it but I don't think that it would represent anything even remotely approaching instability of any kind. The fact that we have signed up for the Good Friday Agreement and the St Andrews Agreement, the Hillsborough Agreement and the Stormont House Agreement, is a very clear indicator that we as Irish republicans want to move forward to the achievement of our primary political objective, which is the reunification of Ireland by purely peaceful and democratic means.'

He refers to 'our community', which traditionally in Northern Ireland consists exclusively of Catholics or Protestants, depending on which side the politician in question originated. But McGuinness makes clear he is referring to people of both religions: 'All of our community, yes.'

On my way in I had noticed one of his staff reading that morning's *Irish Times*, which carried an opinion poll showing Sinn Féin at 24 per cent, the same as Fine Gael and ahead of both Fianna Fáil, on 17 per cent, and Labour, on 7 per cent. McGuinness says this hasn't come about by chance: 'It wasn't something that happened by a fluke or by accident. There was a very clear plan that getting Gerry Adams as our leader into Leinster House, supported by very competent and committed and dedicated TDs, would make an impact on the electorate, and that has come to pass. So none of this is a surprise to me.'

So what does he think is the outlook for Sinn Féin in the South? If I called it 'the Republic' he would doubtless correct me, as Sinn Féin people don't believe the Republic has yet been achieved. Does he ever see them in government there, and under what terms?

'Obviously what I want to see is Sinn Féin emerging as the largest party in the South. In that context then we can dictate terms in relation to the formation of a new government. Symbolically speaking, for Sinn Féin to be the largest party in the South and the largest party in the North would be huge, particularly as we approach the 100th anniversary of 1916.'

Given that Sinn Féin has been under sustained attack from its opponents and critics over such issues as allegations of sexual abuse by IRA members and the killing of Jean McConville, is he surprised that the party's showing is so strong in this poll? 'The difficulty that our political opponents have in terms of their virulent anti-Sinn Féin agenda is that we are dealing with a very intelligent electorate, people who can see through an awful lot of the grandstanding that takes place.'

He doesn't expect any let-up in the political and media barrage: 'As the general election comes closer, the attacks and the demonisation of Sinn Féin will continue. But our opponents will have to calculate whether or not these attacks are, in fact, counter-productive because of the ability and the intelligence of the electorate to see through their grandstanding.'

Given the imminence of the British general election and some speculation that small parties could hold the balance of power, I ask him if abstentionism will always be the Sinn Féin policy. After all, the Scottish Nationalists seem to be using Westminster to promote independence, so why can't Sinn Féin do the same?

> Well, the big difference is that there are far more MPs elected in Scotland than there are in the North of Ireland, and anybody who harbours the notion that any of the parties in the North of Ireland are going to be kingmakers in relation to the next British Government is living in cloud cuckoo land...We are elected on the basis of our abstentionism because they see us as principled republicans who are not prepared to

countenance attending a parliament in London, which in many ways doesn't heed or even take part in many of the debates in relation to the North of Ireland. The real power now rests here, in terms of health and education and so forth. What we need to change is the British Government's attitude towards how to deal with our block grant.

He quotes an audience member on a TV discussion programme who said that four of the five main parties in the North had a policy of taking their seats at Westminster but the only one to get extra money out of the British Government in recent months was Sinn Féin. 'I think he was spot-on,' says McGuinness, adding that this resulted from 'the very strong stand that we took mobilising the other parties through the Stormont House Agreement'.

Based on what he has just said, I ask him if abstentionism was a matter of principle or whether it was just that a party from Northern Ireland, where only eighteen MPs are returned, will never have enough seats to exert real influence?

Well, it is quite clear, in the constituencies from which we gain greatest support, that people vote for us because we are an abstentionist party and because they respect the role that we have played within political life, in terms of the peace process, social justice and so forth. So, they look at politicians who attend Westminster...and they don't see them being in a position to change the British government's agenda in relation to the social and economic circumstances that affect them. I don't know how many photographs I have seen of Northern MPs sitting with their heads down, sleeping.

In describing their different roles in the republican movement, I have often said that Gerry Adams is the architect and Martin McGuinness is the engineer. I ask McGuinness how come he gets on so well with Adams? In a movement where splits are not uncommon, how have they sustained such a cordial working relationship over so many decades? He replies: 'An awful lot of other parties are afflicted by people at that level who want to be the boss. I have never harboured any inclination whatsoever to be President of Sinn Féin.'

So when did they first come across each other? 'I think we first met when we were part of that delegation that went to London in 1972, when we travelled by helicopter from Derry to the military base at Aldergrove airport [*outside Belfast*].'

They were flown from there across the Irish Sea to a secret meeting which took place at Cheyne Walk in London's Chelsea district on 7 July 1972, between leaders of the Provisional wing of the republican movement and the Secretary of State for Northern Ireland, William Whitelaw. The Provo delegation was led by Chief of Staff Seán Mac Stiofáin and other members included Daithí Ó Connell, Ivor Bell and Seamus Twomey, as well as legal adviser Myles Shevlin. The IRA had called a ceasefire and, in the course of the meeting, Mac Stiofáin demanded a British declaration of intent to withdraw its forces from the North within three years and allow the population of the entire island to decide the future of Ireland. Whitelaw responded that, under statute, his government could only change the status of Northern Ireland with the consent of a majority there.[9] The meeting concluded, the delegation went back home and the ceasefire broke down shortly afterwards. For McGuinness, who had just turned twenty-two, it was a surreal experience: 'It was unbelievable and to be met then at RAF Benson on the far side by two limousines to bring us to Cheyne Walk. It was like something out of a movie.'

He highlights the joint efforts of Adams and himself for peace in the past twenty-five years: 'If you want to know who was the key architect of this peace process, then undoubtedly it was Gerry Adams, and Father Alec Reid and, of course, John Hume's contribution also...when you look at the risks that have been taken, when you look at the leadership that he [*Adams*] has provided, when you look at the challenges and the pain and the difficulty that is always associated with a peace process, then what has happened in terms of the Republican contribution to this has been truly remarkable, and Gerry Adams is a truly remarkable leader.'

McGuinness is philosophical about the fact that his party president comes in for heavy and sustained criticism: 'He sure does and he gets it mostly from people who are opposed to Sinn Féin. I am never under any illusions: you expect criticism from other political parties who will go to any depths to criticise Gerry. There will also be some people within the media, not everybody, who are supporters of these parties, even though they describe themselves as impartial journalists, and they are more than willing to write articles every now and again which are critical of Gerry Adams, because they see him as a danger to the status quo.'

When Mary McAleese was coming to the end of her second term as President of Ireland, there was an election for her successor and McGuinness became the Sinn Féin candidate. Why did he do it: hadn't he got enough on his plate as Deputy First Minister? Looking back on it now, how did he feel about the campaign - did he enjoy it?

> Well, it was an incredible experience. I enjoyed travelling through every one of Ireland's 32 counties and meeting some very incredible and wonderful people who were very supportive of my campaign. I was never under any illusions about what I was up against...One of the reasons I took the decision to stand was because I was from the North. There was an Irish presidential election and I was effectively saying, on behalf of nationalists and republicans in the North, that we're as entitled to be here as anybody else – whether or not we get elected will be a matter for the democratically-expressed wishes of the people of Ireland.

Then, of course, there was the notorious episode in the last televised debate between candidates on RTÉ's *Frontline* programme. Independent Seán Gallagher was ahead in most of the polls but got badly tripped-up by a false tweet to the programme which was incorrectly attributed to an official 'McGuinness for President' account. In the end, Labour candidate Michael D. Higgins won the election and McGuinness came third, ahead of the Fine Gael candidate. He comments:

> The Twitter thing had absolutely nothing to do with me whatsoever. I challenged Seán Gallagher in relation to the fundraising activities that he was involved in. Seán I saw, basically, as a front for Fianna Fáil, a party that had plunged the South into economic misery, and I thought it was quite legitimate to challenge him. Unbeknownst to me, then somebody on a false Twitter account put up a message that had absolutely nothing to do with me and nothing to do with Sinn Féin, which effectively then decided the outcome of the presidential election.

But he is happy enough with the result: 'We ended up with a good president'. And as well as having a warm regard for Michael D. Higgins, the former IRA leader famously also regards the British head of state quite highly. Reporting on his first encounter with Queen Elizabeth at Belfast's Lyric Theatre in Belfast in June 2012, I wrote: 'All is changed, changed utterly, and the Provisional republicans have irrevocably gone from the clenched fist to the open hand.'

They shook hands, not once, but twice. Given that the IRA killed Prince Philip's uncle, Lord Mountbatten in 1979 – McGuinness is said to have been chief of staff at the time although he told the Saville Inquiry that he 'left the IRA in the early part of the 1970s' – there was speculation that the Queen's husband might not shake hands, but he did.[10] On the way out, McGuinness declared: 'I'm still a republican'.[11] The meeting with the Queen angered hardline dissident republicans, and he was later told by police that the Continuity IRA considered an attack on him, using a rocket launcher.[12]

Almost two years after the handshake, on 8 April 2014, McGuinness made world headlines when he stood for a toast to the British monarch as an orchestra played *God Save the Queen*. The occasion was a banquet at Windsor Castle which was part of the historic state visit to Britain by President Higgins. The following June, the former IRA leader had a ten-minute private audience with the Queen at Hillsborough Castle in Co Down, their first meeting on a one-to-one basis. Next day, he accompanied the royal couple on a tour of the old Crumlin Road Gaol in Belfast – where he himself was detained during the Troubles. When I ask him how he would describe the Queen's attitude to the peace process, he replied:

> One hundred per cent behind it. I mean, obviously I want to be a Deputy First Minister for everybody. And when the opportunity arose, when the visit was planned for here, I saw it as an opportunity to reach out the hand of friendship to the unionist people of the North. But also the hand of friendship to someone who had all sorts of reasons not to meet with me. And I had many reasons not to meet with her. But I think the fact that we both accept that reconciliation is an essential next phase of the peace process, then, being involved in a very symbolic [event] – and the way the world reported it turned it into a world event – was something that I think sent a very powerful message to everybody about how we all need to move forward. And I have met her twice since that. I was very privileged to be part of the presidential visit to Windsor, which in itself was an incredible experience, and then to meet with her privately and to make up my own mind about her attitude to the peace process. But key to all of what she

does are the people who are around her, and we have a very good relationship with them.

When I ask him if he means the Downing Street people or her personal staff, he replies:

I mean her people and when you look at the way she conducted herself in Dublin and in Cork, the very powerful reverence with which she stood, to honour Ireland's patriot dead, the honour that she bestowed on the Irish language by using it and, probably most powerfully of all, the speech that she made in Dublin Castle when she talked about, and I am paraphrasing it, how we all wish that things could have been done differently or not at all. And she expressed sympathy to everybody who had suffered as a result of the conflict – so there was no hierarchy of victims.

Thinking of the explosion that killed her cousin, Lord Mountbatten, I interject to say: 'She suffered as well.' McGuinness agrees: 'Absolutely, absolutely and I think she knows that I am conscious of that and I also know that she's conscious of Bloody Sunday. So...the argument that I shouldn't meet with somebody who is a very powerful advocate for the peace process: if I was not to meet with her, then why am I meeting with British prime ministers?'

When I remark that he seems to regard the Queen as a greater friend of the peace process than Prime Minister David Cameron, he replies: 'Well I certainly think, in terms of the way that she has conducted herself both in Dublin and here in Belfast and her willingness to meet with myself [*sends out the message*] to everybody, including those people here in the North who give allegiance to her, that the next phase of the peace process has to be about a reconciliation between all of us.'

On a more contentious note, republicans have been under attack over their handling of alleged sexual abuse by IRA members. McGuinness has written to Taoiseach Enda Kenny suggesting a north-south approach to such issues, what does he have in mind?

> Well I think it needs to be approached in an all-Ireland way. Victims of abuse of any description – and this goes right across society – need to be supported in terms of helplines, counselling, access to justice. I am absolutely of the view that the governments North and South need to be working closer together to give as much support as we possibly can. I know that there have been all sorts of wildly-exaggerated stories put about, mostly by our political opponents, aided by some within the media, about the numbers of people involved in all of this. But whatever about the numbers of people involved, if there are people involved in child abuse they should be arrested and brought before the courts and we, as Irish Republicans, like everybody else within society, have a duty and a responsibility to assist both the PSNI and the Gardaí in the apprehension of these people. So I am not behind the door in advocating that Republicans throughout the length and breadth of Ireland, if they have information to give to the police, that should be passed over to them, as Gerry Adams has done in the course of recent times..

Turning to another current issue, does he see the republican dissidents as a growing force, and what about his own personal security?

> Well I have been threatened by them. That's on the public record and it doesn't stop me doing my work. I am buoyed up by the fact that I know the overwhelming majority of the people of Ireland support my role within the peace process and within these institutions, so I am

not going to bend the knee to anybody in relation to changing my lifestyle or in any way capitulating to the threats and intimidation. I am more concerned about the people that they actually attempt to kill, like police officers.

Warming to his theme, he says:

> In my opinion, these people represent nobody. We have had electoral tests with them in recent times. I stood in Assembly elections in Mid-Ulster and myself and the [other] Sinn Féin candidates got 21,000 votes, and a candidate [for Republican Sinn Féin] got 400 votes [in 2007]. And that is in a constituency [comprising] east Tyrone and south Derry, areas that have suffered as a result of the conflict but who are absolutely 100 per cent behind the peace process. No, I think that the danger from so-called dissidents is, obviously, every now and again they attempt to do something, but have they the ability to bring the peace process down? Absolutely not.

Shortly after the Good Friday Agreement was concluded in April 1998, I was walking in Dublin's Parnell Square, where Sinn Féin's head office is located, when I noticed that someone had put up two posters with pictures of Adams and McGuinness and the motto: 'Wanted for Treachery'. McGuinness returned the compliment in March 2009 after dissident republicans had taken the lives of two British soldiers in Antrim and killed PSNI Constable Stephen Carroll at Craigavon, Co Armagh.

Standing beside Peter Robinson and Chief Constable Sir Hugh Orde at Stormont Castle, he said: 'These people are traitors to the island of Ireland. They have betrayed the political desires, hopes and aspirations of all of the people who live on this island. They don't deserve to be supported by anyone.'[13] He also called on members of the public to support the police in combating the activities of dissident groups. As Ed Curran wrote later in his *Belfast Telegraph* column, it was 'a defining moment for this community, and surely most of all, for him'.[14]

Yes, Martin McGuinness has indeed come a long way. The same passion he once devoted to organising armed attacks on the security forces in and around Derry, as well as further afield, is now being applied to community reconciliation and working out with others a joint path to the future for both sides of the community in Northern Ireland. He's not the first Irish republican to go from guns to government. It didn't end well for Michael Collins, and Éamon de Valera never achieved his dream of a united Ireland. Who knows if McGuinness will succeed better than they did, but it is very much a safe bet that he will keep on trying.

5. NOW GET OUT OF THAT: DISOWNING FATEFUL ECONOMIC DECISIONS

UNLESS THE IRISH LABOUR Party goes into government with Sinn Féin – and maybe not even then – it will never cease reminding people that the republicans voted for the Bank Guarantee. For its part, Sinn Féin has continued to stoutly reject this version of events, while Labour points to the record of the Dáil and Seanad by way of response.

The news of the emergency measure that would dominate economic and political discourse in Ireland for years to come first broke on the morning of 30 September 2008. The Irish banks were in crisis, and the Government had decided, in the middle of the night, that six institutions needed state backing: AIB, Bank of Ireland, EBS Building Society, Irish Life & Permanent, Anglo-Irish Bank and Irish Nationwide (the latter two proving the most controversial). Contributing to the eerie atmosphere was the revelation that the Cabinet had held an 'incorporeal' meeting, where the deliberations, such as they were, took place over the telephone, with ministers being woken from their sleep at around 2 am to make the biggest decision since the Anglo-Irish Treaty of 1921 and neutrality during the Second World War.

The initiative was generally described as a 'blanket guarantee' because it covered so many of the liabilities the banks in question might face, to an estimated total of €440 billion. Just two weeks beforehand, New York-based investment bank Lehman Brothers had collapsed and there were fears of a similar disastrous development in Ireland. The Fianna Fáil-Green Party Government, led by Taoiseach Brian Cowen and Minister for Finance Brian Lenihan Jr., proposed the guarantee as a means of ensuring that the Irish financial system would remain intact. There were grave concerns about a possible run on the banks by panicked depositors, as had occurred with the British institution Northern Rock the previous year. Indeed this writer can recall the queue outside Northern Rock's Harcourt Street office in Dublin at the time.[1]

Legislation to establish the guarantee was brought before the Dáil and Seanad, where it received the support of Fine Gael, the main opposition party, as well as Sinn Féin, but Labour voted against it. The divergence between the two smaller parties remains a live issue and, as recently as 7 May 2015, Environment Minister and Labour deputy leader, Alan Kelly, wrote in the *Irish Independent* with reference to Sinn Féin, that 'this is the party that voted for the bank guarantee with Fianna Fáil'.[2] In a TV3 debate on TV3's *Tonight with Vincent Browne* show, between candidates in the impending Carlow-Kilkenny by-election, Labour's William Quinn said: 'Of all the established parties here tonight, the Labour Party is the only party that voted against the bank guarantee... they [Sinn Féin TDs] ran down the steps of Leinster House to vote for the bank guarantee.' Sinn Féin candidate Kathleen Funchion, in line with party policy of drawing on the second time the issue came before the houses of parliament rather than the first, responded: 'We didn't vote for the bank guarantee. That's on the Dáil record. Go check the records for yourself.'[3]

When the guarantee was first put in place there was a wary but broadly favourable reaction in political circles and among the wider public. Later, however, the measure attracted a massive amount of odium, especially when a major controversy developed over the internal workings of Anglo-Irish Bank and its lending in the property market. The Labour Party deployed the issue relentlessly in its battle with the 'Shinners'.

There was a fairly typical example of Sinn Féin's method of dealing with this difficulty when RTÉ screened a party leaders' debate on 14 February 2011, shortly before that year's general election. Reviewing the 'best and worst moments' for each participant, I wrote in the *Irish Times* that Gerry Adams's worst moment was: 'Claiming that Sinn Féin had always opposed the bank guarantee scheme when the party initially supported it.'[4] In a letter published in that paper two days later, the Sinn Féin leader wrote:

> Deaglán de Bréadún does not accurately reflect what I said in the leaders' debate about Sinn Féin's position on the bank guarantee scheme. I clearly and correctly said on Monday night that Sinn Féin had not supported the blanket guarantee to the banks. When the initial vote on the guarantee was taken in the Dáil in September, Sinn Féin sought to protect ordinary bank depositors. When it emerged that the Government wanted a blanket guarantee Sinn Féin voted against this in every subsequent vote.

In a response published with the Adams letter, I wrote: 'The scheme which Sinn Féin voted for in the Dáil and Seanad on 1 October 2008, was commonly known as "the blanket guarantee" and it applied not only to deposits but also to "covered bonds, senior debt and dated subordinated debt (lower tier II)" with the relevant financial institutions, (as stated in a Department of Finance press release on September 30th, 2008).'[5] The term 'blanket guarantee' is the Central

Bank's official description of the legislation that Sinn Féin voted for in the Dáil and Seanad. The bank's website states, under the heading, 'Government Guarantee Scheme', that: 'The government introduced a blanket guarantee of bank liabilities on the 30th September 2008 for a period of 2 years.'[6] On 1 October 2008, while the legislation was still going through the parliamentary process, the term was used by economist Alan Ahearne (who later became an adviser to Brian Lenihan) in an opinion piece published in the *Irish Times*.[7] Three days later, Patrick Honohan – who was appointed Governor of the Central Bank a year later – wrote in the same paper that 'the Government's blanket guarantee is exceptionally generous to the bankers and exposes the taxpayer to considerable potential costs'. Pointing out that the subordinated debt-holders 'had already been earning a premium for the explicit risks they were taking', Honohan added: 'Though reassuring to depositors, this guarantee... should worry taxpayers, given the evidence from other countries, where the introduction of blanket guarantees was followed by heavier ultimate costs to government.'[8]

The Sinn Féin position, as outlined in the Adams letter, is that the party voted for the guarantee solely to protect 'ordinary' depositors, that the sweeping nature of the legislation did not come to light until later and that the party had been opposing it ever since.

Answering questions in the Dáil some hours after the decision was announced, Taoiseach Brian Cowen said that 'the guarantee liabilities are approximately €400 billion' (the generally-accepted figure in the end was €440 billion). In his opening speech to the House that night on the emergency legislation for the guarantee, Finance Minister Lenihan said (my italics):

> The Bill provides a legislative framework to underpin the guarantee arrangement for depositors *and lenders* to Irish financial institutions... The guarantee is also essential to give confidence to depositors *and wholesale lenders* that they can continue to transact their business

as usual with the institutions concerned... In section 3 'relevant date' is defined as 30 September 2008, the day upon which I announced the decision to guarantee deposits in credit institutions and subsidiaries and *to protect the interests of creditors of credit institutions and their subsidiaries.*

Responding to the Minister, Fine Gael's finance spokesman Richard Bruton said: 'It is clear that a different definition is being applied in the legislation from that indicated earlier. This morning it was just deposits and bonds that were to be subject to guarantee, while tonight there is a wider definition that includes the obligations of credit institutions.'[9]

Nearly four years later, when the two parties were on opposite sides in the referendum on the European Stability Treaty, Labour issued an online 'anthology' of Sinn Féin contributions to the Dáil and Seanad debates on the bank guarantee, with the title *Wrong Then, Wrong Now*. The introduction to the chronicle stated: 'Sinn Féin is tortured by the memory of the enthusiastic welcome they gave for the blanket bank guarantee when it was introduced. They have tried to deny it many times, but the facts speak for themselves. On the fateful night of the bank guarantee Sinn Féin welcomed the move and voted the measure through the Houses.'[10]

A typical entry on Labour's list is the statement by Sinn Féin's Economic Affairs spokesman at the time, Arthur Morgan TD, that the Credit Institutions (Financial Support) Bill of 2008 'may well prove to be a move that other states will seek to emulate'. However, the chronicle does not include the reservations that were also expressed by Morgan, who asked: 'What will the Government extract from the banks in return for this legislation? The Bill does not offer the details needed to inform us of the terms and conditions the taxpayer will require.'[11] At the Committee Stage, Morgan backed an unsuccessful Labour amendment seeking to have more information on terms and conditions for the guarantee included in the Bill. He said: 'We are giving the banks a blank cheque, but we are also giving the Minister a complete blank cheque... I do not trust the Government, and with good reason.' His party colleague Caoimhghín Ó Caoláin told the Dáil: 'There are many outstanding questions on the real outworking of this legislation. However, in consequence of what we recognise as a most serious situation facing the economy of this State, there must be a courageous response.'

The frantic pace of events at the time is conveyed in remarks by Fine Gael's Leo Varadkar:

> Our front bench met this morning to discuss what was going on, yet there was no indication at all that legislation would be required. We only found that out at Taoiseach's Questions at approximately 4.30 p.m.. We were summoned back here at 6 pm, 7:30 pm and 9 pm. It was suggested by the Taoiseach that we should discuss a draft Bill that had not even been published, and we returned here at 10 pm. We have been told that markets and banking operate on confidence, but I do not have a lot of confidence in a Government that does its business that way. We finally got the Bill — and it is still warm, believe it or not — at 9:45 pm. We have been asked to read it but it is like being asked to read the Lisbon Treaty in fifteen minutes. Apart from being stand-alone legislation, it also amends four other Acts: the Competition Act, two Finance Acts and the Companies Act. We have a national crisis and, on this side of the House, we are doing our best to offer responsible and patriotic opposition. As a result and because this Bill changes other legislation, we are by and large supporting this Bill on trust.

Morgan said at the time that Sinn Féin, which then had four TDs and one Senator, was not notified in advance about the Government's intervention, unlike other Opposition parties: 'I don't know if it was fatigue on the part of the Department's senior officials and the Minister, perhaps because of the late nights they were enduring, or if it's some kind of change in tack.'[12]

The Dáil debate went on until 2 am and, having been approved by 124 votes to 18, the Bill went to the Seanad, where the sole Sinn Féin representative was Pearse Doherty, who later won a by-election to the Dáil in Donegal South-West. He said: 'I intend to support this Bill as my party colleagues did in the Dáil, when the vote was taken there in the early hours this morning. We do this because the Bill is in the national interest, but we do so with reservations because we know that the Bill could be much better... My party understands that the Government must intervene to stabilise the economy and the financial system and that is why we will support the Bill... As the media speculated, other states may well follow this move by our state.'

Doherty complained about a lack of detail on the terms and conditions the banks would be expected to fulfil, in return for being saved by the State. He was approaching the nub of the matter when he said: 'We do not know what the budget-sheets of the major banks look like and what liabilities Irish taxpayers now undertake.' Presumably he meant 'balance-sheets'. His Seanad speech was virtually word-for-word the same as the one Morgan had already given to the Dáil. When the sitting finally came to an end, Doherty said: 'I am glad I was able to support the Bill, which is in the national interest. However, I harbour a number of reservations.'

The Seanad debate concluded at 8 am. The Bill had to be brought back to both the Dáil and Seanad that same day to secure approval for two amendments accepted by the Government. It was signed into law by President McAleese at Áras an Uachtaráin in the afternoon. Labour leader Eamon Gilmore said that the Government had failed to address his party's anxieties: 'In the early hours of this morning, the Labour Party stood here alone to oppose the passage of the Bill because we were not given those assurances that we sought. Even so,

I hope the Bill works and that the financial markets in Ireland will be stabilised, that Irish banks will succeed and that there will not be a requirement to draw down the guarantee that has been provided for in the Bill.'

Sinn Féin's Ó Caoláin said it had been 'an important but also a difficult debate, particularly for Members on the left'. He added: 'Sinn Féin did not take its position in supporting this Bill lightly. We have our concerns and reservations but we decided to support the passage of the legislation because we believed it is about more than the banks. It is about offering security to ordinary citizens, to investors and Irish businesses which means, in turn, the protection of Irish jobs.'

Despite its opposition to the Bill, Labour facilitated its passage by withdrawing an amendment in the Seanad seeking the terms and conditions of the guarantee. Finance Minister Lenihan said it would lead to a delay in dealing with the crisis: 'The Bill is necessary to allow the State to act urgently and decisively in respect of a complex issue when markets are volatile...The purpose of the Bill is to enable prompt, effective and expeditious action. Accepting the amendment would defeat that purpose and mark a departure from standard reporting procedures.' However, a similar amendment from Labour in the Dáil was debated at very considerable length and rejected. Labour Senators pressed ahead with other proposed amendments in the Upper House.

Later, in his *Irish Times* column, Political Editor Stephen Collins wrote: 'The past week was one of the most extraordinary in the Dáil for a long time. Not since the Arms Crisis [when ministers were sacked after allegedly importing arms for use by the IRA] has the Oireachtas sat all through the night. Just as Irish democracy was on the line in May 1970, the Irish economy was teetering on the brink this time.' Commenting on the performance of the main opposition parties, he continued: 'Fine Gael has shown that it is capable of being an alternative government... Labour opted to take a more populist line... Sinn Féin took the opposite view to Labour and, while it criticised the banks and the Government, the party voted in favour of the Bill. That decision could mark an important step by the party into the political mainstream and help transform it into a potential coalition partner in whatever scenario emerges after the next election.'[13]

This was a perspective I shared myself at the time but, when I said to a leading Sinn Féin figure, on the plinth at Leinster House, that the party had made itself a more acceptable partner in a future government, the reply I got indicated there was considerable internal disagreement on the coalition issue. In an article for *An Phoblacht* under the heading 'Why Sinn Féin supported the Dáil legislation: State guarantee needed but banks must be controlled', Micheál Mac Donncha wrote:

> The emergency legislation rushed through the Dáil and Seanad last week was supported with strong reservations by Sinn Féin. The five Sinn Féin Oireachtas members accepted that this major intervention was needed and they supported the passage of the enabling legislation, the Credit Institutions (Financial Support) Bill 2008. However they demanded that the banks be reined-in and strictly controlled and that the economically vulnerable must be protected.[14]

Despite the party's monolithic reputation, internal differences were openly aired in the following week's edition under the heading, 'Was Sinn Féin right to support Dáil banks guarantee?' Answering in the affirmative, Donegal County Councillor and future TD Pádraig Mac Lochlainn wrote: 'Sinn Féin TDs supported this Bill with gritted teeth... they were presented with a real-time decision reflecting the potential collapse of the banking sector in the 26 Counties. Whatever our ideological reservations about the international capitalist system, of which Ireland is part, the implications of a wholesale banking collapse for a small island economy are unthinkable.' The party's leading ideologue on the left, Eoin Ó Broin from Dún Laoghaire, took the No side. He wrote: 'That Fianna Fáil could concoct a scheme that rescues the banks while jeopardising the taxpayer and economy is hardly surprising. What gets me is that Sinn Féin would support a proposal that is both economically and politically reckless. What on earth were we thinking?'[15]

Two weeks after the original legislation, Lenihan sought Dáil support for a motion to approve the detailed operation of the new scheme. Recalling how Sinn Féin had supported the legislation a fortnight before, Arthur Morgan had no doubts about the fundamental correctness of the stance the party had taken: 'We did so because we believed it was necessary to stabilise the State's banking system. Our judgment has been proved correct. Since its implementation, Ireland has not lost a bank or been forced to bail out a bank with cash.' But he expressed grave disappointment with the operational details that were now being presented. On this occasion the party voted with Labour against the combined forces of Fianna Fáil, Fine Gael and the Greens, and Marie O'Halloran wrote in the *Irish Times* on 18 October: 'Sinn Féin did a U-turn on its surprise original decision "in principle" to support the Government's bank guarantee scheme. It obviously came to the conclusion that opposing rather than supporting Government is safer ground.' There is no record of Sinn Féin voting on the issue when it came before the Seanad. Three years later, at the launch of Sinn Féin's manifesto for the February 2011 general election, Caoimghín Ó Caoláin said, in response to Labour's continuing taunts about the guarantee: 'The reality of the situation back in September 2008 is that the Labour Party, with no more information than any of the other Opposition voices, were very happy to burn ordinary bank depositors.'[16]

The issue came up again in the Dáil on 29 September 2011, when Fine Gael (and later Independent) TD Peter Mathews pointed out that it was the third anniversary of a guarantee 'that has left the country on its knees and in pain'. Pearse Doherty, who was now a TD and the party's new finance spokesman, sought to correct him by saying: 'It came into effect two weeks later when the terms and conditions were presented to the House – which Sinn Féin voted against, something which other Members choose to forget.' There was immediate uproar from the Labour benches and Eamon Gilmore, who had at this stage become Tánaiste (deputy prime minister) in a Fine Gael-Labour coalition, said: 'I remind Members that one of the loudest enthusiasts for the guarantee was Deputy Doherty.'

In November of that year, noting that the Minister for Finance in the new Fine Gael-Labour coalition, Michael Noonan, had extended the guarantee scheme for a second time, Pearse Doherty said:

> While Fine Gael always supported the banking guarantee, the decision of the Labour party to support its extension, not once but twice, must be the most brass-necked U-turn to date. Despite all the bluster when in opposition, Labour are now enthusiastic supporters of this catastrophic Fianna Fáil policy failure... Eamon Gilmore, Joan Burton and their cabinet colleagues are imposing this reckless guarantee on the taxpayers again. Not only has the government no exit-strategy from this disastrous guarantee, but they are clearly committed to implementing the failed banking policy of the previous government. Sinn Féin opposed the legislation that gave legal effect to the blanket guarantee [on] 17 October 2008. We have consistently opposed the guarantee in all its incarnations since.

Having originally said he was glad, despite reservations, to support legislation which was 'in the national interest', Doherty was now condemning the scheme as 'this catastrophic Fianna Fáil policy failure' and describing the guarantee as 'reckless' and 'disastrous'. He was speaking a year after Ireland proved unable to meet the cost of propping-up the banks and had to request a €64 billion bailout from the 'Troika' of the European Commission, European Central Bank and International Monetary Fund. Meeting the terms of the bailout involved massive tax increases, cuts in social welfare and reductions in public sector pay and pensions. Labour at this stage had joined Fine Gael in a coalition government which was implementing the terms of the bailout.

Gerry Adams has persisted in his denials that Sinn Féin voted for the guarantee. In a TV debate on RTÉ's *Claire Byrne Live* on 26 January 2015 with Joan Burton, who had succeeded Gilmore as Tánaiste and Labour leader, there were two exchanges on the matter. The first went as follows:

JB: You voted for the Bank Guarantee.

GA: No, we didn't vote for the Bank Guarantee.

JB: You voted for the Bank Guarantee on the night.

GA: You have renewed the Bank Guarantee twice.

JB: We renegotiated it.

Adams remained in denial mode for the second exchange:

JB: What have we done in relation to the banks? We have exited an incredibly difficult situation that we inherited and that his [GA's] party actually voted for on the night of the guarantee.

GA: We didn't.

JB: Well, the records of the Dáil show that you did.

GA: No we didn't.[17]

Sinn Féin's critics would say the party should have known that the original legislation it supported in the Dáil and Seanad was very sweeping in nature and was, in fact, a blanket guarantee. Labour behaved more shrewdly – some might say opportunistically – by engaging in risk-free opposition to a Bill that was always going to be passed by a huge majority. When Sinn Féin realised it had given a major advantage to its rivals on the left, critics would say it should have defended the initial decision on the basis that it was an emergency situation, rather than attempting to rewrite history, when the facts are set down in black and white on the record of the Dáil and Seanad.

But as well as the exchanges with Joan Burton on the bank guarantee, another issue came up on the same TV programme, in an exchange between Adams and Claire Byrne herself. When the presenter said to the Sinn Féin leader: 'You talk about increasing corporation tax...' he replied immediately: 'We have never talked about increasing corporation tax – never'.[18] This appears to be a further example of the strategy whereby denial is felt to be better than explanation, which has also applied in the case of the bank guarantee. In politics, as in other spheres, it seems that, 'If you're explaining, you're losing.'

Drawing multinationals in with low taxes on their profits has been a central part of the Republic of Ireland's industrial strategy for decades. The current 12.5 per cent rate of corporation tax has applied since 1 January 2003. In a 'well-received' address to the Dublin Chamber of Commerce on 21 April 2004, Adams indicated that his party wasn't particularly happy with the situation, but didn't intend to do anything about it: 'Sinn Féin opposed the cutting of corporation tax to 12.5 per cent, especially as minimum wage workers were in the tax net. So we're not in principle opposed to higher taxes, though we have no plans to increase them. Instead, we want a comprehensive reform and overhaul of the tax system... We believe tax cuts should be incentive-driven. That means linking low corporation tax to good environmental practices, to the provision of childcare, to investment in worker training and education' (The address wasn't quite so well-received on the republican left.)[19]

Fianna Fáil remained in government with the right-of-centre Progressive Democrats after the 2002 general election but, three years into that term of office, Taoiseach and Fianna Fáil leader Bertie Ahern moved to deprive Fine Gael and Labour of the argument that a vote for his party in future was a vote for Sinn Féin, because that's who would end up in government with Fianna Fáil. He issued a statement in mid-November 2005 ruling out any arrangement with

Sinn Féin after the next general election. He said the economic policies of the two parties were incompatible, adding that Adams had proposed on RTÉ's *Prime Time* current affairs programme on 3 November that corporation tax should be increased to 17 per cent from its current 12.5 per cent.[20]

But it wasn't official party policy just yet. In the *Irish Times*, Mark Hennessy reported that a review of Sinn Féin's economic policies, headed by party chairman Mitchel McLaughlin, had been in progress for over a year, and that it favoured increasing corporation tax to 17.5 per cent. The party was in an upbeat mood, and Hennessy wrote: 'Sinn Féin is confident of winning 14 seats in the next general election and may want to take part in a coalition, the party's Cavan-Monaghan TD Caoimhghín Ó Caoláin said.'[21]

At the start of 2006, Hennessy reported extensive details of the document, which would be debated the coming weekend at a party conference, with the final draft to be put before the following month's ardfheis:

> 'Sinn Féin challenges the view that the 26-County State would not be competitive, and the economic boom would not have occurred but for the low level of corporation tax, now less than half the EU average,' the document said. Multinationals were 'siphoning' €25 billion out of the Republic's economy 'which could have been used to tackle the State's infrastructure deficit, to invest in education, and training or to subsidise research and development'. Low corporation tax imposed 'hidden costs' on the economy because it eroded the 'ability of the State to pay for public services, imposing a disproportionate tax burden on the poor, thus aggravating poverty and undermining R&D [research and development] essential to the economy's future... Sinn Féin will not reduce corporation tax or even allow it to remain as minimal as at present. We will raise it, but

in tandem with other measures that create a supportive enterprise [environment],' the document said.[22]

In a media briefing at the conference, McLaughlin was asked whether an increase in tax would drive out foreign investors. He said that he 'flatly rejected' such an argument, and added: 'We recognise some well-paid jobs have been created by Foreign Direct Investment but we also recognise global trends. We are concerned that in the past year that 100,000 jobs were created in this State, and yet you still find that the VAT [Value-Added Tax] receipts are in excess of the receipts of income tax. So that would indicate that the type of jobs created in our economy are low-paid jobs, and are not long-term jobs.'[23]

A report on the conference in *An Phoblacht* said it was 'an important milestone' in the development of the party's economic policy: 'Sinn Féin members, activists and public representatives from across the country, discussed a detailed draft policy document prepared by the party's Economic Policy Review Group... The paper proposes a five per cent increase in corporation tax in the 26 Counties, from the present 12.5 per cent to 17.5 per cent. It also [*proposes*] the harmonisation of corporation tax on an all-Ireland basis.'[24]

Fianna Fáil were watching developments closely and, in a letter to the *Irish Examiner* on 20 January, Pat Carey TD wrote: 'The prospect of a government with a Sinn Féin hue raising corporation tax to 17.5% sends out a signal that our economic policy cannot be trusted and that Ireland is not a place to make long-term relocation plans. No wonder the Taoiseach said Sinn Féin's economic policies would "surrender Irish workers to unemployment and emigration" and that he took the sensible step of ruling out any coalition arrangement with that party.'[25]

Fianna Fáil clearly saw this issue as an Achilles heel for their republican rivals, but Sinn Féin sailed blithely onward. In his ardfheis speech the following month, Adams declared: 'Sinn Féin would increase taxes on capital gains, property speculation and corporate profits.'[26] And in April 2006, McLaughlin, in his role as Economy Spokesman added: 'Sinn Féin is proposing the gradual harmonisation of corporation tax on an all-Ireland basis. In the immediate term we would plan to lower the corporation tax rate in the six counties to 17.5% for smaller companies with profits up to 300,000 euro, and to raise the rate from 12.5% to 17.5% in the 26 Counties.'[27]

At the end of that year, as part of its pre-budget submission on 23 November, Sinn Féin recommended bringing corporation tax from 12.5 per cent up to 17.5 per cent.[19] The issue was again cited by a leading figure in Fianna Fáil as a barrier to government partnership. In an interview with myself for the *Irish Times* in December 2006, then-Minister for Foreign Affairs, Dermot Ahern, rejected any prospect of Fianna Fáil going into coalition with Sinn Féin because of what he saw as their hard-left stance on economic and European issues: 'They want to put up corporation tax to 17 per cent. They want to put capital gains tax back up.'[28] In the first of a two-part series on Sinn Féin's approach to economic issues, the party's National Director of Policy, Shannonbrooke Murphy wrote in *An Phoblacht* on 22 March 2007:

> We have proposed interim rates for the purpose of harmonising corporation tax on the island, involving a small decrease in the Six Counties rate for SMEs [Small and Medium-Sized Enterprises] from 19% to 17.5% and a sustainable increase (according to the ESRI, CORI and ICTU economists) in the 26 Counties from 12.5% to 17.5%. This proposed rate is still significantly less than the lowest personal income tax band in the 26 Counties.[29]

But elsewhere on the political scene, the 12.5 per cent rate had become the Irish equivalent of protecting the British crown jewels.

In April 2007 I reported a claim by then-Minister for Finance Brian Cowen, who said: 'Our corporation tax regime is safe only in the hands of this party.' He added that Fianna Fáil was giving a guarantee that corporation tax would be kept at the current level, so that Ireland could remain 'a preferred location for the world's most value-creating profitable businesses'. Cowen expressed doubts about the commitment of the Labour Party, especially its then-leader, Pat Rabbitte, on this issue, and Cowen's colleague, Micheál Martin, claimed the Green Party had an ambivalent history in this regard. In its response, Labour flatly rejected Cowen's charge and pointed out that, when the party was last in government, Rabbitte had helped to negotiate the 12.5 per cent rate. The Greens conceded that in the 2002 general election they had called for a 15 per cent rate but their policy since 2006 had been for 12.5 per cent.[30]

To all outward appearances, Sinn Féin's commitment to a five per cent increase could hardly be more emphatic. However, there was a dramatic but unannounced change of tack by the party when, on the morning of 30 April 2007, Taoiseach Bertie Ahern called a general election for 24 May. As a political correspondent, I attended a Sinn Féin news conference held the same day for the launch of a policy document entitled *Workers' Rights for an Ireland of Equals*. When asked if the 17.5 per cent rate was still Sinn Féin policy, Mary Lou McDonald said: 'The 17.5 per cent is not in our manifesto.' Commenting on declarations by Bertie Ahern that Sinn Féin would not be an acceptable coalition partner due to its economic policy, she said: 'We now have an electoral contest, and the people in their very great wisdom will cast their votes and they will decide the composition and the balance of forces in the next Dáil.'[31] The Labour and Green election manifestos both included a commitment to retain the 12.5 per cent rate. The Labour document said that 'a competitive tax regime has been, and will remain, vital in encouraging employment, entrepreneurship, investment and exports'.[32]

Calling for a hike in corporation tax had clearly become

politically toxic. Commenting in a piece headed 'EU battle on corporate tax looms', Kathleen Barrington wrote in the *Sunday Business Post* four days before the election: 'Sinn Féin and the Labour Party have decided to hop on the low corporation tax bandwagon... Sinn Féin made the most spectacular U-turn when it abandoned recently-formulated plans for a five per cent hike in corporation tax to 17.5 per cent. Labour also moved quickly to reassure the business classes it had no plans to reach further into their companies' pockets. Now, all the left-wing parties, including the Green Party, agree with Fianna Fáil, the Progressive Democrats and Fine Gael that our 12.5 per cent corporation tax is broadly a good thing.'[33]

The election was a major disappointment for Sinn Féin. Having publicly set a target of 14 Dáil seats (see above), the party ended up with only four, which was one less than it had on setting out. The reality is that, if it had not buried the demand to raise corporation tax, it might have come back with even fewer TDs. Economic policy was seen as one of the factors in the party's poor performance. Sinn Féin failed to connect with the mood of the electorate in a period when the Celtic Tiger boom was at its height. As I wrote at the time for the Belfast-based *Fortnight* magazine:

> The party's manifesto... came across as curiously old-fashioned, like a piece of work that some Soviet state theoretician had cranked up for a satellite regime in the middle of the Cold War... Like it or not, it has to be admitted that traditional state-led socialist or nationalist economics did not create the Celtic Tiger. The South's openness to foreign investment and its tiny rate of corporation tax were a major factor... Sinn Féin's policy document failed to acknowledge this in any meaningful way... Sinn Féin also got it wrong on corporation tax. The party formerly advocated a five per cent increase in the current rate, from 12.5 up to 17.5 per cent. It was very difficult indeed to get a straight answer to the

question as to whether this policy still stood, but it didn't appear in the manifesto and seems to have been quietly dropped. At a time when all parties in the North are trying to get the 12.5 per cent extended to the whole island, it didn't make sense to be seeking an increase in the South. Besides, an increase like that would almost certainly lead to widespread factory closures and large-scale job-losses. Meanwhile, other countries are eyeing our corporation tax-rate with great envy and there are moves in Brussels to bring about 'harmonisation', which means bringing Ireland up to a higher level. It's an issue of sovereignty and the old political masters in Fianna Fáil presented themselves as the only party that could be relied upon to fight the good fight on this issue. Sinn Féin used to understand the issue of sovereignty as well, but seemed to have forgotten it in some pseudo-leftist ideological miasma.[34]

In a wide-ranging analysis under the heading 'Where it all went wrong for Sinn Féin', Colm Heatley wrote in the *Sunday Business Post*:

Undoubtedly one of the biggest problem areas for the party is its economic policies, which are at best confusing and, at worst, scaring off voters. The party's willingness to ditch its corporation tax policy just weeks before the election suggested desperation. Privately, Sinn Féin acknowledges that getting its economic policies in order is a key priority. Economic policies were never central to Sinn Féin strategy and while the party is beginning to address its shortcomings, its commitment to left-wing policies means it will always be vulnerable to accusations that it will damage the Celtic Tiger.[35]

In a further examination of Sinn Féin's difficulties in this regard,

Heatley wrote in the same paper at the end of 2007: 'Sinn Féin's move towards the centre on economic issues also exposed a fault-line between the northern and southern wings of the party. Whereas Sinn Féin members in the Republic were prepared to go along with the leadership wishes on issues such as decommissioning and policing, they are more reluctant to accept the dilution of left-wing economic policies.'[36]

The accuracy of this assessment was very apparent at the party's ardfheis in the spring of the following year, where a heated debate on taxation took place. Mark Hennessy reported: 'The party's ardchomhairle produced a cautiously-worded motion on tax policies which said that taxes would be "increased only where demonstrably necessary. Tax rates should be decided on the basis of what is needed to meet social goals and other spending demands"'.

But the motion came in for sharp criticism from several speakers, among them Dublin South-Central TD Aengus Ó Snodaigh, who said: 'We believe that Sinn Féin does not have a credible tax policy. We are unable to explain how we would fund the kind of public services and government programmes contained [*in it*]... The ardchomhairle motion avoids difficult issues like corporation tax, capital gains tax and a third band for high earners.' Sinn Féin Dáil leader Caoimhghín Ó Caoláin denied that the tax policy was vague or that the party had dithered on the issue in the previous election: 'Make no mistake about this: Sinn Féin made no U-turns. What it did do was *change the presentational emphasis.*' (My italics.) The ardchomhairle motion was passed.[37]

The voter-repellent policy of seeking an increase in corporation tax was now well and truly buried, but Sinn Féin did not make a song-and-dance about it. A year later, in an article on the launch of the party's pre-Budget proposals and headed, 'Sinn Féin does U-turn on raising corporation tax', the *Irish Examiner* reported: 'Sinn Féin confirmed yesterday it is not in favour of raising corporation tax — a reversal of its previous policy on the issue. The party said businesses are under extreme pressure at the moment and "you couldn't be asking them to pay any more than they already are"... The party had previously called for dramatic rises in the rate of corporation tax. This policy was dropped last year and the party did not state its position on the issue.'[38]

There remained a sense that Sinn Féin was bowing to political reality rather than acting out of deep conviction. The party's alternative Budget for 2013, entitled *Making the Right Choices*, reflected this: 'The headline tax rate of 12.5% on profits made by companies in Ireland is fiercely protected by the Department of Finance, where officials say the rate has become so entrenched it would be difficult to move it up or down. Sinn Féin believes that the 12.5% must be protected, but also that the issue of the effective tax rate has to be addressed.' The issue of multinationals using such tax-avoidance schemes as the 'Double Irish' and other reliefs and loopholes was coming to the fore, and Sinn Féin was seeking the fullest possible disclosure in this regard. The document continued: 'Sinn Féin supports the 12.5% corporation tax rate. We do not want to change it and we are not asking struggling companies to pay more tax. However, the effective rate of tax on profits must be addressed.'[39]

Life must have seemed much simpler in the days when the primary focus was on the IRA campaign of bombing and shooting to 'get the Brits out' of the North. The path to power through the democratic process can be complicated and circuitous. Principles tend to be diluted by pragmatism, but unless a party gets the votes, it will never be able to implement even a modified version of those principles. Sinn Féin is not the first, nor will it be the last, political organisation to change its tune on major issues. What sets it apart is a greater tendency to distance itself from past decisions which may have made sense at the time but have since become politically unpopular. Since the record is there for all to see, this approach damages the party's credibility to a significant degree.

6. TURNING SWORDS INTO PLOUGH-SHARES: GOOD FRIDAY AND ITS AFTERMATH

BY THE TIME THAT the abstentionist policy towards Leinster House was abandoned, the Provisional IRA campaign had been in progress for sixteen years. The cherished dream of a united Ireland did not seem any closer. The failed ceasefire of the mid-1970s showed that, while there might be occasional loose talk and speculative notions within the British political and administrative system, they had no serious intention of pulling out of the North. The Provos did not have the capacity to drive them out either and the British, in their turn, could contain but not crush the Provos. The IRA might still have a role in defending Catholic ghettos from loyalist assault, but it had no mandate for an all-out offensive campaign. It could all be summed-up in a single word: stalemate.

I first met Gerry Adams in October 1986, shortly before

abstentionism from the Dáil was jettisoned. He gave me an interview for the *Irish Times*, and I remember being disappointed that he went on so much about local issues in his constituency of West Belfast, where he was the (non-attending) Westminster MP at the time. But if he failed to impress on our first meeting, over time I arrived at a greater appreciation of his talents. The assessment in my 2001 book on the Good Friday Agreement applies to his role in the peace process rather than in the southern political arena:

> Even his enemies would acknowledge that Adams looks at the Big Picture. Everything he says and does in politics is connected with a grand plan or strategy. His pronouncements are often enigmatic and hard to fathom at the time but this may be because he is so many jumps ahead of everyone else. His enemies and critics call him Jesuitical. His intellectual and tactical subtlety sometimes confuses and irritates people but he has brought the republican movement a long way down the peaceful road, in the process helping to create a large and powerful political consensus stretching from the White House to Leinster House.[1]

The Anglo-Irish Agreement, signed in November 1985 at Hillsborough Castle, official residence of the Secretary of State for Northern Ireland, had been a major development, although its significance and implications were not widely appreciated at the time. In the first place, the most virulently anti-Provo Prime Minister, Margaret Thatcher, had allowed the Irish Government a say in the administration of Northern Ireland, complete with a base for Dublin's civil servants at Maryfield, on the outskirts of Belfast. The 'Iron Lady' was responding to pressure from US President Ronald Reagan, who was, in turn, influenced by the charismatic Irish-American politician T.P. 'Tip' O'Neill. Secondly, the massive wave of unionist outrage and hardliner Ian Paisley intoning 'Never,

never, never, never!' failed to move her. Like a good many observers at the time, I was inclined to underestimate the importance of the deal between the two states. A wake-up call came when I met some Kurdish nationalists from Turkey who spoke in envious terms about the pact. A very senior and distinguished figure from the Irish civil service, who was now retired but had played a major role on north-south issues in the past, expressed the view to me that the Anglo-Irish Agreement was a 'gunna chun cleamhnais' for the unionists. This was an Irish-language version of the gun in a shotgun wedding. Peter Robinson lamented that 'We are on the window ledge of the Union' and poet Tom Paulin wrote *The Defenestration of Hillsborough*, evoking the memory of Jan Masaryk, the Czech foreign minister allegedly pushed to his death from a windowsill in Prague after the Communist *coup d'etat* in 1948.

In his 1996 memoir, *Before the Dawn*, Adams writes that, following Sinn Féin's electoral successes, 'The establishment became seriously concerned that the SDLP could be displaced' and the Agreement was 'an attempt to counter the rise of Sinn Féin.'[2] All the more reason, then, to get involved in politics in the South: no wonder abstentionism was duly consigned to the dustbin twelve months later, in November 1986. The dramatic change of tack was facilitated by the fact that the IRA campaign continued apace, aided by an estimated four enormous shipments of arms and explosives from the Libyan dictator Colonel Gaddafi – a fifth consignment was intercepted on its voyage from Tripoli, giving rise to the suggestion that British intelligence had finally been tipped-off from inside the Provos. Ensuring the IRA was well-nourished kept the militarists happy, but disasters such as the horrific Enniskillen bombing of 8 November 1987, when ten civilians and one police officer were killed, did nothing to enhance the standing of Sinn Féin.

The political isolation of the 'Shinners', from the mainstream on both sides of the border as well as internationally, cried out to be tackled. In an interview with the music and current affairs magazine *Hot Press*, Adams declared: 'I would be prepared to consider an alternative, unarmed struggle, to attain Irish independence. If someone would outline such a course I would not only be prepared to listen, but I would be prepared to work in that direction.'[3]

The description of the 'someone' in the Adams interview equated perfectly with the attributes of SDLP leader and long-time advocate of peaceful political action, John Hume. With the Redemptorist priest Father Alec Reid acting as an intermediary, a meeting took place between Hume and Adams on 11 January 1988. The Hume-Adams dialogue, which gradually broadened into a wider peace process, had begun. It was arguably the most significant development in Irish politics since the 'New Departure' of the nineteenth century, when the revolutionaries of the Fenian movement made common cause with constitutional nationalists under Charles Stewart Parnell. There were parallel developments taking place in South Africa, where the racial injustice of apartheid was still the order of the day, and in the conflict between Israel and the Palestinians.

Whereas the Anglo-Irish Agreement served, among other things, to benefit the SDLP, the process initiated between Hume and Adams had the opposite effect in the long run. Hume's admirers and detractors can both say that he sacrificed his party, at least in the short term, to achieve the peace we now have. When his dialogue with the Sinn Féin leader came to light he was excoriated at great length by some in the media. But he ploughed ahead regardless, single-minded in his pursuit of the ultimate goal of peaceful democratic politics, where difficulties and differences would be resolved with talks around a table instead of prolonged and intensified with bombs, bullets and various forms of repression.

The contact with Hume enabled Sinn Féin to escape the pincer movement between the British Tories and the Fine Gael-led coalition in Dublin that was represented by the Anglo-Irish Agreement. But the process needed to be broadened. Fianna Fáil was back in power in Dublin – could it be persuaded to throw its weight behind the new initiative for peace? Not as long as Charles Haughey was in charge, it seemed. While still in opposition, he was invited to meet Adams, but refused. When he became taoiseach again in March 1987, he authorised two secret meetings in Dundalk between a Fianna Fáil delegation and Sinn Féin, but made it clear he would disown them if the news leaked out. That was in 1988, and there were no further contacts, as far as is known, until Haughey left office in 1992. It has been suggested to me by a well-placed source that Haughey was concerned the 'Brits' might leak embarrassing details of his personal finances, which later became matters of major controversy in a different political context. He also carried a lot of 'baggage' from the period of the 1970 Arms Crisis and subsequent trial, when he and others were ultimately acquitted on charges of attempting to import arms for the IRA which, at the time, was seen as a defender of the nationalist communities in the North. In addition, Haughey did not fully trust Adams and Co. and he was in government with the right-of-centre Progressive Democrats (PDs), who were even less well-disposed to Sinn Féin than he was himself.

Whether through timidity or excessive caution, Charles Haughey missed his appointment with history. Cometh the hour, cometh the man: exit Haughey and enter Albert Reynolds, rightly described by Adams in a complimentary sense as 'a buccaneer', such was his swashbuckling dash and daring. 'Who's afraid of peace?' was his clarion-call. 'Who's afraid to take risks for peace?' In truth, many people were, not least at the higher levels of government in Dublin and London. I covered the triumphant return of the new Fianna Fáil leader and taoiseach to his home county. An open-air platform had been set up outside the Longford Arms Hotel and, as Reynolds was speaking, I was very much struck by his sincerity and determination on the issue of peace in the North, a change from the usual ticking-the-boxes rhetoric of southern politicians. His words pierced the chill February air: 'I know there must be a better way forward, there *is* a better way forward and I will work day and night, go anywhere with any of my colleagues, to work out that new path for peace.' [4]

In his previous role as Minister for Finance, Reynolds had built-up a friendship with his British counterpart, Chancellor of the Exchequer John Major. Now the two of them were heading up governments on either side of the Irish Sea. Reynolds told the cheering crowd in Longford that he had already spoken to the Prime Minister on the phone for 'about fifteen minutes' and he added: 'I told him I would be looking for an early get-together.'[5] The urgency of the situation was reflected in the fact that, the night after the Reynolds homecoming, four IRA members with an average age of twenty-one – were shot dead by members of the SAS special forces regiment in response to their attack on a police station in Coalisland, County Tyrone, with a machine-gun mounted on the back of a truck. Clearly the British had very good intelligence, which they were prepared to use quite ruthlessly. The four were only born at the start of the Troubles, and the mother of one of the deceased was reported as requesting that the IRA and Sinn Féin not attend her son's burial. They didn't. At the funeral of another victim, Father Liam McEntagart said: 'To those paramilitary leaders who sent him out to die I say it is not right; it is not just; it is not moral.' He added: 'To those security forces who shot him dead, I likewise say it is not right; it is not just; it is not moral.'[6] Questions have been raised since as to why they were not arrested instead of being shot down.[7] The British side could say, of course, that the attack on the police station was a shoot-to-kill operation.

In short order, Reynolds authorised his special adviser and expert on Northern Ireland issues, Dr Martin Mansergh, to meet Gerry Adams face-to-face on a regular basis.[8] Much time had been wasted, but now things were moving at last. The Downing Street Declaration, signed by Reynolds and Major on 15 December 1993, repeated the statement by Secretary of State Peter Brooke, three years before, that Britain had 'no selfish strategic or economic interest in Northern Ireland'. The document continued:

> Both governments accept that Irish unity would be achieved only by those who favour this outcome

persuading those who do not, peacefully and without coercion or violence ... parties which establish a commitment to exclusively peaceful methods and which have shown that they abide by the democratic process, are free to participate fully in democratic politics and to join in dialogue in due course between the Governments and the political parties on the way ahead.[9]

A senior Irish official close to the negotiations on the Declaration privately expressed the view that the document was 'suffused with the psychology of withdrawal'. But there was still a long way to go before the IRA could be persuaded to call another ceasefire, especially given that the truce in the mid-1970s was seen as such an abject failure. Rightly or wrongly, the Provisional IRA regarded its campaign as a means of putting pressure on the British to pull out of the North, and was not going to set it aside unless there were very persuasive political alternatives.

What must be seen as a massive step along that road was taken in January 1994, when US President Bill Clinton granted a US visitor's visa to Gerry Adams to attend a New York conference. Major felt 'astonishment and annoyance'. He refused to take phone calls from Clinton for a number of weeks,[10] former Irish ambassador to Washington, Seán Donlon, said later: the initiative began with John Hume and was taken up by US ambassador to Ireland Jean Kennedy Smith, who persuaded her brother, Senator Ted Kennedy to lobby Clinton on the issue.[11] Irish-American journalist Niall O'Dowd was another key figure in securing the Adams visa.

On 31 January when Adams arrived in the US it was, as Conor O'Clery has pointed out, the world's biggest news story on the day.[12] In a front-page piece, the *New York Times* described the Sinn Féin chief as 'an articulate and enigmatic partisan leader in a centuries-old struggle' – a far cry from the descriptions in most British and Irish media. A profile on the paper's opinion page by author Edna O'Brien compared Adams to the legendary Michael Collins and, noting that the Sinn Féin leader's hero was Nelson Mandela, she added: 'No doubt on his journey from violence to the negotiating table he sees parallels.'[13] O'Clery reported in the *Irish Times* how the Sinn Féin leader arrived for a rally at a New York hotel to the tune of *A Nation Once Again* played by pipers from the Emerald Society Police Band who were 'dressed in kilts but with revolvers strapped to their waists'.[14]

Prospects of an IRA ceasefire appeared to suffer a very serious setback when a conference of 800 Sinn Féin delegates, called to discuss the Downing Street Declaration at Letterkenny, decided that, although the document marked 'a further stage in the peace process', it contained 'negative and contradictory elements'. But Albert Reynolds remained optimistic, insisting there were 'some positive signals' from the conference.[15] The Taoiseach clearly 'knew more than his prayers', as the saying goes. As a political reporter for the *Irish Times*, I got reliable word on 24 August that an indefinite ceasefire would be called by the end of the month and the paper ran it as a lead story next day. Sinn Féin sources in Belfast were reported as dismissing the story and a leading journalist from the North expressed the opinion that the Irish Times was 'flying high' – but a similar story appeared in the *Irish Independent* the same day. I wrote in my report: 'There will be no time limit on the IRA ceasefire, and its announcement will be followed by a major drive by Sinn Féin to enhance its political position, particularly in the US. It is understood that a US visa for the party president, Mr Gerry Adams, is likely to be issued within weeks of the ceasefire announcement.'[16]

The conduct of the anti-apartheid struggle in South Africa was a template for the IRA at the time. My report continued: 'The ceasefire will represent a new stage in the republican movement's "unarmed strategy". The step-by-step approach, republicans claim, is closely modelled on the strategy adopted by the African National Congress after its leader, Mr Nelson Mandela, was released from prison. They point out that the ANC reserved the right to resume "armed struggle" if peaceful efforts to end the apartheid regime were unsuccessful.'[17]

And so it came to pass on 31 August that the IRA announced 'a complete cessation of military operations'. The statement continued: 'We believe that an opportunity to create a just and lasting settlement has been created... We note that the Downing Street Declaration is not a solution, nor was it presented as such by its authors. A solution will only be found as a result of inclusive negotiations.'[18] Could it really be all over? I was at the All-Ireland Hurling Final in Dublin's Croke Park, a few days after the announcement. When Albert Reynolds arrived, the crowd stood in his honour as the band played the traditional salute to the Taoiseach, which is titled *Amhrán Dóchais (Song of Hope)*. It was a poignant moment, and I wondered if there would ever be a day when a unionist leader would attend such an event – that would nowadays be a relatively unremarkable occurrence.

The paramilitaries on the other side of the divided community, under the Combined Loyalist Military Command, announced a reciprocal ceasefire on 13 October. But the peace process wasn't the only game on the island, and other issues were bubbling away in southern politics. Eleven weeks after the historic breakthrough he had worked so hard to bring about, Reynolds was forced to resign as taoiseach. Tensions with his Labour partners in government came to a head, and the same stubborn strength of will and refusal to be deflected that made him so effective in helping to secure the ceasefire proved to be his downfall as head of the coalition. Labour went into another partnership under a new taoiseach, John Bruton of Fine Gael, who was a hardworking and committed politician, but sharply-critical of Irish republican ideology and never likely to develop the same rapport with Sinn Féin.

Negotiations between Dublin and London continued, leading to the publication of documents in February 1995 entitled *Frameworks for the Future*, which set out the administrative structure as well as proposals on north-south relations that might underpin a political settlement. Then the British Government threw a hand grenade into the process when it insisted that partial decommissioning of IRA weapons and explosives was required before Sinn Féin could be admitted to multi-party talks. As far as the republicans were concerned, calling a ceasefire was the sole precondition for talks, and prior decommissioning wasn't part of the deal.

Gerry Adams drew headlines when he told a Belfast rally that the IRA 'haven't gone away, you know' in August that same year. A month later, David Trimble, who was perceived as a hardliner, was elected leader of the Ulster Unionist Party. The ceasefire finally broke down on 9 February 1996 with a massive bomb at London's Canary Wharf that killed two people, injured more than 100 others and caused massive structural damage. The challenge for the British and Irish governments was to restore the cessation, and build on that to achieve a settlement. But it wasn't going to happen under the existing governments in Dublin and London. The arrival of Tony Blair at No. 10 Downing Street and Bertie Ahern's election as taoiseach in a Fianna Fáil-led government in Dublin set the scene for a resumption of the ceasefire in July 1997. Sinn Féin was admitted to multi-party talks two days after the announcement.

Playwright and IRA activist Brendan Behan famously said once that the first item on any republican agenda was always the split. Given the tumultuous events at the time and the journey republicans had travelled, it was inevitable that cracks would appear in the Provo edifice. It was said that about 100 delegates attended an IRA convention in County Donegal in early October 1997. There was clearly a fork in the road, with non-violent constitutional politics in one direction and a resumption of armed struggle in the other. The hardliners would have won a majority, it was said, if one of their number – a woman activist who was originally from Belfast – hadn't launched a bitter personal attack on the role of Martin McGuinness. This was counterproductive, we are told, because his track-record meant that he remained in high esteem, even among those who were sceptical about the political course he was now taking. The breakaway group became known as the Real IRA. A political counterpart called the 32-County Sovereignty Movement was later established, although, as per usual in republican politics, there was no formal connection between the two.

Meanwhile, the multi-party talks, chaired by former majority leader in the US Senate George Mitchell, continued at Stormont's Castle Buildings. In front of as well as behind the scenes, Ahern and Blair were putting a colossal effort into achieving a settlement. Against all expectations, the Good Friday, a.k.a. Belfast, Agreement was concluded on 10 April 1998. It provided for a 108-member elected Assembly in the North, with a power-sharing Executive or cabinet drawn from both sides of the community; modification of the Republic's constitutional claim to the North; cross-border bodies headed by a North-South Ministerial Council; republican and loyalist prisoners convicted of terrorist offences to be released within two years; a commission on establishing a cross-community police force; a British-Irish Council of eight national, devolved and regional administrations; and a commitment by participants in the talks to use their influence to achieve the decommissioning of paramilitary weapons. Sinn Féin makes much of the fact that the Government of Ireland Act, which instituted partition, was being repealed – although the border, of course, remained in place.

Far from having a problem with residual abstentionist sentiment in the party, a month later at a special ardfheis in Dublin, the Sinn Féin leadership got 96 per cent support from delegates for taking seats in the proposed Northern Ireland Assembly. In the course of the proceedings there appeared to be some activity outside the hall at the RDS. When I went outside, who should appear but the Balcombe Street Four, arguably the most formidable and fearsome IRA unit since Michael Collins's 'Squad' in the War of Independence. They were in the twenty-fourth year of their prison sentences, and had been given leave, along with two dozen other republican prisoners, to attend the event (the four were fully released in 1999). The place pulsated with emotion, and some delegates with a very formidable history in the Troubles were seen to wipe away a tear. As

I wrote in the *Irish Times*: 'It was uncannily like dead people coming to life: these were the subversives from beyond the Pale who were locked up and the key thrown away.'[19]

There was a time when the Sinn Féin annual conference was considered a matter for reporters covering the North and/or security issues, or perhaps general news, rather than the political correspondents based in Leinster House: Sinn Féin was not regarded as a genuine political party. But now it was hard to find an empty seat in the area reserved for the media. The newly-politicised Sinn Féin had echoes of Fianna Fáil at the time of its foundation in 1926, when it is said that, in some cases, units of the 'Old' IRA converted into party branches overnight. Twelve days after the ardfheis, a referendum in the North approved the Agreement by 71.1 to 28.9 per cent, on a turn-out of 81 per cent, although the vote among the Protestant community was estimated at 55-45 for Yes. In the South, where constitutional change was also being voted on, the score was 94.4 per cent Yes and 5.6 per cent No, although the turn-out was lower at 56 per cent.[20]

In the week leading up to the ardfheis there had been widespread coverage of the fact that the activists who split away from the Provisionals had set up a new paramilitary organisation – later to become known as the Real IRA. There was considerable speculation as to its prospects of developing a campaign to match the body from which it had sprung. Nobody had the slightest expectation that this offspring of the Provos would perpetrate the greatest horror of the entire Troubles when a car-bomb exploded on a busy street in Omagh on a sunny Saturday afternoon on 15 August 1998. It killed twenty-nine people including a woman pregnant with twins. It was by no means the first horrific atrocity of the Troubles, but everyone hoped it would be the last. People noted that the victims came in equal numbers from both sides of the community divide. You had to wonder what the bright shining vision of Wolfe Tone, Robert Emmet and Thomas Davis had to do with blowing-up teenagers and shop assistants. Few believed that the mass slaughter of ordinary people was the bombers' actual aim, but even to place them at risk was considered reprehensible in itself. The high drama of hope mixed with tragedy in the North meant that little attention was being paid to Sinn Féin's tentative steps on the road to political power on the southern side of the border. The party had not taken part in elections to the Dáil since 1961 – although most of the H-Block candidates in 1981 would have been Sinn Féin supporters. In February 1982, Sinn Féin put up four candidates on an abstentionist basis. Three of them ran in border constituencies, where they got between six and nine per cent of the vote; Christy Burke ran in Dublin Central, where he achieved 3.2 per cent. There was another general election at the end of that year, but Sinn Féin didn't stand any candidates. Abstentionism in Dáil elections was dumped at the 1986 ardfheis and, in the following year's general election, Sinn Féin fielded no less than 23 candidates. None of them got elected, and the party's overall share of the vote was only 1.9 per cent. The contenders nevertheless did reasonably well in border constituencies. The party ran again in 1989 and 1992, without success. The breakthrough finally came in the 1997 general election, when Caoimhghín Ó Caoláin made it into the Dáil, having topped the poll in the border constituency of Cavan-Monaghan with 11,541 votes (19.4 per cent of first preferences), a major advance from the 4,197 votes or 7.7 per cent that he secured the previous time in 1992.

The party came close to winning three other seats: Martin Ferris in Kerry North, Seán Crowe in Dublin South-West and Pat Doherty in Donegal North-East all did well. Sinn Féin achieved only 2.5 per cent of the total general election first preferences, but this was an advance on the 1.6 per cent figure for 1992.[21]

The climate for Sinn Féin had improved even further when the next general election in the South came to pass in 2002. The media were awash around this time with allegations of corruption among the political establishment, primarily Fianna Fáil. A poll in the Dublin-based *Evening Herald* showed that Adams was the most popular party leader, at 57 per cent.[22] In an interview with Mark

Hennessy of the *Irish Times*, the Sinn Féin leader claimed that 'we certainly retain the idealism and the sense of public service that some others had, but which they have lost'. When Hennessy pointed out that others would find it nauseating to be lectured by Sinn Féin in light of the thirty-year IRA campaign, Adams replied: 'We're not lecturing.' [23]

When the votes were counted in the general election of May 2002, Sinn Féin emerged as the fourth-largest party, with 6.5 per cent of first preferences, ahead of the Progressive Democrats at 4 per cent, and the Greens at 3.8 per cent. But the republicans still won only five seats, whereas the PDs went from four to eight TDs and the Green Party's Dáil representation rose from two to six.[24]

Sinn Féin's expectations were high going into the next general election in 2007. This was despite what Britain's Queen Elizabeth would have called an *annus horribilis* in 2005, when almost every conceivable type of bad news story was appearing about members of the republican movement, including a massive bank robbery and particularly brutal and appalling murder outside a pub in Belfast. In addition, Taoiseach Bertie Ahern's role in the peace process was highlighted by a speech he gave to a joint session of the British houses of parliament shortly before the election. And in a party political broadcast by Fianna Fáil, British Prime Minister Tony Blair, former US President Bill Clinton and former US senator George Mitchell all praised Ahern's contribution to peace in the North.

Far from increasing its Dáil representation, Sinn Féin went down from five TDs to four, with the loss of Seán Crowe's seat in Dublin South-West. Mary Lou McDonald, the party's rising star, who had already been elected to the European Parliament in 2004, failed to win a Dáil seat in Dublin Central where she had been chosen to run instead of long-time republican activist Nicky Kehoe, who had come very close to getting elected in 2002.

The four Sinn Féin TDs were competing with twenty Labour Party deputies on the Opposition benches. Party leader Gerry Adams was not a member of the Dáil, whereas Labour's Eamon

Gilmore was sweeping all before him with his attacks on the Fianna Fáil-Green Party government. An *Irish Times*/Ipsos MRBI poll showed Labour as the most popular party in the State for the first time ever, at 32 per cent, and some Labour-friendly phrasemaker said there was a 'Gilmore gale' blowing. There was no favourable wind at the time for Enda Kenny and his party, which had dropped to 28 per cent. The poll helped to generate a heave against the Fine Gael leader, which ultimately proved unsuccessful.

The Sinn Féin contingent in the Dáil went up from four to five when Pearse Doherty won a by-election in November 2010. Doherty had failed to win a seat in 2007, but subsequently got elected as a Senator. The election of Fianna Fáil's Pat 'the Cope' Gallagher to the European Parliament in June 2009 created a Dáil vacancy in Donegal South-West, though the deeply-unpopular Fianna Fáil-Green Party Government was in no rush to hold a by-election to replace him. Doherty sought a judicial review and, on 2 November 2010, the High Court ruled that the delay was unreasonable. The government was forced to allow the contest, which Doherty won by a substantial margin. He was barely two months a TD when the Dáil was dissolved for a general election, to take place on 25 February 2011. Labour's attitude to Sinn Féin as a potential partner in government had already been made clear to reporters at an event in Enniscorthy, County Wexford, where the leader of that party, Eamon Gilmore, was addressing local supporters. Adams had been making political advances to Labour, but Gilmore said a coalition of the two parties was 'mathematically impossible. It's really not a runner'. Not only that, but there was also the question of Sinn Féin's economic policies: 'Insofar as we do understand what they are, I can't see how it would be possible to negotiate a programme for government with them.' While he was at it, Gilmore – surprise, surprise – pointed out that Labour was the only party in the Dáil that voted against the bank guarantee. The room where the rally was held in the Riverside Park Hotel on the banks of the River Slaney was packed to capacity, and nobody even giggled when Gilmore said Labour was going to lead the next government.[25]

Ireland was in the throes of a massive financial crisis, and the government of the day was widely perceived as being part of the problem instead of the solution. This was reflected in the opinion polls ahead of election day. Fianna Fáil scored an average of 15.3 per cent in seven surveys carried out in the lead-up to the election, whereas Fine Gael was on 38.3 per cent, Labour scored 19.3 and Sinn Féin was just below 11 per cent. Most attention was focused on Labour, which ran its most ambitious campaign since 1969 when it adopted the slogan, 'The Seventies will be Socialist'. In response, Fianna Fáil had successfully employed 'red scare' tactics, alleging communist influence. Labour actually went down by one seat, and the cynics reworked the Labour mantra to read: 'The Socialists will be Seventy.' This time around, Labour deployed the slogan 'Gilmore for Taoiseach'. Referring to the bailout terms set for Ireland by the Frankfurt-based European Central Bank, the European Commission and the International Monetary Fund, Gilmore declared that the choice facing voters was 'Frankfurt's way or Labour's way'.[26]

Sinn Féin probably benefited from being out of the limelight, and it did not have to contend with the same quantity of 'scare stories' as in the previous election. Adams stepped down as Westminster MP and Member of the Legislative Assembly for Belfast West to run for the Dáil in Louth, where the party's sitting TD, Arthur Morgan, had stepped aside.

The party's manifesto was launched in Dublin on 10 February under the slogan, 'There is a better way – *Tá bealach níos fearr ann*'. The document suggested – despite Eamon Gilmore's defiant words on the subject – that the bigger parties were sticking too closely to the terms of the bailout, and that they were maintaining a 'consensus for cuts'; the mainstream parties in turn accused Sinn Féin of fantasy economics. But there were no surprises in the Sinn Féin manifesto as there had been in 2007, when the proposal to cut corporation tax was left out. The 40-page bilingual document in 2011, proposed a third tax-rate of 48 per cent on individual incomes over €100,000 per annum, a wealth tax on assets worth over €1 million, restructuring bank debts, capping the salaries of TDs and ministers and exemption of low-earners in the 'no-tax' bracket from the Universal Social Charge introduced under the outgoing government's austerity policies.

Adams told a press conference that the purpose was to create 'an Ireland of equals' and I wrote, in an analysis-piece at the time: 'Sinn Féin's election manifesto is like a *Late Late Show* giveaway: there's something for everybody in the audience... "Burn, baby, burn" was a slogan used by African-American militants in the destructive riots of the 1960s and it has been adapted, consciously or otherwise, by Sinn Féin as "Burn the bondholders". The establishment throws up its hands in horror at the consequences of such an approach but it has undoubted doorstep appeal with those who wonder, "Why should we pay for the debts incurred by those feckless bankers?"... It hardly needs saying that Sinn Féin would restore the minimum wage to €8.65 an hour and restore social welfare and child benefit to last year's levels. Stimulus, not hardship, is the way forward. Spend, baby, spend!'

Among other proposals, Sinn Féin wanted all 18 MPs from the North – nationalist, unionist or otherwise – to be given 'membership' of the Oireachtas, whereby they would be able to attend and speak at Leinster House, but without having a vote. And of course the manifesto called for a referendum on Irish unity.[27]

Fianna Fáil went into the election with 71 TDs, and came back with 20. It was the most severe drubbing any party had suffered since the foundation of the State in 1922. The Greens, their minority coalition partners, were completely wiped out and lost all six seats. Fine Gael, which had overcome its internal tensions of the previous year, went up an extra 25 seats, from 51 to 76. Labour rose from 17 to 37, becoming the second-largest party in the Dáil.

Having embarked on the campaign with five TDs, Sinn Féin came back with fourteen. If one were to accept that this is essentially the same party that opposed the Treaty, then it was the highest total

1. Sinn Féin 2013 ardfheis in Castlebar (l/r): Trevor Ó Clochartaigh, Pearse Doherty, Gerry Adams, Mary Lou McDonald, Martin McGuinness and Sandra McLellan. (pic: Brenda Fitzsimons, *Irish Times*)

2. Gerry Adams (left), Ruairí Ó Brádaigh (seated) and Martin McGuinness, at the Sinn Féin Wolfe Tone Commemoration at Bodenstown, June 1986. (pic: Peter Thursfield, *Irish Times*)

3. Partners for peace (l/r): Gerry Adams, Taoiseach Albert Reynolds and SDLP leader John Hume shortly after the IRA ceasefire of August 1994. (pic: Matt Kavanagh, *Irish Times*)

4. The Chuckle Brothers: Northern Ireland First Minister Ian Paisley and Deputy First Minister Martin McGuinness at a press conference in Dublin, February 2008. (pic: Dara Mac Dónaill, *Irish Times*)

5. Mary Lou McDonald with Gerry Adams at the general election count centre in the RDS in May 2007, when she failed to win a Dáil seat in Dublin Central. (pic: Dara Mac Dónaill, *Irish Times*)

6. Mary Lou McDonald TD addresses the Sinn Féin Ard Fheis in Derry, March 2015, with Senator Trevor Ó Clochartaigh in the background. (pic: Dara Mac Dónaill, *Irish Times*)

7. Sinn Féin TDs Caoimhghín Ó Caoláin and Martin Ferris at Leinster House, October 2009. (pic: Eric Luke, *Irish Times*)

8. Sinn Féin's 14 TDs assemble at Dáil Éireann after the February 2011 general election. (pic: Cyril Byrne, *Irish Times*)

9. Sinn Féin's new generation: Senator Kathryn Reilly from Cavan, July 2013. (pic: Dara Mac Dónaill, *Irish Times*)

10. Lynn Boylan celebrates her election to the European Parliament after topping the poll in Dublin, May 2014. (pic: Dara Mac Dónaill, *Irish Times*)

11. Sinn Féin MEPs meet party leaders at Leinster House, June 2014 (l/r): Liadh Ní Riada, Matt Carthy, Mary Lou McDonald TD, Martina Anderson, Gerry Adams TD and Lynn Boylan. (pic: Brenda Fitzsimons, *Irish Times*)

12. Sinn Féin Lord Mayor of Dublin, Críona Ní Dhálaigh lays a wreath for the 40th anniversary of the August 1975 killing of three members of the Miami Showband by loyalists. (pic: Eric Luke, *Irish Times*)

13. Theoretician and activist Eoin Ó Broin addresses the 2012 Sinn Féin ardfheis in Killarney. (pic: Alan Betson, *Irish Times*)

14. Windsor Castle chat (l/r): Prime Minister David Cameron, Taoiseach Enda Kenny and Deputy First Minister Martin McGuinness at the banquet hosted by Queen Elizabeth and Prince Philip for the state visit by President Michael D. Higgins, April 2014. (pic: Alan Betson, *Irish Times*)

15. Martin McGuinness and Gerry Adams carry the coffin of veteran republican Joe Cahill in Belfast, July 2004. (pic: Dara Mac Dónaill, *Irish Times*)

16. Pearse Doherty arrives at Leinster House after his November 2010 by-election victory in Donegal South-West. (pic: Eric Luke, *Irish Times*)

17. Sinn Féin abortion rebel and Meath West TD Peadar Tóibín. (pic: Dara Mac Dónaill, *Irish Times*)

achieved by republicans since 1923. The party ran 41 candidates, the same number as in 2007, but this time a third of them were elected. Sinn Féin's share of the overall vote went up by 77,251 to 220,661, or three percentage points to 9.9 per cent of the overall total of first preferences, and it had only six seats fewer than Fianna Fáil, the largest party on the opposition benches. In three of the constituencies, Sinn Féin ran two people: Cavan-Monaghan on the Border, Carlow-Kilkenny and Mayo – no extra deputies came out of this approach, but there might be benefits in the future.

For obvious reasons, Sinn Féin tends to do best in the border counties. In 2011 it got TDs elected in each of the five constituencies along the dividing-line with Northern Ireland and could arguably have brought in two deputies in Cavan-Monaghan if there had been better vote-management. But despite taking four seats in Dublin, the level of support there was below what it achieved outside the capital city. There was clearly an issue to be addressed here: Sinn Féin's vote in Dublin was only one per cent higher than in 2007. The capital and its environs accounted for 12 of the forty-three constituencies, and 47 of the 166 Dáil seats.[28]

Given the generally friendlier attitude towards left-sounding candidates in Dublin, Sinn Féin might have been expected to do better – but this was Labour's hour in the sun. At least Mary Lou McDonald finally won her seat in Dublin Central, and the party got one other woman TD elected: Sandra McLellan, in Cork East. They became the first female deputies for Sinn Féin since 1927; Fianna Fáil's 20 TDs in the new Dáil were all male.

I was reporting from the count-centre in Dundalk when Adams was elected at the head of the poll. He declared that the Sinn Féin gains were part of the 'reconquest of Ireland by the people of Ireland,' and recalled that the following Tuesday was the day that Bobby Sands started his hunger strike. His success in getting elected on the first count, following a campaign marked by constant questions about his grasp of economic issues and precise role in the republican movement, surprised some observers. Martin McGuinness was on hand to celebrate the victory of his long-time comrade, whom he compared to legendary Ulster hero Cuchulainn. Instead of the traditional '*Tiocfaidh ár lá*' (Our day will come), republican supporters chanted, 'Top-the-poll, top-the-poll' as they toasted their leader with plastic glasses of Prosecco. A win is a win is a win.[29] Adams had achieved the third-highest vote of any candidate, behind Independent contender Shane Ross in Dublin South and, in first place, Taoiseach-to-be Enda Kenny in the Mayo constituency.[30] Now that the party had more than seven TDs it could take part in Leaders' Questions, generally the high point of Dáil business, as well as other parliamentary activities from which it had previously been excluded.

Despite a very creditable performance, Labour's dream of being the biggest party failed to become reality, and nobody was surprised when it went into coalition as the minority partner. Fine Gael could, in theory, have coalesced with Sinn Féin, but the republicans were identified with the conflict which had so recently ended in the North, while Fianna Fáil was completely untouchable – the entire election had for many people been a case of getting that party out of power. An alliance between Fine Gael and a range of Independents was also possible, but would probably have lacked the discipline required for dealing with the economic crisis. Adams replaced Caoimhghín Ó Caoláin as leader – of what I termed at the time, with unconscious irony, 'the Sinn Féin parliamentary party'.[31]

The party now had almost enough TDs to appoint a front bench to monitor the activities of the fifteen members of the Cabinet on a one-to-one basis. Mary Lou McDonald was named as Deputy Leader, and Spokeswoman on Public Expenditure and Reform. Pearse Doherty from Donegal became Finance Spokesman – his grasp of economic issues had clearly lifted an immense burden from the shoulders of the party leader. Other appointments in Sinn Féin's 'shadow cabinet' were: Michael Colreavy – Agriculture, Food and Marine; Seán Crowe – Education and Skills; Dessie Ellis – Transport and Housing; Martin Ferris – Communications, Energy and Natural Resources; Sandra McLellan – Arts, Heritage, Tourism and Sport;

Pádraig Mac Lochlainn – Foreign Affairs and Trade; Jonathan O'Brien – Justice, Equality and Defence; Caoimghín Ó Caoláin – Health and Children; Aengus Ó Snodaigh – Social Protection; Brian Stanley – Environment, Community and Local Government; Peadar Tóibín – Enterprise, Jobs and Innovation, and the Gaeltacht.

Announcing the list, Adams claimed that Sinn Féin was now the 'main opposition party' because of the 'sameness between the Fianna Fáil party, Fine Gael and Labour in terms of their support for austerity packages and policies.' At the same press conference he was asked for his views on the situation in Libya (which was in turmoil at the time) and he replied: 'We think the Gaddafi administration is wrong in the way it has been treating its own citizens.' It is not known whether Colonel Gaddafi read those comments before his brutal demise the following October but, if he did, the longtime supplier of the sinews of war to the republican movement may have felt that, in politics and revolution, there ain't no gratitude.[32]

At around the same time that Gaddafi was overthrown, Ireland was also changing its head of state, but in a more gentle fashion: through a presidential election.

At the Sinn Féin ardfheis, which took place on the second weekend of September that year in Belfast, Martin McGuinness was asked if he would be interested in running for the presidency and he replied: 'I haven't even thought about it.'[33] As well as McGuinness, the names of Michelle Gildernew and Caoimhghín Ó Caoláin were being speculatively mentioned. Adams and Mary Lou McDonald both ruled themselves out.[34]

With Fianna Fáil sitting this one out the field was clear on the opposition side, and Sinn Féin seized that opportunity. It was announced that McGuinness would be the party's candidate and take a break from his role as Deputy First Minister in the North for the duration of the campaign. Assessing the McGuinness candidacy, Gerry Moriarty wrote in the *Irish Times*: 'The IRA killed some 1,800 people throughout the Troubles, and regardless of his protestations or elisions, he is viewed both in the Republic and in the North as an

IRA figurehead... He will be asked once again, as was alleged eighteen years ago, whether he encouraged alleged IRA informer Frank Hegarty to return to his home in Derry in 1986, only to be murdered by the IRA? He will be asked about the circumstances of how in 1990 the IRA in Derry turned a civilian, Patsy Gillespie, into a human bomb, and how that bomb was detonated, killing Gillespie and five British soldiers – an action the retired bishop of Derry, Edward Daly, termed as Satanic. He will be asked many more questions, including, as was also alleged, whether he doubled as a British agent during the Troubles?'[35]

McGuinness caused a minor stir early on, in an interview on the Newstalk radio station, when he said that there were 'West Brit elements' in the Dublin-based media who were linking his candidacy to the activities of the IRA over the years. Talking to reporters later that day, when he was lodging his nomination papers at the Custom House later that day, he was asked if he could understand why people might have difficulty believing his assertion that he left the IRA in 1974. He replied:

> I went to prison on two occasions for membership of the IRA, in 1973 and 1974, on the word of a Garda superintendent. I was never, ever charged with membership of the IRA after that, except on one occasion in 1976 when I was brought to Castlereagh interrogation centre in Belfast and they threw down a sheaf of newspapers in front of me, and that was their evidence... and the case collapsed within a few days.[36]

In a debate chaired by Seán O'Rourke on RTÉ Radio a week later, McGuinness continued to hold to the position that he had left the IRA in 1974: 'The reality is that I was convicted of IRA membership in 1973 and in 1974 and never after that ... But I have never denied my past in the IRA: the circumstances that existed on the streets of Derry with our citizens being treated as second-class citizens, treated like dirt.'[37] McGuinness told reporters in Dublin that he had 'no role whatsoever' in the death of Frank Hegarty (45), whose body was found on a border road near Castlederg, County Tyrone, on 25 May 1986, and who is believed to have been shot by the IRA as an alleged informer.[38]

Fine Gael Minister for the Environment Phil Hogan said that the election of a 'former terrorist' to Áras an Uachtaráin would jeopardise foreign investment. Government Chief Whip Paul Kehoe claimed on Twitter that McGuinness had the proceeds of the Northern Bank robbery of December 2004 at his disposal.[39] Speaking on TodayFM, McGuinness was unable to name the Republic's environment minister, or to say how many TDs were in the Dáil.[40] In a candidates' debate on TV3, moderator Vincent Browne produced a pile of eight books containing assertions that McGuinness had been an IRA member after 1974.[41]

The McGuinness campaign was punctuated by drama. Canvassing in Athlone on 10 October, he was confronted by David Kelly, a son of Irish Army Private Patrick Kelly who was shot dead, along with Garda Gary Sheehan at Derrada Woods, County Leitrim, on 16 December 1983, while trying to rescue businessman Don Tidey who had been kidnapped by the Provisional IRA. David Kelly held up a picture of his father as he told McGuinness: 'I want justice for my father. I believe you know the names of the killers of my father and I want you to tell me who they are. You were on the Army Council of the IRA.' It was a searing episode, captured on television. McGuinness denied knowing the names, insisting as well that he was not a member of the Army Council, and pointed out that he had 'been at the heart of a very important peace process in the North over the last twenty years which has brought conflict and violence and death to an end'.[42]

The IRA connection resurfaced in a debate among the contenders on RTE's *Prime Time* programme conducted by Miriam O'Callaghan, who asked the Sinn Féin candidate: 'How do you square, Martin McGuinness, with your God the fact that you were involved in the murder of so many people?' McGuinness replied: 'I think that's a disgraceful comment to make.' Later in the programme she asked McGuinness if he went to confession, and she challenged his constant assertion that he left the IRA in 1974: 'We're not going to argue that fact that absolutely everyone thinks you were there, longer, after 1974.' When she went on to ask why he had not named those who killed Private Kelly in 1986, McGuinness said that he didn't know who they were. O'Callaghan replied: 'But you're a republican, you know everyone in the republican movement.' McGuinness responded: 'I think that's a stupid statement for you to make.' McGuinness later asked for a one-to-one meeting where he complained directly to the presenter.[43] Whatever was said didn't prevent them having a 'friendly conversation' when they met again the following week at a function in the Mansion House.[44]

Given the political climate at the time, the Sinn Féin candidate was never going to win the election but he did play a significant role in determining the outcome. Independent candidate Seán Gallagher, who had a Fianna Fáil political background, had become the frontrunner in the race. Three days before the election, four different opinion polls showed him between ten and fifteen points ahead of his nearest rival, Michael D. Higgins. A senior Labour Party source told me later that the mood in the Higgins campaign was 'very downbeat' over the gap in the polls: 'It's not something you can recover in the last week, so a lot of people were very upset.' It looked like Gallagher was coasting to victory. All changed, however, when the candidates appeared that night in a debate on RTE's current affairs programe, *The Frontline*. McGuinness was in attack mode and declared he had been contacted before the show by a man who said he had been one of a group of thirty to thirty-five individuals, invited by Gallagher, who paid €5,000 each to be photographed with Brian Cowen at an event in a Dundalk hotel, when the latter still held the office of taoiseach. McGuinness said the man told him it was arranged by Gallagher, who then brought the photos to his house and collected the cheque from him. Gallagher denied collecting the cheque, and said he had invited 'perhaps two to three people' to meet Cowen. Presenter Pat Kenny referred to a message that had just appeared on what he described as 'the Martin McGuinness for President Twitter account' and he added: 'Sinn Féin are saying they are going to produce the man who gave you the cheque for five grand' (The actual name of the account was @mcguinness4pres and the message read: 'The man that Gallagher took the cheque from will be at a press conference tomorrow'; earlier, respected blogger David Cochrane tweeted: 'A SF person has told me they have the person who gave the 5k cheque to Gallagher and are likely to roll him out tomorrow.') When Kenny asked him if he knew who the man was, Gallagher said it was a convicted fuel-smuggler who had rented out an office to Gerry Adams in the recent general election, but that he had 'no recollection of getting a cheque from this guy'. Kenny asked: 'You went around to a fuel-smuggler... and invited him to a Fianna Fáil do?' Gallagher said: 'If he gave me the cheque it was made out to Fianna Fáil headquarters and it was delivered, and that was that. It had nothing to do with me.'[45] A tweet from the real McGuinness campaign, @Martin4Prez2011, which pointed out that it was not the source of the earlier bogus message, was received twenty-six minutes before the end of the programme, but was not mentioned on the air. The Broadcasting Authority of Ireland, which is the regulatory body in this area, later upheld a complaint by Seán Gallagher that the broadcast of a tweet from what had been erroneously described as the 'Martin McGuinness for President Campaign' was unfair.[46]

When the votes were counted, the poll figures from the previous weekend were reversed. Labour's Michael D. Higgins was just below 40 per cent of first preferences, while Gallagher got 28.5 per cent. McGuinness secured 243,030 votes, or 13.72 per cent, on the first count, which was more than double the figure for Fine Gael's Gay Mitchell, in fourth place.[47] While the Sinn Féin candidate did not win, he played a significant role in determining the result. It is a matter of debate whether someone with a less-contentious history would have been a better choice for Sinn Féin. The McGuinness candidacy did revive many controversial past issues, but giving them an airing might prove beneficial to the party in the long run.

In contrast to the South, Sinn Féin's path to power in Northern Ireland since the Good Friday Agreement has been relatively straightforward, although there were difficulties along the way about issues such as the decommissioning of IRA weapons. The party won 18 seats out of 108 in the elections to the new power-sharing Assembly in June 1998, compared to 24 for the SDLP, 28 for the Ulster Unionist Party (UUP) and 20 for the Democratic Unionist Party (DUP).[48] In the next Assembly elections in November 2003 the positions of the nationalist parties were reversed, with Sinn Féin winning 24 seats this time, and the SDLP coming home with 18. The DUP also passed out the UUP, by 30 to 27 seats.[49] The third elections to the Assembly, which took place on 7 March 2007, reflected the growing dominance of the DUP, with 36 seats and Sinn Féin with 28, compared to 18 for the UUP and 16 SDLP seats.[50] On 5 May 2011, ten weeks after the Republic had gone to the polls, Assembly elections in the North saw the DUP win 38 seats, with 29 for Sinn Féin, while the UUP got 16 and the SDLP, 14 seats.[51]

UUP leader David Trimble and Séamus Mallon, deputy leader of the SDLP, were elected First Minister and Deputy First Minister respectively, on 1 July 1998. Five months later, as part of the d'Hondt mechanism to ensure power-sharing between the parties, McGuinness became Minister for Education, and his Sinn Féin colleague, Bairbre de Brún, was appointed Minister for Health. Mallon was succeeded by his SDLP colleague Mark Durkan in November 2001. Trimble's term of office ended in October 2002, when the Assembly was suspended for five years because of the Stormontgate scandal, in which an IRA spy-ring was alleged to be operating in the Parliament Buildings. Sinn Féin's group administrator at Stormont, Denis Donaldson, was one of three men arrested at the time: he later admitted having been a British agent for more than twenty years, but unwisely remained in Ireland and was shot dead in County Donegal in April 2006. Three years after that, the dissident Real IRA claimed responsibility for the killing.

By the time devolution was restored in May 2007, the Provisional IRA had formally declared an end to its campaign, and was adjudged to have decommissioned its weapons, while Sinn Féin had accepted the Police Service of Northern Ireland. DUP leader, the Rev Ian Paisley, became First Minister, with Martin McGuinness as Deputy First Minister – this was the period of the 'Chuckle Brothers', reflecting the amiable public interaction between the pair. Paisley stood down in March 2008, and was succeeded by Peter Robinson.

When Queen Elizabeth visited Northern Ireland in June 2012, the Deputy First Minister met her at Belfast's Lyric Theatre, as mentioned in Chapter Four, where they shook hands in an historic gesture. We reporters were waiting outside and, when he emerged, McGuinness said: 'I'm still a republican.'

In parallel with its efforts to get elected to Dáil Éireann, Sinn Féin was throwing its hat in the ring for the European Parliament. Elections are held every five years, and the party started out on this path in 1984 when Danny Morrison came fourth in the three-seat constituency of Northern Ireland with 91,476 votes. This was a respectable total, given that he was up against a giant of the political scene, SDLP leader John Hume, who won a seat with 151,399 votes. The party also ran in the four Euro-constituencies south of the border, but without much impact.[52] Morrison ran again in 1989 but the political climate was less-favourable and his vote dropped to 48,914, down from 13.35 to 9.15 per cent. Sinn Féin ran in the South this time also, but without attracting much support.

It seemed to be set in stone in the North that the three seats would be divided between Ian Paisley of the Democratic Unionist Party, John Hume of the SDLP and a third contender from the Ulster Unionists. This was the outcome again in 1994, when Sinn Féin put up three candidates in the North, who polled a respectable total of 55,215 between them. But the soil on the other side of the border remained barren: the party ran in all the Euro-constituencies but all of its candidates, bar one, were below the 10,000 mark. The 1994

European contest took place in early June and, at the end of August, the IRA declared its ceasefire. This was interrupted in February 1996 but resumed in July 1997. These cessations, and the peace process in general, clearly benefited Sinn Féin. The party got its strongest support so far in a European election in 1999 when Mitchel McLaughlin nearly took the third seat in the North from Ulster Unionist Jim Nicholson. The mood was much improved in the 'Free State' constituencies as well, where the total Sinn Féin vote went up from 33,823 to 88,165.

Fast forward to 2004: John Hume retired from politics in February that year and, in the June European elections, Sinn Féin's Bairbre de Brún won the 'nationalist' seat with 144,541 votes – a total worthy of the SDLP leader in his prime. Sinn Féin was on a roll: Mary Lou McDonald took the last of the four seats in Dublin; in the North-West (formerly Connaught-Ulster) constituency, Pearse Doherty received the second-highest number of first preferences at 65,321, but got squeezed-out on the fifth count by others who got more transfers.

Five years later, in 2009, Bairbre de Brún topped the poll as she took a seat in the North but Mary Lou McDonald lost out in Dublin, which had gone down from four seats to three. Coming in the wake of her failure to get elected to the Dáil two years before, it was a difficult time for her. In Ireland South, Toiréasa Ferris, daughter of leading republican and Sinn Féin TD, Martin Ferris, got the third-highest total of first preferences but failed to win any of the three seats, due to the vagaries of the Proportional Representation system.

Labour was still in opposition in 2009, and making the most of the economic difficulties the Fianna Fáil-Green Party Government was facing at the time. The party won three of the twelve seats in the Republic's constituencies, whereas it only had one going into the election. Five years on, when the next European contest took place, Labour had been in coalition with Fine Gael for three years. It also bore the brunt of criticism for that government's austerity policies which, in many voters' eyes, did not appear to be much different from those of its predecessor.[53]

Israeli diplomat Abba Eban is supposed to have said of his Arab opponents that they 'never miss an opportunity to miss an opportunity'. Whatever the truth of his words in that particular instance, the same could not be said of Sinn Féin in the 2014 European elections. It was no great surprise when Martina Anderson stormed in ahead of the rest in the North to take a seat for Sinn Féin on the first count. But the South was where the real news was developing. It had been generally taken for granted that Sinn Féin would do well, but the party exceeded most expectations when it took a seat in each of the three constituencies – Ireland East and North-West had by now been replaced by a single unit called Midlands-North-West. Lynn Boylan topped the poll for Sinn Féin in Dublin, Liadh Ní Riada came second in South and Matt Carthy took third place in Midlands-North-West.

Sinn Féin's first-preference vote in the South totalled 323,300, which was a 57 per cent increase on the 2009 European elections. Figures for the island as a whole were: 483,113 in 2014; 331,797 in 2009 and 146,148 in 1984. Nearly half-a-million voters, north and south, chose Sinn Féin in 2014.

The 2014 European and local elections in the Republic were held on the same day. Sinn Féin increased its city and county council seats from 54 to 159. The number of Sinn Féin first preferences in the local elections was over a quarter of a million, an increase of more than 100,000 on the last time in 2009. An *Irish Times*/Ipsos MRBI poll shortly beforehand, on people's voting intentions in the local elections, had Sinn Féin on 19 per cent support but the actual score at the ballot-box was 15 per cent, which probably reflected an uneven level of organisation at grassroots level. The republicans got 19.5 per cent of first preferences in the European elections, where a local support network is less important. The challenge now was to build up the organisation in the Dáil constituencies in time for the general election.

7. MEMBERS, CRITICS AND OBSERVERS

FOR MOST KERRYMEN, WINNING an All-Ireland senior medal in Gaelic football represents the summit of achievement. Sinn Féin's Martin Ferris has an All-Ireland medal at Under-21 level and, if he hadn't gotten caught up in revolutionary politics, might have reached the heights of sporting glory with the senior team. On the rain-soaked day in 1973 when the Under-21 final was held, there were two other future TDs on the pitch. Ferris's Kerry team-mate Jimmy Deenihan went on to win five senior medals, as well as getting elected as a TD for Fine Gael and becoming a cabinet minister. John O'Mahony played for Mayo, the losing team, but went on to great success as a team manager as well as getting elected to the Dáil for Fine Gael in 2007. Many members of Kerry's Under-21 line-up from 1973 went on to play in the senior team's famous victory in the All-Ireland final two years later. Ferris might have made that team but he was incarcerated in Portlaoise prison for his republican activities by that stage: 'I watched it in Portlaoise in '75 when Kerry beat Dublin. I would like to know – would I have been good enough or not? But my commitments were elsewhere.'[1] Expert football opinion in Kerry is quoted as saying Ferris would have won many senior medals if he had given the game his full concentration.[2]

Like Martin McGuinness in Derry, Ferris's parents were not involved in the republican movement. The Sinn Féin TD, who hails from Ardfert, outside Tralee, describes his mother as a 'very strong' Fianna Fáil supporter and his father as a non-aligned voter. But the young Martin was very close to Jack Ferris, a first cousin of his father's, who had been imprisoned for four years by the De Valera government during the Second World War and taken part in a number of hunger strikes. However, it was events on the ground at the start of the Troubles that played the key role and he recalls in an interview for this book at Leinster House: 'The real influence on why I became actively involved was the civil rights movement in the North and the optics of seeing that on television, with them being beaten off the streets, and then at Burntollet Bridge and all of those things that happened. That was the real motivation.'

Ferris has spent at total of almost thirteen years behind bars. He goes through the list: 'I was in on two occasions in the seventies. One was for a twelve-month sentence, one was for an eighteen-month sentence, both for membership of the IRA. And I went back in, in September 1984, and I was released in September 1994.' The second stint included a 47-day hunger strike over prison conditions. His next jail term came after he was arrested with two others off the south coast of Kerry in September 1984 for attempting to import seven tons of explosives, arms and ammunition on the fishing vessel Marita Ann. The notorious James 'Whitey' Bulger was involved in the original shipment out of Boston but Ferris has denied knowing anything about the gangland connection.[3]

Looking back on his prison time now, he says: 'The first two occasions I was in, I was young: when you are young there is a lot of romanticism about the struggle, about being in prison and all of that. And there was a huge turnover in Portlaoise at that point. You had people coming and going the whole time. And then I wasn't married, I had no ties as such. The third time I went in, from '84 to '94, I was married. We had five children when I went in; my wife was pregnant with our sixth child. But I was fortunate in being married to a very strong woman and we had a great support base from all shades of political opinion in the area where I live, and it made things very easy – for me anyway. It was okay: I suppose if you have the political conviction that's required to get you through it, you'll get through it.' He was allowed out on parole for three days in 1989 when his mother died: 'I got out in '91: my son was playing in an All-Ireland final, I got twelve hours. I got out for a confirmation and a communion in '92 and '93. I got out for Christmas one year as well.'

He makes no apologies for his IRA activities, nor does he accept that going on to take the peaceful, democratic road constituted a sell-out. He sees the two phases as complementary: 'I firmly believe that the earlier part of my life from 1970, when I became involved in militant republicanism, was necessary. I remain convinced of that to this day. I believe ... the ceasefire of 1994 and in particular the negotiation of the Good Friday Agreement, created a platform where we can address the outstanding difficulties within our country and also address the national question as well, and the people of Ireland are in the position to address that at a future date.'

Kerry is a republican heartland, so how was his transition from revolutionary militant to political activist received there? He replies: 'The best way to judge it is that over 90 per cent of the republican membership in Kerry supports the Sinn Féin project.' He points out that the party went up from two to five county councillors in Kerry in the May 2014 local elections. Martin's daughter Toiréasa Ferris has been a councillor since 2003.

He first entered Dáil Éireann in 2002, as one of five Sinn Féin candidates who won seats in that general election. But this wasn't a sufficient number, under standing orders, to play a proper role in parliamentary life: 'It was quite soul-destroying because we didn't have any speaking rights as such, we had no party status. Then we went down to four in the 2007 election, and you didn't believe you were achieving anything here during that period. But since the election of 2011 where we now have fourteen TDs and three Senators, you can see that the efforts of the past in the electoral-political process are now starting to pay dividends.'

Listening to him, it almost sounds as if his prison terms weren't quite as bad as those early years in Leinster House. But all that has changed and Martin Ferris is looking forward to the time ahead: 'I'm very confident that there's a very encouraging future for Sinn Féin as a political party but more importantly I think we're moving towards the inevitable goal of a United Ireland.'

TO FIND out more about the internal workings of the party, I talked to Ken O'Connell, who is the Political Director for Sinn Féin in the South. He points out that people can join as individual members or they can choose to be part of a cumann or branch, which involves a greater level of activity. The membership subscription is €10 in the South for employed persons and €5 for unwaged (the same figures apply in sterling, north of the border). There is a three-month probation period.

When rock star Sinéad O'Connor applied to join at the end of 2014, O'Connell and a party colleague, Sinéad Ní Bhroin, met her to discuss the application. In an interview with the present writer, he recalls the type of advice he gave the singer at the meeting:

> Being a member of Sinn Féin would probably hold her back: she wouldn't be able to speak freely, she'd have to follow party policy on all policy issues, she couldn't be out there [and] accept one part of it and not accept another part of it, and that's what membership entails. If you sign up to be a member, that's what you are, you take on the policy. It doesn't mean you have to support it completely yourself. There are things in Sinn Féin policy that I possibly wouldn't 100 per cent agree with, but I wouldn't be speaking out against them. If the party makes a decision at our ardfheis, that's it, you're bound by the decisions of the ardfheis. And that it would probably constrain somebody like herself in terms of

doing that and there's other ways of actually getting to
people if she feels so strongly around the united Ireland,
if she felt so strongly around the [1916] Proclamation,
all of that sort of stuff.[4]

As regards her observation on Facebook that the Sinn Féin
leadership should step down in favour of a younger generation,
O'Connell says: 'Sure that doesn't matter, that's an opinion.' But he
continues that, 'It is hardly compatible with somebody coming in
and saying, "I accept the policy of the party, I accept the democratic
nature of the party but I don't accept the leadership of the party as
democratically-elected at an ardfheis", as Gerry is every year.'

That particular issue didn't arise in discussion with Sinéad
O'Connor, but O'Connell says he made the point to her that, if she
was involved in her local cumann in Bray, County Wicklow, the
members would be out in the evening, 'probably giving out leaflets
on water-charges or housing or unemployment... and you'd have to
accept that and be part of doing all of that'. The singer withdrew her
application after the meeting and wrote on Facebook: 'They
persuaded me that I'd be bored shitless, pretty much waiting for them
to get into government before being able to help generate any
national discussion on the issue of ending partition.'[5]

As regards the claims, in some quarters, that Sinn Féin is the
political equivalent of a monastic sect whose members are afraid to
talk out of turn, O'Connell says: 'It's nonsense... There isn't a sense
that everybody is controlled, the party doesn't do that. It would take
far too long and far too much time to actually go about doing that.
You've been at ardfheiseanna, there's a very healthy debate, and
different points of view are taken. Sinn Féin is probably better than
some of the other parties in terms of actually getting out there and
debating policy issues.'

O'Connell first became active in his native Bray as a teenager in
the 1970s. Shortage of housing, high unemployment and public
access to beaches on the Wicklow coast were live issues at the time:

some of them are still on the agenda. Asked if he was ever a member of the IRA, he replies: 'No, I was never a member of an illegal organisation.' He has been working full-time for the party since 1985 and previously held such positions as Munster Organiser and Regional Organiser.

Sinn Féin has 'roughly around 8,500' members in the South and 'probably in or around 3,000-4,000' north of the Border. 'You're probably looking at around 11,000 members altogether.' Asked how many candidates Sinn Féin will run in the next general election, he replies: 'We're hoping to run up to sixty.' (The latest figure is 46.)

LIKE Eamon de Valera, Eoin Ó Broin attended Blackrock College. Both of them went on to become active republicans. But Ó Broin considers himself distinctly to the left of the 'Long Fellow' who set up Fianna Fáil. The leading voice on the left in Sinn Féin and the party's most prominent theoretician, Ó Broin is the author of a book on Sinn Féin's place in the left-republican tradition.[6] Reviewing it for the *Irish Times*, Professor Richard English found it 'impressive and provocative... compelling, lucid and intelligent'.[7] The magazine *History Ireland* carried a review by Dr Emmet O'Connor, who said it 'ought to be read by all who are interested in the left, where it's come from and where it should be going'. [8]

Ó Broin has also written a book about the *matxinada* or rebellion in the Basque country.[9] Born on 6 January 1972, his background is solidly middle-class. He recalls: 'There was no politics in the family when I was growing up.'[10] Leaving the warm embrace of south Dublin in 1991, he took a degree in Cultural Studies (politics, history and political theory) at the University of East London. During his sojourn by the Thames he became involved in the politics of the local Irish community, got to know people from the North of Ireland and followed coverage of the North in the British media. Ironically, the level of anti-republican insulation in south Dublin was more effective than its equivalent in the British capital.

When he returned to Dublin, one of the first things he did was join Sinn Féin. In September 1995, he moved to Belfast and worked for the party there. In 2001 he was elected to Belfast City Council for the Oldpark Ward in North Belfast – quite an achievement for a Blackrock boy. In 2004 he became the party's Director of European Affairs. That was the year in which Sinn Féin got two candidates elected to the European Parliament – Mary Lou McDonald in Dublin and Bairbre de Brún in the North.

He moved back to Dublin in 2006, and took three years out to work for the charity Focus Ireland as a policy officer. He was co-opted to South Dublin County Council in October 2013 for Clondalkin and kept his seat when he topped the poll for the area in the local elections of May 2014. Ó Broin has been selected to run for the Dáil in the Dublin Mid-West constituency, which includes Clondalkin, Lucan and Palmerstown. His partner Lynn Boylan was elected MEP for Dublin in the May 2014 European elections with 24 per cent of the first preferences, nearly 29,000 votes ahead of her nearest rival. Sinéad Ní Bhroin, mentioned earlier in this chapter, is also a prominent Sinn Féin activist and a sister of Eoin's.

In the course of our interview, Ó Broin denied that he was ever in the IRA. But he's an important voice in post-IRA Sinn Féin, and has strong ideas on the future path the movement should take. He holds forth in *An Phoblacht*, writes a blog entitled *Another View* and makes regular appearances in the opinion pages of the *Sunday Business Post*. In a set of eight theses at the end of his book on left-republicanism he warns against allowing social and economic change to take second place to the cause of national reunification. And he says the party cannot grow unless there is real internal democracy as distinct from the highly-centralised and vertical command-structure of the decades prior to the peace process. Instead of taking the road that will lead to a coalition with Fianna Fáil on the centre-right, his 2009 book says Sinn Féin should seek to organise an alternative alliance with parties of the left, trade unions and other progressive forces.

Despite its authoritarian image, Sinn Féin has been tolerant of his opinions: 'I've never been treated differently for holding contrary views.' As far as he is concerned, 'you can be loyal and well-disciplined and still have varying views from the party at various stages'. When I put it to him that he appears to have at least a difference of emphasis with some others in the party on the issue of coalition, he replied: 'Well, not now. I was one of a number of people who, over the last year or so, was arguing very strongly that we should take a really clear position, well in advance of the election, of not being willing to participate in a Fianna Fáil- or Fine Gael-led coalition.'

He points out that this was unanimously accepted at the March 2015 ardfheis in Derry, but I draw attention to the section of that motion which 'commits Sinn Féin to form broad alliances with like-minded parties and independents... to maximise the potential for an anti-austerity government in the 26 Counties'.

Ó Broin comments: 'We would still have to be the largest party. We wouldn't participate in a coalition that's led by Fianna Fáil or Fine Gael.'

But what if Sinn Féin was the largest element in a left alliance which was larger than Fianna Fáil but FF still had more seats than Sinn Féin? Ó Broin replies: 'I think you're reading too much into the motion, I don't think that's the conscious intention of it. I think the view is, if you had a situation where Sinn Féin was the dominant party around the cabinet-table, if Sinn Féin was the Taoiseach and in a position to [set] the main direction of economic and social policy, that's really the substance of the motion. And obviously if you could have Sinn Féin plus a collection of Left deputies, that would even further strengthen that position. I don't think you would have a situation where Fianna Fáil could be the larger party but would concede the dominant position in the coalition because we have an alliance with X number of non-aligned Left deputies.'

When I say that I have been getting the impression that there is another view that it might be nice to be in government, north and south, for the centenary of the 1916 Rising, he comments: 'I've never heard internally, in any debate or discussion – and we've had very detailed discussion around it – anybody arguing [*for*] the merits of that.' Nor does he think the party would have significantly greater influence on Northern Ireland policy as a minority element in a Dublin coalition.

He points to the fate of the Labour Party, the Greens and the Progressive Democrats, who, he says, could not implement the core objectives that got them elected, due to the fact that they were only junior partners in government. 'In terms of your ability to deliver, you really need that dominant position. So for us, it's not even about wanting the position of Taoiseach, it's about the arrangement that would allow you to deliver significant portions of your policy agenda and, as we can see from this coalition and the previous one, that requires you to be the larger party,' says Eoin Ó Broin.

PEARSE Doherty is the product of a mixed marriage, in Irish political terms. In an interview for this book, he said: 'My late father would have been a Fianna Fáil supporter and indeed would have canvassed on the odd occasion with Pat the Cope Gallagher.'[11] Something of a legend in Donegal political circles, 'Pat the Cope' (his middle name refers to a family connection with a local agricultural cooperative) was a Fianna Fáil TD for twenty-three years, and gave up his seat in 2009 to serve as a Member of the European Parliament, but lost that position in the 2014 European elections. However, Fianna Fáil wasn't the only political perspective in the house when the future Sinn Féin TD and finance spokesman in the Dáil was growing up, as his mother supported Fine Gael, albeit the 'republican element' in that party.

Emigration to Scotland is a long-standing feature of Donegal life, and Pearse Doherty was actually born in Glasgow, on 6 July 1977, in the shadow of Ibrox Stadium, home of the Glasgow Rangers soccer club. The location has a certain irony, since Irish republicans invariably support that club's age-old rival, Glasgow Celtic. But the family was back in Donegal before young Pearse had a proper chance to deliberate on the issue: 'I was only three-and-a-half or four when we came back to Ireland. My uncle had an accident and he subsequently passed. My Mum and Dad came back when he was sick. We weren't supposed to stay but we ended up staying.'

That was in Gweedore, still one of the strongest outposts of the Irish language: 'We were brought up with Irish... Mum and Dad were fluent Irish-speakers.' In the same year that young Doherty started as a pupil at Bunbeg primary school, headmaster Dinny McGinley was elected as a TD for Fine Gael and, at the time of writing, the two of them, teacher and pupil, are members of Dáil Éireann. Doherty went on to attend the community school in Gweedore, where he had what he calls his 'first brush with politics'. As a participant in a schools drama festival, he was invited to Áras an Uachtaráin in Dublin's Phoenix Park to meet the then-President, Mary Robinson, at her official residence.

He reckons it was 1991 or 1992, when he was about fourteen or fifteen years of age, that he became interested in Sinn Féin. It stemmed initially from a joint project with pupils from a school in Germany and, sophisticated beyond his years, young Doherty suggested a comparative study of Northern Ireland and the collapse of the Berlin Wall. He grins as he recalls how he ended up phoning the home number of the Sinn Féin vice-president at the time and current Westminster MP for West Tyrone, Pat Doherty (no relation): 'He probably thought it was bizarre that a fourteen-year-old was asking, "Do you have any information on Irish reunification?"'

About a year later, the eager young tyro applied to join the party: 'I got a letter back, saying that the nearest branch was 45 kilometers (28 miles) away in Letterkenny.' There was no car in the family, so

Doherty didn't see this as a practical option. But he organised fund-raising activities in the locality for republican prisoners – the Provisional IRA campaign was still in progress at the time – putting up a placard at the end of the lane at home with a slogan calling for their release. He was about sixteen when his new affiliation became known to his parents, after a friend of his father's said he had seen Pearse on a TV news channel talking to Martin McGuinness at a Bloody Sunday commemoration in Derry: 'I used to work in the local butcher's shop at home after school and at weekends, so I pretended to my parents that morning that I was going out to work, but I actually hitched out to Derry.'

His parents' main concern was for his personal security. This was prior to the Good Friday Agreement, and Sinn Féin Councillor Eddie Fullerton had been shot dead by loyalist paramilitaries at his home in Buncrana, Co Donegal, in May 1991.

After secondary school, Doherty was off to the big city as a student at the Dublin Institute of Technology, where he helped to set up a branch of Sinn Féin with others of his age-group, including Matt Carthy, later elected to the European Parliament in May 2014. Doherty was also one of the founders of the youth wing of Sinn Féin in 1997. He qualified as a civil engineer technician after two years. There was some controversy later when he was running for the Dáil, and his election material described him as a fully-fledged civil engineer. He says he was upfront when asked about his qualifications, and recalls the episode now with some amusement: 'They likened me, I think, to a porter in a hospital pretending to be a consultant.'[12]

He ran for the Dáil in the 2002 general election, and scored just less than 2,700 first preferences, to come fifth in the race for three seats in Donegal South-West.[13] In the European elections of 2004, Doherty got the second-highest number of first preferences in the sprawling Ireland North-West constituency, with 65,321 votes. But he failed to win a seat due to the usual Sinn Féin problem in attracting transfers under the Irish proportional representation system. Having served as a member of Donegal County Council from 2004 – he got the second-highest vote in the Glenties electoral area – Doherty made another run for the Dáil in 2007, and trebled his vote since the previous general election. It still wasn't enough, but he did get elected as Sinn Féin's first-ever Senator as part of a voting pact with Labour (most of the seats in the upper house of the Irish parliament are filled by the votes of local councillors.)

The election of Pat the Cope Gallagher to the European Parliament in 2009 left a Dáil vacancy in Donegal South-West. The economic crisis was in full flow and the embattled Fianna Fáil-Green Party government of the day was in no rush to hold a by-election. As things dragged on, Doherty inquired about the prospects of a successful legal challenge. 'It's a slam dunk,' a party colleague told him. Despite some nervous moments after that, he won the case when the High Court ruled that the sixteen-month delay was unconstitutional.[14] The by-election was held on 25 November 2010 and Doherty romped home, with nearly 40 per cent of first preferences compared to 21 per cent for the Fianna Fáil candidate and 19 per cent for the Fine Gael contender. It was a famous victory and he comfortably held the seat in the general election that followed three months later.

Doherty is generally seen as a success in the role of Sinn Féin Finance Spokesman in the twenty-six counties. A delegate at the 2015 ardfheis described him as a 'finance rockstar', and even his opponents would agree that he expresses his views with a confidence and coherence that his party leader could never muster in this particular area.[15] Adams usually holds his own on issues relating to the peace process, but has never been comfortable with economics, particularly in a southern context. When I asked Doherty what fundamental conditions Sinn Féin would set on economic issues before going into government with anyone else, he replies: 'There will be no Sinn Féin coalition government without water charges being abolished; there will be no Sinn Féin coalition government without property tax being abolished. And that's very clear from our point of view.'

The party would prioritise investment in public services such as health and education: 'We wouldn't cut taxes for the highest earners in society; instead what we would do is lift those at the bottom out of some of the tax-net by abolishing the Universal Social Charge for those earning below the minimum wage.'

Doherty was to the fore in urging support for the ardfheis motion in March 2015 which ruled out Sinn Féin participation in a government led by either Fianna Fáil or Fine Gael.[16] In his interview he says this is a challenge both for Sinn Féin and for the voters:

> The public need to decide what they want here: in other countries you can have a different type of social and economic model where you don't have hundreds of people per day lying on hospital trolleys or a thousand people in emergency accommodation because they're homeless ... We're really putting it up to the public: "Well, look, if you want something different, then, yes, you have to take a risk with Sinn Féin, because we haven't been tested in government here in the South. But we've made it very clear that we will implement our commitments to you. And if you're happy enough with the status quo, then Sinn Féin isn't for you." ... A lot of people fear change and a lot of people are comfortable with what they know.

Along with others such as Mary Lou McDonald and, in the North, Conor Murphy, Deputy Doherty has been spoken about as a potential future leader of Sinn Féin. Asked if he would be interested, he replies:

> At this point in time, I find it really challenging to deal with the responsibilities I have politically, while trying to balance them with the responsibilities I have as a

father and as a husband and as a family man. And that's something that I personally, privately battle with all the time, because politics isn't what defines me. I didn't, as a younger person, want to be a politician or a political activist, but I always wanted to be a father.

Róisín and himself have four children, aged between three and nine years: 'So the answer to your question is, at this point in time, I would not be able to take on any other responsibilities, because that internal kind of battle that I have going, the scales would completely tip in one direction, which wouldn't be sustainable.'

It's a four-hour journey from his home in Co Donegal to Leinster House: 'You're leaving early on Tuesday, and you're here till Thursday ... My aim is to try and get in the door before midnight on Thursday. And then, on Friday, you're gone, you have to do other meetings. Just because you're in Donegal doesn't mean you're necessarily at home.'

YOU GET the strong feeling that the late Harry Holland would have been extremely proud to see his daughter Sarah getting elected as Mayor of South Dublin. It happened on 26 June 2015, but Harry was already dead for the previous eight years, having been stabbed in the head with a screwdriver in West Belfast on 12 September 2007. The judge in the case said the deceased was clearly a 'well-known and much-loved' personality. It was not a sectarian incident: the sixty-five-year-old greengrocer was attacked by a group of youngsters from within his own community as he tried to stop them stealing his delivery van. One of the attackers got a twelve-year sentence, another was given four years.[17]

Sarah Holland represents Rathfarnham, where she lives, on South Dublin County Council. She was also chosen as a Sinn Féin candidate for Dublin South-West in the next general election along with the party's sitting TD Seán Crowe, whose political base is in Tallaght. But she was born in Belfast on 28 April 1978 and grew up on Norfolk Drive, in the heart of a district that includes Ballymurphy, Turf Lodge and Andersonstown, place-names that regularly featured in news coverage of the Troubles. She came from a republican family and recalls how 'Daddy would have been a Sinn Féin member but then he fell out with them'. In his later years she says he moved to the left and was attracted to the politics of the Communist Party.[18] Even in leafy Rathfarnham, she retains stark childhood memories of the Troubles, especially the turmoil in West Belfast in March 1988 when an IRA funeral was attacked by the loyalist Michael Stone, and then the equally-horrific aftermath at another funeral when two British soldiers in civilian attire were killed. Another memory concerns a police raid on the family home: 'That was kind of frightening, the police dog came bounding into the room and that was how we were awakened. It felt like the middle of the night, and they let the Alsatians run through the house. And we were all afraid of dogs.'

Later, after she had finished her education, she met her partner James, who hails from Limerick, when they were both working in the Netherlands, and the pair moved to Dublin in January 2003. Despite her republican family background, she only formally joined Sinn Féin in January 2012. She ran in the May 2014 local elections when Sinn Féin won nine of the forty seats on the Council: 'I've never really been someone who likes the spotlight and I had to challenge myself to stand up and do public meetings and media interviews.'

Brian Hayes, Fine Gael TD for Dublin South-West, got elected to the European Parliament at the same time, and a by-election to replace him in the Dáil was scheduled for 7 October 2014. She was in the running to be the Sinn Féin candidate and Councillor Máire Devine was also a contender, but, in the end, the party opted for Cathal King, leader of the Sinn Féin group on the Council. He was widely seen as a certainty to win the by-election but the entry to the race of the Trotskyist Paul Murphy, who had just lost his European seat, seemed to throw the Sinn Féin camp into confusion. Murphy's opposition to the government's water charges included non-payment, whereas Sinn Féin sent out conflicting signals in that regard. King was still 748 votes ahead of Murphy on the first count but when the Fine Gael candidate and an Independent were eliminated on the eighth count, the socialist got twice as many transfers as the republican and was deemed elected.

Despite having her political base in a solidly middle-class area, Holland says she encounters little outright opposition to Sinn Féin: 'People do have concerns about the past and about what happened.' She herself found the Mairia Cahill case difficult: 'Yeah I did and I still do, actually, struggle with that. She was treated terribly.'

She has given up her job in the pensions sector to work full-time as Mayor. Her motivation is rooted in the tragic experience of her father's death and its aftermath when she felt 'shut off' from the system that was meant to be implementing justice: 'You shouldn't have to shout and yell to have access to your rights. But you do unfortunately, you know.'

THE WINNER in Dublin South-West, Paul Murphy, of the Socialist Party, who ran under the banner of the Anti-Austerity Alliance, also gave an interview to the author of this book.[19] Recalling the contest, he says it was a big help that the feeling against water charges developed into a state-wide mass movement in the course of the by-election campaign.

He believes this was more of a boost to people like himself, on what he calls the 'radical left', than to Sinn Féin, because the left-wing activists are more deeply-embedded in the movement against the water charges. But he adds: 'They made big mistakes and, if they hadn't made big mistakes, again we couldn't have won. Initially, they didn't give a commitment to abolish the water charges. Then, under pressure from us, maybe a third of the way through the campaign, they gave a commitment to abolish the water charges. But we emphasised a very clear message: opposition, but also using our position and the election to try and build non-payment, a massive movement of protest in order to defeat the water charges. Whereas, all through the election campaign, they emphasised the dangers of non-payment. Their candidate indicated that he wouldn't pay, but all their leading figures at that stage were paying.'

Murphy continues that Sinn Féin changed its tune when the votes were all counted and the result was announced: 'After the election, then, they said they weren't going to pay. But a few days before, they said that they were.'

He says it also worked in his favour when someone faked a Facebook conversation with him in which Murphy was falsely shown to be stating that he had misrepresented Sinn Féin's position on water charges. Murphy claims it was perpetrated by a Sinn Féin member, but this was denied by the party.

As for the theory that he finally won the seat with the aid of transfers from Fine Gael voters who find 'Trots' less repellent than 'Shinners', he comments: 'That was a particular line put out by Sinn Féin at a particular time, to diminish their defeat and the reasons for their defeat, which is about their weak position on water charges.'

Murphy doesn't regard Sinn Féin as a left-wing party, even though it has left-wing members: 'It's fundamentally a nationalist organisation that, in the South of Ireland, uses left-wing rhetoric and slogans, basically a left kind of social-democratic programme, but in the North implements austerity together with the DUP, et cetera, and their primary goal is what they would see as a resolution of the national question, and a strategic step towards that is being in government, north and south.'

Essentially, he sees Sinn Féin's professed radicalism on social issues as skin-deep. Even if Sinn Féin was able to form a government without the conservative parties, Murphy doesn't believe it would carry out a genuine repudiation of Ireland's bank debt and a true reversal of austerity measures: 'I think it's likely that Sinn Féin wouldn't agree to what would have to be a strategy of confrontation with the EU authorities. I just don't think that's the direction that they would go.'

There are basic differences between the Socialist Party and Sinn Féin on the North and the national question: 'The entire strategy of the IRA and Sinn Féin to defeat British imperialism was mistaken. Obviously many heroic, brave people got involved in the IRA for admirable reasons like fighting against imperialism. But we think it was always a road to nowhere because it was premised on the idea that you could force the British State out militarily, when I don't think you ever could and the reality was that the bigger block was the attitude of the Protestant slight majority in the North. And so, instead, our strategy was always the idea of building a united struggle of working-class people, Catholic and Protestant, around key economic demands for better wages, better living standards, etc.'

He would like to see an independent Ireland as part of a federation with Scotland, Wales and England in a larger socialist confederation of Europe. The right of Protestant workers in the North to autonomous self-government in that context, if such was their wish, would also be recognised.

Protestant working-class fear of a united Ireland is not irrational in his view: 'Take the example of Sri Lanka where the British left and effectively the terms of repression were reversed, where the British had previously rested upon the Tamils as opposed to the Sinhalese people – the Sinhalese were the majority. The British left, the Sinhalese took control and then there was vicious chauvinism and oppression against the Tamils.'

ANOTHER trenchant critic of Sinn Féin, but from a different political perspective to Paul Murphy, is former tánaiste (deputy prime minister) and justice minister in the Fianna Fáil-Progressive

Democrat government of 2002-07, Michael McDowell. For one thing, the former PD leader does not believe Gerry Adams's denial of IRA membership. But he accepts that the IRA campaign is over and that 'the great majority' of its weapons were decommissioned.

McDowell says that, even if Adams were now to change his tune and admit that he had been in the IRA after all, this would leave him open to accusations of deceiving the public: 'He is sort of hoist on his own petard, he has to stick with it.'

Asked if he sees anything positive about the party, he replies by comparing Sinn Féin's transition into democratic politics to the acceptance of the Anglo-Irish Treaty by Michael Collins and Eamon de Valera's break with republican abstentionism by setting up Fianna Fáil: 'They have, in fact, curiously, done what Collins did in '21 or Dev did in '26, they have crossed the line and they said they are now going to pursue democratic politics and seek a democratic mandate. You can't deny them that and you can't deny them the support level they have.' However, he still retains doubts about the level of internal democracy in the party, given the power of Adams and those around him.

Looking ahead to the general election, due in late 2015 or early 2016, he believes that Labour's Dáil representation could be greatly reduced: 'If Sinn Féin becomes the party of the left in opposition it would be very hard for Labour to recover from that position.' He anticipates that Sinn Féin, which currently holds fourteen Dáil seats, could come back with more than thirty TDs, with Fianna Fáil rising to a similar figure from its current representation of twenty-one deputies: 'It is inconceivable they [*Sinn Féin*] could get into government at this election but they could force Fine Gael and Fianna Fáil together, if Labour does very badly.'

As for Sinn Féin's political programme, he says: 'They are populist policies. I'm perhaps a cynic but I believe that Middle Ireland is fundamentally bourgeois in outlook and the bourgeoisie will not allow an anti-bourgeois government to get into office, that the price of power in Ireland is to become bourgeois.'

He believes that Sinn Féin will eventually pay that price: 'There will be a post-Adams generation, it has to happen. How far they will move into the shoes of Labour is something which is very hard to predict at this stage, but will they become social democrats and admit to being social democrats? I'd say that is fifteen years off.'

FORMER adviser to the Dublin government on the North, Dr Martin Mansergh, is a close observer of Sinn Féin from the outside. He was one of the key figures in the peace process and played a major role in developing contacts between Fianna Fáil-led governments and Sinn Féin. He was elected as a TD for Tipperary South in 2007 and became a junior minister in the Department of Finance for three years from 2008 before losing his seat, like so many others in Fianna Fáil, at the 2011 general election. In an interview for this book, he assessed the future prospects for Sinn Féin as follows:

> The next election poses them with a few conundrums,
> given that they are conscious of the fact that, if you go
> into government as a minority party you put your
> future at risk. Leaving aside the regular experience of
> Labour, not to mention the fate of the Progressive
> Democrats and the Greens, look abroad: Mitterrand
> finished off the French Communists when he brought
> them into government in 1981; a similar fate befell
> [*Joerg*] Haider's party in Austria. They [*Sinn Féin*] are
> saying it would have to be a Sinn Féin-led government:
> but who else, bar a few odds and strays of
> Independents, is going to support a Sinn Féin
> government?[21]

Pointing to the cautious approach of Irish voters over the decades, he says: 'The electorate has proved over the last ninety years to be quite conservative. The Irish voters are always conscious of what they have to lose as well as what they have to gain. The recent phase of austerity has been very disruptive for many individuals, families and groups but, taking Irish society as a whole, not deep-dimension disruptive.'

Turning to the situation on the other side of the border, he says: 'As for the North, Martin McGuinness is very pragmatic. I would have thought it is very much in Sinn Féin's interests to keep the show on the road. Bringing down the power-sharing executive isn't going to impress the electorate in the South. I would hate to see Sinn Féin overturn what has been achieved in the North, [in order] to further their political interests down here. If you are in government in the North and opposition in the South, that creates as many difficulties as opportunities. Oppositions often propose things they would not implement in government, but their job is to put the other point of view.'

Our interview took place in Dublin in June 2015 and Dr Mansergh – holder of an Oxford PhD in pre-revolutionary French history – said that he didn't anticipate Sinn Féin being in government on *both* sides of the border anytime soon. 'It isn't going to happen in the short term. I would be simply amazed if Sinn Féin were in government after the next election here: perhaps five to ten years hence, when there is a new generation of Sinn Féin politicians, few of whom had been directly involved in the Troubles. Sinn Féin would like it as a step towards a United Ireland but they would find that it scarcely advanced them a jot in that direction and was more of a marketing tool in reality.'

When asked if Gerry Adams would be acceptable as a member of a government in Dublin, he replied: 'That depends on the necessity of the circumstances. After another five years he would scarcely be going into government anyway. He may be a Moses figure who won't personally step into the Promised Land.' As for Sinn Féin itself being an acceptable government partner, he said:

When Bertie [Ahern] was leader of Fianna Fáil he was horrified at the notion of Sinn Féin in government here. It was nothing to do with their past, or their policies on the economy and European issues. It was to do with their method of doing business: it tends to be crisis-ridden decision-making, their instinct all the time is to hang tough and play hard-ball. Bertie had deep experience of this in the peace process. It was in contrast with the Social Partnership [with employers and trades unions] where you had stand-offs, but there was fluidity, and deals were done.

Elaborating on this theme, he said:

The perception is that all the important Sinn Féin decisions are taken by a sort of politburo, a group of eight to ten people. Adams and McGuinness don't take decisions on their own. It's not necessarily a fixed group. I am not convinced it's formalised and it's not the Army Council of old, as it includes people who were never involved in the IRA or are too young to have been involved; if it's the Army Council, it's a civilian version. They look at things as a group. They are quite cautious in terms of making any moves. The feeling that the Sinn Féin people sitting at the cabinet table wouldn't actually have the power to make definitive and in principle irreversible decisions, that is what other parties would find uncomfortable about working with Sinn Féin.

Then there's the issue of media coverage: 'If you had Sinn Féin in government in the South, you would have a substantial section of the media who would not give either the Government or Sinn Féin in that government any peace from Day One. They would be trying to yank Sinn Féin out of it.'

Looking ahead to the next election and beyond, he said: 'I have no doubt that the Sinn Féin strategy is to keep building up – and opposition is the best place to build up. But people don't vote for parties to be in opposition. Sinn Féin has to pretend or at least argue plausibly that it could be in government after the next election. Fianna Fáil will have to argue the same thing in regard to their own party.'

❀

BRIAN LEESON was unhappy with what he saw as Sinn Féin's inexorable move to the political centre, so he resigned in February 2006 and, two months later, helped set up Éirigí (Irish for 'Rise Up!') where he holds the position of cathaoirleach (chairperson). He wasn't just any Sinn Féin member: Leeson had occupied a key post as National Organiser with the party. Born in 1974, he was only fifteen years of age when he first became politically active: 'I started selling *An Phoblacht*, which was a fairly traditional entry-point, in the summer of '89, outside the GPO... I would have been with the movement from '89 till 2006.'

In the 2002 general election, he was joint campaign manager for Seán Crowe's successful bid to win a Dáil seat in Dublin South-West. Shortly afterwards he started as National Organiser. His duties included attending numerous meetings where Gerry Adams was present. Leeson was 'underwhelmed' by his party leader: 'He just didn't impress me the way I thought he would. Perhaps I had unduly high expectations. There were others – Ted Howell, Aidan McAteer, Leo Green, et al., who were far more impressive as strategists and in their contributions (even if I disagreed with their arguments).'[22]

As for the party's future vice-president, he says: 'At that point in time Mary Lou was a relative newcomer without any meaningful history in the republican struggle – and as such, very few people could have foreseen her rising to her current position. So while she was clearly bright, articulate and educated, she just wasn't seen as a likely contender for leadership. At that time the likes of Conor Murphy, Gerry Kelly and others were the names that people were discussing.'

Up until the time that he left, at least, he says the party was firmly under northern control: 'I don't know [*about*] now but there was no toleration of any kind of a strong southern axis or cohort.' The party was run by what he calls the 'kitchen cabinet' and he continues: 'It was a parallel think-tank – there would have been a cohort of people around, almost exclusively northern, who, in my opinion, were the real leadership of the movement.'

Although these were 'extremely capable, intelligent people', he found himself disagreeing with their outlook: 'For me, the core problem was they were not ideologically anchored in a Left analysis. They were anchored in – *no* analysis, outside of social democracy, that I could see. Civil rights for the Catholics and, you know, get into power. And possibly be like the Labour Party: try and modify the more repugnant aspects of a capitalist system.'

As he sees it, that's the difference between Sinn Féin and Éirigí: 'We are clearly anchored in that radical-left type of territory.' Role-models for Éirigí include such historical figures as James Fintan Lalor and James Connolly and, more recently, the left-republican Séamus Costello who died in a republican feud in 1977. Charting his disillusionment with Sinn Féin, he recalls:

> They used to have a great expression, that everything was 'for the optics'. Essentially whatever was the latest dramatic reversal of a position, or line in the sand that had been walked through, it was a case of: 'Don't worry about that, that's only for the optics, that's only for the media.' From the first IRA cessation, the second cessation, putting the weapons beyond use, all those different stages were all sold to the base, on the basis that, 'Don't be worrying; that's just for the consumption of the media, and we remain committed to our revolutionary intent.' But in truth it turned out that we were the gobshites and not the other way round, that

what was being put out for mass consumption was the actual position and what people were being briefed in private was actually just horseshit really, just fantasy. But it took a few years for that to dawn.

Getting votes was the priority: 'Essentially what it became was a shameless rush for popularity, not the popularisation of a set of core politics but just simply increasing the popularity of the party or the brand.' He came to the conclusion that Sinn Féin was not part of the revolutionary left:

> Very late in the day it dawned on me, and I think many others who left, that it really was more of a sort of Catholic Defenders organisation that emerged, that morphed, out of the 1970s, not really terribly rooted in any sort of radical, revolutionary tendency... I would have believed that the cause of conflict in the North was the British occupation, and that would have been the Provisional position for many, many years. But in truth it appears that the cause of conflict was the denial of civil rights of Catholics and, once those civil rights were extended, the cause of conflict disappeared and by and large the conflict has disappeared, and it's kind of hard to get away from that logic that the Provisionals were essentially a Northern organisation which came into existence as a result of the denial of basic civil rights for the Catholic population.

In addition, he says that there was little enthusiasm among the leadership to build a radical republican movement in the South: 'It was only seen in terms of adding leverage to the negotiation in Stormont. It wasn't seen as a project with its own legitimacy – hence my belief that essentially the Northern-dominated leadership saw the role of the South and Southern activists as simply to provide logistical and political support to the Northern end of it.'

A variety of factors contributed to his eventual decision to quit, beginning with the party's cooperation in the watering-down of Articles 2 and 3 of the South's constitution as part of the Good Friday Agreement, and culminating with the realisation that Sinn Féin was about to recognise the Police Service of Northern Ireland: 'For me, it wasn't one simple issue: "That's it, I'm storming off in a huff here". It was a general pattern over a fifteen-year period of moving away from challenging the British state in any meaningful way, challenging capitalism or the rule of the elite in the South in any meaningful way... In my opinion Sinn Féin at this point, ideologically, don't know what they are.'

He says that his disillusionment was shared by many others who dropped out of the movement as well: 'Now, they've obviously been replaced by new people, so essentially the numbers haven't necessarily dropped, and obviously popular support has increased.'

Summing it all up, Leeson says: 'Someone else has coined the phrase that, "The republicans were too clever to admit they'd lost and the loyalists were too stupid to realise they'd won". And I think there's some merit in that.'

IF KILLIAN FORDE had stayed with Sinn Féin, he could well have become a major player. A rising star in the party at one time, he topped the poll in his local electoral area of Donaghmede at the elections to Dublin City Council in 2004. There was speculation he could win a Dáil seat in Dublin North-East in the 2007 general election, but he wasn't on the ticket. In the 2009 council elections, Labour had a wind at their back and topped the poll in Donaghmede, yet he still got in on the third count with a drop of only one per cent in his share of first preferences. But he was not a happy Shinner at that stage; he moved over to Labour and then resigned his council seat, which reverted to Sinn Féin.

Forde originally joined in 2001 when he was a mature student at Trinity College Dublin. Then aged thirty-one, he had been an aid worker in the Balkans for five years and was impressed with the way Sinn Féin was handling developments in Northern Ireland: 'I thought that the peace process, in comparison to what I had seen in the Balkans, was an amazing piece of work, I really admired Adams and McGuinness.' He had also held republican sympathies in his schooldays.[23]

But he soon found the Trinity branch wasn't for him because, he says, members were unduly concerned about rivalries with Trotskyist groups like the Socialist Workers' Party and the Socialist Party. So he ended up joining a local branch, the Patrick Cannon cumann, named after a twenty-year-old IRA member from Raheny who died in a premature explosion on the Border in 1976, along with twenty-four-year-old Peter McElchar from Donegal.

Working with long-time Sinn Féin activist Larry O'Toole in north-east Dublin, Forde became chair of a new cumann in the area. He approached a number of former republican prisoners about running in the 'locals' in 2004 but they turned him down flat: 'And then at some point I was asked to run and I said "Oh yeah, yeah, I'd love to run" but I didn't think I'd actually get elected.' In fact he breezed in, making a dream-start to his political career.

He was one of ten Sinn Féin candidates elected to Dublin City Council on that occasion but he says the group was not as effective as it might have been. Years later he met a former top official on the Council who said the bureaucracy was 'surprised at how little impact we had between 2004 and 2009'. But the level of commitment was high: 'We could outwork everybody else. Genuinely I could ring ten people on a Tuesday night and get them to distribute 10,000 leaflets and they'd be [delivered] for the next day.'

Hostile media coverage strengthened the members' resolve: 'The press was pretty much always negative and that only reinforced the victimhood that we [felt] internally. It was us against the world.' Forde stayed in Sinn Féin till 2010. Asked to describe the internal life of the organisation in those years, he recalls how there was what he and his friends called a 'Bobby Sands Factor' and that the spirit of the IRA hunger striker who died in 1981 was constantly being invoked:

> The Bobby Sands Factor was that you can motivate people to do anything on the basis that Bobby Sands made the ultimate sacrifice. And people are prepared to put up with a very strict, authoritarian, top-down approach... In Sinn Féin you don't whinge; the culture is one of not complaining, of doing what you're told. They are very, very strict on discipline, in terms of, if you're drunk, if you get into a fight, if you take drugs, all that. This is the irony of it; they're really, really clean in all that kind of stuff.

He himself sat on a number of disciplinary boards which expelled party members. The biggest no-no for Sinn Féin was any expression of racism: 'They just wouldn't tolerate it.' Indeed he believes the strong anti-racist stance taken by Sinn Féin in the communities where it is active has prevented the growth of a right-wing, anti-immigrant party in Ireland. Forde believes the work ethic of the party could be diminished when Gerry Adams finally steps down:

> He's a very strange man to be in a meeting with. He says very little and then, what he does say, everybody agrees with it. And the problem for Sinn Féin, I think, is that when Adams leaves, I don't see how they can maintain that 'pleb' work ethic, that authoritarian thing, under the leadership of somebody who hasn't been at war. Their strongest suit is the culture of the organisation, they can get people to work really hard for very little money – for no money, mostly. They keep people on message, but it's done on the basis of the hunger strikes, it's done on the

basis of the [past] riots, it's all that. So how do you maintain that, if somebody like Adams goes? Do you think people in Finglas are going to get out on a Tuesday morning in November for Mary Lou?

He lists General Secretary Dawn Doyle and National Chairperson Declan Kearney as key figures in the party. As for the successor to Adams, he doesn't subscribe to the usual speculation about Conor Murphy in the North, Mary Lou McDonald and Pearse Doherty in the South: 'I think, if there's enough time, Eoin Ó Broin. He's incredibly talented, he's respected, he's probably the only person who can pull it off [on] both sides of the border. But he hasn't got a [Dáil] seat yet. So if Adams stays on and Eoin is elected to the Dáil then I think there's a significant chance Eoin will be the next leader.' Surprisingly perhaps, he doesn't see Mary Lou McDonald in the role: 'She's never demonstrated any leadership skills. She's a fine Dáil performer; on organisation, she's very weak. She was chairperson of the party, didn't really do it.' (His favourable assessment of Ó Broin is not reciprocated, judging from a column in *An Phoblacht*, after Forde left Sinn Féin for Labour, in which Ó Broin sharply criticises his former party colleague over the move.[24])

Forde says there is no pressure on Adams to vacate the leadership – quite the contrary: 'He's venerated. If he goes anywhere it's like a rock star has turned up, and people get their picture taken with him.' But the chemistry between himself and the party leader was poor: 'The funny thing is, I don't know anybody who knows him. It's not that I find him intimidating but I would find him uncomfortable to be with, because he's physically imposing, you feel that he's constantly assessing you and then he keeps on trying to speak to me in Irish, which I can't speak. And he doesn't say an awful lot; he doesn't do small talk. Martin McGuinness, no problem, you can have the craic [Irish for 'fun'] with him. But Gerry Adams is a very serious man.'

As regards the party leader's denial of IRA membership, Forde says: 'Nobody believes that. It's considered a joke.' He confesses bewilderment as to the motivation behind it, speculating that it could be a 'technicality' whereby, during the wild and hectic days at the start of the Troubles, the formal process of being signed-in as a member of the organisation could not be implemented. Forde says that he himself was never approached to join the IRA, which was leaving the stage during the years that he was in Sinn Féin.

The greatest period of internal tension during his time in the party occurred when Sinn Féin was about to accept the Police Service of Northern Ireland, which eventually took place at a special ardfheis on 28 January 2007. Key people in Dublin were uncomfortable with the way the party was going and they also tended to be more left-wing than the Belfast leadership. People arrived in Dublin from the North – some of them with a long history of activity in the republican movement – to re-organise things and Forde says many of the leading locally-based activists either quit the party or were eased-out, with a fair number of them ending up in the left-republican group, Éirigí.

He says he became 'deeply unhappy' in Sinn Féin, partly because so many people he liked and admired had left: 'They'd either gone to Éirigí or quietly resigned... For a lot of people, policing was the one that was kind of enough. But they quietly left and it was actually quite polite.' Policing wasn't a sore point for him[25] but he moved across to Labour on the Council in 2010, then dropped out a year later ('I never really engaged') and went to work for the Integration Centre, a non-governmental organisation for assisting refugees and immigrants, where he spent the next three years.

As well as being a Sinn Féin member of Dublin City Council, Forde wrote for the *Irish Times* on a regular basis about skiing. He also did radio broadcasts about the sport for *Newstalk*. Asked now if he considers Sinn Féin a left-wing party or a populist movement like the early Fianna Fáil, Forde replies: 'I think they're both.'

❀

VETERAN of the 1950s Border campaign by the IRA and currently national treasurer of the Workers' Party, Seán Garland regards Sinn Féin as an 'establishment party' at this stage: 'They talk about progressive politics but really it's hard to find any aspect of their political philosophy which would put them on the left. They're very far from a socialist position.'[26] Whatever others may think, Garland does not regard Sinn Féin as a left-wing party: 'Frankly I don't, no. There may be some elements who are [on the] left, but in the main their support and their membership is broad and, at the same time, very narrow in regards to politics.'

Back in 1972, the 'Official' wing of the republican movement, supported by Garland, called a ceasefire in the North (except for self-defence) and opted for an exclusively political approach, but the 'Provisional' wing kept its campaign going till the mid-1990s. As he sees it, the only outcome of Provo violence was 'thousands of deaths and destruction and really alienating the loyalist, Protestant population'.

He believes the Provisional IRA campaign was on the verge of collapse at the start of the 1980s but was given a new lease of life by the Iron Lady: 'They were, by the time of the hunger strikes, at the point of closing down but Mrs Thatcher, through her dogmatic and stupid ideology, breathed life into them again. The deaths of hunger strikers certainly revived their fortunes and made it possible for them – because you can see yourself in Irish history the effect that hunger strikes can have – to mobilise tens of thousands of people who were not Sinn Féin supporters but they became involved through the hunger strikes.'

But the Provos are not true republicans in his view: 'Tone's concept of the United Irishmen, the unity of Catholic, Protestant and Dissenter is very far removed from the mentality of Sinn Féin.'

From 2005 onwards, Garland was the subject of attempts by the US authorities to secure his extradition through the courts in relation to an alleged Marxist conspiracy to undermine the US currency by distributing fake dollars printed in North Korea. He denied this and a campaign against his extradition gathered support from across the political spectrum in Ireland and elsewhere. An application for his extradition was refused by the High Court in Dublin and the case was referred in January 2012 to the Irish Director of Public Prosecutions. In his interview for this book, he acknowledges the support he received from 'many members of Sinn Féin' when he was fighting extradition. 'We were thankful for it because it was genuine support,' he says, but it doesn't affect his attitude to Sinn Féin's politics and he recalls that he also got backing at the time from members of Fine Gael, Fianna Fáil and Labour.[27]

Asked if he would give Sinn Féin a vote, he replies: 'No, I would not.' Nor can he foresee a situation where, if the Workers' Party had a number of TDs, it would go into coalition with Sinn Féin: 'To me it's not a question that we would even consider.'

THERE IS a rather different perspective from Jonathan Powell, who was formerly chief of staff to Tony Blair and the prime minister's principal adviser on Northern Ireland and has since become CEO of the charity Inter Mediate, which works on the resolution of armed conflicts. Given his international brief, Powell takes a broader view of the Northern Ireland conflict and the subsequent emergence of Sinn Féin as a political force. In a telephone interview from London for this book, he cites examples from Latin America to show how former guerrillas can have considerable success in politics, but the process takes time: 'If you look at Colombia for example, the M19 guerrillas gave up fighting in the very early 1990s and they didn't have any political success immediately but now they have had one of their people elected as Mayor of Bogota. They have had other people elected mayors elsewhere. In El Salvador, the FMLN guerrillas, for a long time, were the opposition party, even after they laid down their weapons, and now finally they have won the Presidency.'[28]

A key issue in ensuring long-term success is to find and promote what Powell calls 'successor leaders' to take over from the guerrillas-turned-politicians in due course: 'Guerrillas who lay down their weapons, they usually have leaders who become politicians and they can have success to start with, then you need to find a new generation to take over from them. So there are the heroes of the war and then there is someone else.'

On the performance of Gerry Adams and Martin McGuinness in the move from the Armalite to the ballot-box, he says: 'They made a rather successful transition from physical force republicanism to political republicanism. Not everyone can make a transition like that. If you look at Sri Lanka – one of the big problems was that Prabhakaran, the leader of the Tamil Tigers, couldn't make the transition from armed violence to politics. But in the case of Adams and McGuinness, they did make that transition and it has been remarkably successful in terms of longevity. I can't think of many other politicians who are still going, who were around when they were. So if you look at Blair, he's gone; Bertie [*Ahern*] is gone, but they [*Adams and McGuinness*] are still going, so they've clearly had some success.'

Based on his considerable contact with Sinn Féin in the Blair years, what does he think of the widespread suggestion that the party is really run by a 'kitchen cabinet' or 'think-tank' behind the scenes? Powell, who has referred to this phenomenon in *Great Hatred, Little Room*, says: 'Yes, certainly when we were dealing with them it was, as I said in the book, a brains trust that was running things.[29] There was Adams and McGuiness, which was a very interesting partnership. They are different sorts of people; and then around them a small group who did the work and got into the detail. That's not unusual for political parties around the world. The same thing has been said of Tony Blair in No 10, that it was a small circle of people who were making the decisions. It becomes a problem only if it becomes a funnel or bottleneck in which you can't get decisions made.' When asked if he agrees with the SDLP's Séamus Mallon[30] that the Good Friday Agreement and, by implication, the peace process in general was a case of 'Sunningdale for slow learners', he says:

> Yes and no. In fact I go around quoting Séamus on this point everywhere I go ... what is interesting is that, you quite often build a successful peace on a series of previous failures. In the case of Spain that certainly was the case, a whole series of failures that eventually led to the end of the [*Basque*] conflict in 2011. If you look at places like Indonesia and Aceh, there were a series of failures of peace agreements and then the final one. The final one doesn't come from nowhere, it is built on all the agreements that went before. So we had Sunningdale which failed, we had the Anglo-Irish Agreement which failed, we had the Downing Street Declaration which failed, then we had the Good Friday Agreement, but it didn't come from nowhere. It was built on those previous successes. The thing that is particularly striking, and that is what Seamus is pointing out, is that the provisions in the Good Friday Agreement on power-sharing were pretty much identical to what was discussed in Sunningdale. But that again is not too surprising because there are a limited number of ways you can solve the problem of power-sharing. What did strike me at the time of the Good Friday Agreement was how quickly those provisions were agreed. As I remember, in one day they resolved all the issues on power-sharing, partly because the work had been done earlier under George Mitchell. While we were actually sitting there, that wasn't the big problem, that was easy to solve: the problems were things like prison sentences and, of course, decommissioning of weapons. So Séamus is right, it is a shame we had to go on fighting for another two-and-a-half decades. If we could only have settled it at

Sunningdale: but unfortunately Sunningdale didn't arrive at a settlement and indeed Sinn Féin weren't even included then, so you wouldn't have had an inclusive agreement. So he is right and he is wrong at the same time.

IN ADDITION to the comments he made to the author on various issues, as reported elsewhere in this book, Gerry Adams took the time to respond in writing to questions about the current political situation and prospects for the future.[31] First of all, given the strong solidarity Sinn Féin has displayed towards Syriza and, in light of the way things turned out in Greece and at European Union level, how did he see the implications for Sinn Féin in the coming Irish general election? He replied:

> The EU's treatment of the democratically-elected Government of Greece has been disgraceful. They effectively closed down the Greek banking system and held the Greek Government and people to ransom... Irish people are concerned at this turn of events. The sympathies of most Irish people are with the people of Greece at this time of crisis. To its shame the Irish Government took the side of the strong against those in need of support and solidarity. It is obscene for Fine Gael, Labour and Fianna Fáil to lecture the Greek people while generations of Irish people will be paying off debts that are not of their making. The Irish Government's stance throughout this crisis is not in line with the views of the vast majority of Irish people. The deal which the Greek Government has struck with its creditors could have been a better deal if the Irish Government had stood with the Greeks to deliver debt relief. Sinn Féin has stood by the people of Greece.

They have fought a good fight and stood up for their
rights. I believe that most Irish people understand this
and that it reflects their views also.

I also raised the issue of the dissident republican groups which have
become more active in recent times and asked Adams what response
he would make to claims by such groups that physical force is the
only way to achieve Irish unity. He responded:

There are a number of very small militarist factions,
claiming to be republican, who oppose the Peace Process
and Sinn Féin's peace strategy. They have negligible
support, no political strategy and no ideas. They are in
fact enemies of Irish unity because their actions are
entirely counterproductive to that noble objective. Many
of these groups are involved in criminality and there is
clearly a high level of influence there by British agents.
Their actions suit the agenda of securocrats within the
British system. Both wish to turn back the clock and
remilitarise the North. But there is no chance of that
happening. The situation in the North has been
transformed. The war is over and there is now an
entirely peaceful and democratic route to Irish unity.
These groups need to recognise the reality of Ireland in
2015 and cease their activities. Irish unity is now a live
issue on the political agenda. The Good Friday
Agreement was an historic compromise between Irish
nationalism and unionism. It allowed for a level political
playing field. It specifically provided for a mechanism to
bring about Irish unity. Sinn Féin's role is to argue and
convince ever greater numbers of people that this is a
worthy and achievable objective and to campaign to
bring it about. Sinn Féin is committed to securing, in the
time ahead, a referendum on Irish Unity so that each and

every one of us, working together, can build our country. Such a referendum should not be seen as threatening to any section of our community. All political objectives in Ireland can now be pursued peacefully and democratically and in mutual respect. That is the great success of the Peace Process.

Turning to the situation in the South, I pointed out to the Sinn Féin leader that there was now an 'alphabet soup' of different parties and alliances on the political stage. In that context, what was his perspective on the aftermath of the next general election and his own party's prospects of being in government in Dublin for the 1916 Centenary? Adams replied:

What you are seeing, in advance of the general election is an inevitable consequence of the way many people feel about the old way of doing politics. Fianna Fáil and Fine Gael, often with the support of the Labour Party, have run this State since Partition. The result has been the perpetuation of inequality and conservatism. Following the calamity of the economic crash under the last Fianna Fáil-led Government, a Fine Gael/Labour coalition assumed office with a huge mandate for political change. But as citizens have learned to their cost, nothing has changed... Citizens desperately need, for the first time ever in this State, a Government that is not led by Fine Gael or Fianna Fáil. More than that, they need a progressive Government that will pursue real and viable alternative policies based on equality, not austerity, and rights, not privilege, and that will govern in the interests of citizens and not the elites. The result of the Marriage Equality referendum was a significant advance for the cause of equality in Ireland. The experience of that referendum, in which many people with no previous experience of political activism, became involved in campaigning for equality, must now be built upon to secure support for equality in other aspects of Irish life. We need economic and social equality. That, too, must be fought for, campaigned for. Sinn Féin is very clear that we seek to lead a progressive, anti-austerity Government to further the objective of a united Ireland and an equal society. However, to do that we have to receive a mandate and to agree a programme for government with others. So, the focus of the party has to be to win the largest possible vote in the election for Sinn Féin in government.

On a more personal level, I raised various controversies over his own role which had received widespread media coverage, referring specifically to: the Mairia Cahill and Paudie McGahon allegations; his brother Liam's court case; Jean McConville's disappearance and death; continuing scepticism about the Sinn Féin leader's denial of IRA membership; and alleged bad taste in his Twitter account. He replied as follows:

> First of all it is worth noting that a number of media outlets have had to correct the record and clarify misleading and inaccurate statements about me on several of these issues. I have also been vindicated by the Police Ombudsman and the PPS [*Public Prosecution Service*] in the North in relation to false and entirely malicious allegations of wrongdoing regarding my brother's case, which were made by the DUP [*Democratic Unionist Party*]. I have dealt with each and every one of these issues publicly and in considerable length and detail over the past year and at this stage have nothing further to add.

8. IN THE EYE OF THE STORM

CONTROVERSY IS TO SINN Féin what rain is to the Irish weather: a fresh outbreak is possible at any time. The more the party's political influence has grown, the greater the intensity and duration of the storms that break over its head. This is understandable because the activities of a marginal party are of less interest to the media, the political class and the general public than the conduct of an organisation that could be in government in the Republic, and already is in the North. But there has never been an episode to compare with the avalanche of criticism and condemnation that developed over the allegations of sex abuse made by Belfastwoman Mairia Cahill.

A grand-niece of Joe Cahill, founding member of the Provisional IRA, Mairia Cahill claimed that, at the age of sixteen years, she was subjected to a twelve-month cycle of sex abuse by a member of the IRA, beginning in August 1997.[1] In 1998, she complained to four female members of the republican movement, and says that the IRA questioned her for months in 1999 about the allegations, in what has been described as a 'kangaroo court'. Ms Cahill says she was brought face-to-face with her alleged abuser in March 2000, but that the IRA came to no decision on the matter, and that her alleged abuser left Northern Ireland. She says that in the years 2000-06 she had a number of meetings with Gerry Adams about the issue.

In January 2010, she gave an interview to the *Sunday Tribune*. The following April, she made statements to the Police Service of Northern Ireland about her alleged rapist and subsequent alleged IRA 'interrogators'. In April and May of 2014, cases against the alleged rapist and 'interrogators' collapsed after she withdrew evidence. The prosecution told the court that she was in 'fear' of testifying against her alleged rapist.

On 14 October 2014, she repeated her allegations about rape and IRA questioning, on a programme in the *BBC Spotlight* current affairs series. Ms Cahill said that in the first of several meetings with Adams, he told her that abusers could be extremely manipulative and that he added: 'Sometimes they're that manipulative, that the people who have been abused actually enjoy it.' This was sharply denied by the Sinn Féin leader in an interview with RTÉ shortly afterwards: 'I am personally horrified at the allegation that I would make the comments Mairia has attributed to me... I would never make such remarks to anyone, much less an alleged victim of abuse.'[2] He wrote in the pages of *An Phoblacht* and on his blog:

> Maíria alleges she was raped and that the IRA conducted an investigation into this. The IRA has long since left the scene so there is no corporate way of verifying this but it must be pointed out that this allegation was subject to a police investigation and charges were brought against some republicans who strenuously denied Maíria's allegations. They insist they tried to help her. They were all acquitted by the court. Maíria has also accused Sinn Féin and me of engaging in a cover-up. That is untrue. When I learned of the allegation that Maíria was the victim of rape I asked her grand-uncle, Joe Cahill, a senior and widely-respected republican, to advise her to go to the RUC [Royal Ulster Constabulary]. He did this but Maíria did not want to do so at that time. When Maíria subsequently did go to the police, I co-operated with the police investigation.[3]

What are we to make of the statement by Gerry Adams that the Provisional IRA 'has long since left the scene'? Former Tánaiste (deputy prime minister) and Justice Minister in the Dublin government and a political opponent of Sinn Féin, Michael McDowell says it is still in existence, although it may be no longer in the public eye. In an interview for this book, he said: 'I don't know what has happened to the Army Council, I don't think it's ever dissolved itself.' As for the IRA itself, he said: 'It hasn't ceased to exist formally, it hasn't disbanded.' He continued: 'There was never a convention to disband it and it can't disband because it is in its own mind the repository of the legitimate authority of the people of Ireland going back to 1916.'[4]

A solicitor representing four people who had been acquitted of charges relating to the alleged IRA questioning of Maíria Cahill, complained that they were being subjected to 'trial by the media'. Peter Madden of Belfast solicitors Madden and Finucane said the fallout from the *BBC Spotlight* programme meant that his clients' acquittals 'have been either ignored or devalued'. Pointing out that Ms Cahill, as the main prosecution witness, was to be cross-examined about her version of events, which was not accepted by his clients. The letter continued: 'She refused to allow this to take place and would not participate in the normal method of giving evidence at a trial, where the truth of her version of events would be tested by cross-examination. My clients were therefore found not guilty of these offences.'[5]

A longtime observer of Sinn Féin and its progress along the political path, Andy Pollak, expressed the view that, for all the political skills Adams had shown in persuading the IRA to accept the Good Friday Agreement, the Sinn Féin leader had one major weakness – he would continue to be dragged into the past by various episodes. Adams's other problem was his lack of credibility – few believed his denial of IRA membership, for example. But Pollak continued:

Potential Sinn Féin voters in the South and nationalists in the North will feel one thing in common when they look at how the Mairia Cahill affair has been dealt with in recent weeks in the Republic. They will wonder about the sincerity of mainstream political parties and media, which normally have little or no interest in what happens north of the Border, working themselves into a frenzy about this issue.[6]

News reports that Ms Cahill had previously been national secretary of the Republican Network for Unity (RNU) group did not reduce the heat on Sinn Féin. On its current website, the RNU condemns the Good Friday Agreement as sectarian and partitionist and opposes the police services in both parts of the island.[7] She said she had only held the post for 'a period of a few hours' in 2010 and added: 'I was opposed to "outside influences", in what was a perfectly legal pressure group, and was extremely vocal in this regard. Indeed, this was the reason that I left. I am on record consistently as being opposed to illegal armed actions.'[8]

In late October 2014, Sir Keir Starmer, former Director of Public Prosecutions for England and Wales, was asked by the North's DPP, Barra McGrory, to conduct an independent review into how the Public Prosecution Service (PPS) in Northern Ireland dealt with the allegations that Ms Cahill and two other women were sexually abused by an IRA member when they were in their teens, between 1997 and 2000.[9]

The report, jointly written by Sir Keir Starmer and barrister Katherine O'Byrne, was issued on 6 May 2015. It found that there was 'a lack of strategic thinking and management by the prosecution team'. The authors considered it regrettable that delays in the prosecution for sexual abuse 'were not more robustly opposed'. There was a failure of communications and, in overall terms, the three women 'were let down by the PPS and counsel'. Given the failings in the handling of the case, it was 'almost inevitable' that the three individuals would pull out of the process: 'Each of them was prepared to support their allegations at the outset, but as their cases became increasingly weakened and delayed, their willingness to continue understandably diminished.'[10]

Separately, the Police Ombudsman, Dr Michael Maguire, was investigating Ms Cahill's complaints that the police failed to deal with the case adequately.

Meanwhile, a second sex abuse controversy broke out in March 2015 when forty-year-old Paudie McGahon from County Louth said on another *BBC Spotlight* programme that he was raped by an IRA man in the early 1990s at the age of seventeen years. This had taken place, he said, in his own family home, which was often used by IRA activists as a 'safe house'. Mr McGahon said republicans who questioned him over his claims had offered to shoot the alleged perpetrator. On one occasion, he said, the IRA brought a psychiatrist along to offer him counselling but McGahon declined the offer.[11]

Responding, Gerry Adams said: 'Paudie McGahon clearly feels badly let down'. The Sinn Féin leader added: 'Nothing that I may say will change this but it is a matter of deep regret to me. I hope that justice is served and support delivered to Mr McGahon. Sinn Féin's priority is to support victims of abuse whether that abuse is historical or contemporary and we will support victims in their efforts to get truth and justice.'[12]

Adding to Sinn Féin's woes was the long-running saga of Liam Adams, a younger brother of the Sinn Féin president, who had appealed against his conviction for the sexual abuse of his daughter Áine between the ages of four and nine years. On 5 May 2015, the Court of Appeal in Belfast upheld the conviction and the sentence of eighteen years, two of them on probation.

In October 2013, a jury of nine men and three women, by an eleven to one majority, had found Liam Adams guilty of all ten charges against him – three counts of rape, three of gross indecency and four of indecent assault. A previous case in April collapsed over an issue of disclosure. Gerry Adams, who gave evidence in the first trial, 'was cross-examined at length with regard to his credibility', but was not called to give evidence in the second trial.[13]

Issues were raised for the Sinn Féin leader in both the first and the second trial. It turned out that, as far back as 1987, he was aware of the allegations against his brother. Gerry Adams confronted him on the matter in the same year at Buncrana, County Donegal, but Liam Adams denied the allegations. The case did not proceed at the time because Áine retracted her evidence and complained that some members of the RUC seemed more interested in her Uncle Gerry as a leading republican than in the abuse issue itself. In 2006, she repeated the allegations to the Police Service of Northern Ireland (PSNI), successor to the RUC. In 2007, Gerry Adams went to the police to give a statement, but did not mention that, during a 'walk in the rain' in Dundalk in 2000, Liam Adams admitted sexually assaulting Áine on one occasion, although he denied raping her. The Sinn Féin leader told the police about it in 2009 and, in the first trial – which was to collapse for legal reasons – defence counsel Eilis McDermott QC said Gerry Adams only gave the 2009 statement because he knew UTV's *Insight* programme was about to screen a documentary on the case. She also accused Gerry Adams of being untruthful when, in 2009, he said that, after 1987, Liam Adams was 'out of my life more or less for the next fifteen years'. The barrister showed the Sinn Féin leader photographs of himself and Liam Adams together in 1991, 1996, 1997, 1998 and 2003, at family and political events. She questioned how it was that Liam Adams worked in youth clubs in west Belfast and Dundalk, County Louth – even after the 2000 admission. Adams insisted he was endeavouring to deal with the situation in an informal, family context: 'I was trying my best to resolve these matters in a way which helped Áine but, also, if I may say so, in a way which allowed Liam to get rid of these demons... but I always had said to Áine that if she wanted to go to the police I would support her in whatever stand that she took... I was acting as Áine wanted me [to] in terms of getting her father to acknowledge what he had done. She became increasingly dissatisfied with the failure of that process and then she went to the police and that brought it into a totally different arena.'[14]

Speaking elsewhere, the Sinn Féin president claimed that, outside the court, he was being subjected to a media witchhunt: 'I am a public figure and subject to scrutiny and that is fair enough. But the despicable manner in which this issue is being dealt with by the DUP [Democratic Unionist Party] and others, and by some cynical elements of the media, has become trial by media.' He also referred to the fact that in 2009 he had disclosed that his father, Gerry Adams Senior, abused family members emotionally, physically and sexually for many years.[15]

In June 2015, a month after Liam Adams lost his appeal against the jail sentence, the Northern Ireland Attorney General, John Larkin, QC, issued a report on the issue of whether Gerry Adams should have been prosecuted for allegedly withholding information about the sexual abuse of his niece. In his 48-page report, Mr Larkin found that the North's PPS 'correctly formed the view that the evidential test for prosecution could not be satisfied in relation to Gerry Adams'. However, Mr Larkin did suggest that the PPS should have obtained a further statement from Áine Adams, also known by her married name of Dahlstrom, to clarify what exactly she had told her uncle. Did she inform him at Buncrana in 1987 that she had been raped by her father, or had she just made the less-specific allegation of sexual abuse?

Mr Larkin said in his report: 'I consider that there was sufficient information regarding Gerry Adams's state of knowledge to at least merit obtaining a further statement from Áine (Adams) concerning the issue of what she had told her uncle.'

But the North's deputy Director of Public Prosecutions, Pamela Atchison, said after the report was issued that Áine Adams had informed the PPS that she had nothing further to add to her statements and did not wish to see the matter pursued any further.[16] In his report, Mr Larkin also made the point that it should be open to the PPS, in the public interest, to treat people who could offer evidence for the prosecution as witnesses rather than suspects. Gerry Adams gave evidence in the first trial, but when that collapsed and a second trial took place, he was not called. This was for 'technical reasons' which were not disclosed by the PPS.[17]

It didn't end there. The North's Police Ombudsman Dr Michael Maguire had also started an investigation after receiving a complaint that the police had failed to fully investigate Gerry Adams for withholding information on the sexual abuse and that a recommendation against prosecuting the Sinn Féin leader was politically motivated. A report issued by Dr Maguire on 7 July 2015 found that the PSNI acted properly and was not influenced by political considerations in its decision against prosecuting Adams for allegedly withholding information about the sexual abuse.[18]

If Gerry Adams was off the hook over the case of his brother Liam, there was another unresolved issue stretching back even further. In 2014, the Sinn Féin leader was questioned by the PSNI for four days over the disappearance and killing of 38-year-old Jean McConville in 1972. The police sent a file to the PPS, and a decision on what action to take on it, if any, was expected to be made in the summer of 2015, but it seemed to be taking longer.

A recently-widowed mother of ten children, Mrs McConville was abducted from the Divis Flats, an IRA stronghold in west Belfast, on 7 December 1972. The number of deaths in the Troubles that year was 479, by far the highest of the entire conflict – the nearest was 1976 with 295 deaths.[19] Originally from a Protestant background in east Belfast, she converted to Catholicism when she married Arthur McConville, an ex-British Army soldier, who died of cancer in early 1972. After the IRA undertook as part of the peace process to help find the bodies of the so-called 'disappeared', a number of searches took place in remote border areas for the remains of Jean McConville and others. A member of the public found her body when out for a walk at Shellinghill Beach, on the Cooley Peninsula in County Louth in August 2003 – heavy rain had unearthed her remains. She had been shot in the back of the head, and a post-mortem also found evidence that she might have been beaten, or even tortured.

Why was she kidnapped and killed? It was suggested that she had helped a wounded British soldier, and that she was passing information via a secret radio transmitter. An IRA statement issued on 8 July 2006 said: 'Following a public request from the family of Jean McConville the IRA carried out a thorough investigation into all the circumstances surrounding her death. That investigation confirmed that Jean McConville was working as an informer for the British army.'[20] Brendan 'The Dark' Hughes (1948-2008), a leading IRA figure in his day, made a similar claim. But an investigation carried out in 2006 by the Police Ombudsman of Northern Ireland found no evidence to back up this allegation.[21]

Hughes was interviewed for the Boston College Oral History Project whereby participants in the IRA and the Ulster Volunteer Force talked about their past activities, on the understanding that nothing would be published while they were still alive. After his death, it was revealed he had alleged that Gerry Adams, formerly a close friend, had ordered the killing and disappearance of Jean McConville. He also stated that McConville had admitted to being an informer. Hughes's version of events was repeated in a newspaper report of an interview with Dolours Price, in 2010, three years before she died. Imprisoned after the 1973 bombing of the Old Bailey in London, Dolours Price had also been interviewed for the oral history project but the contents have not been made public at time of writing. The PSNI won a legal battle to obtain any Boston College interview material which specifically referred to McConville. Six people were subsequently brought in for questioning, including Adams.[22] In a speech after his release, Adams denied any involvement in the McConville abduction, killing or burial, and said he had notified the PSNI two months earlier that he was available to meet them, in view of the latest wave of media coverage received by the case.[23] He added, however: 'I was concerned about the timing, given that Sinn Féin is involved in very important EU and local government elections across the island of Ireland.' He continued: 'I rejected all the allegations made about me in the Boston Tapes.'[24]

There are other issues for the Provisional republican movement in general. On 9 June 2015, BBC Northern Ireland screened a programme in the *Spotlight* series, in which reporter Darragh McIntyre gave details of the case of Caroline Moreland. The lone parent and mother of three was shot dead by the IRA as an alleged informer the month before the August 1994 declaration of a ceasefire. The programme featured a tape recording of the victim admitting that she had become an informer because she feared a long jail sentence for IRA activity that would take her away from her children. Her daughter Shauna blamed both the IRA for carrying out the shooting and the British intelligence services for failing to prevent it. The programme said the order almost certainly had to come from the IRA Army Council. Once again, the name of Freddie Scappaticci – also known as 'Stakeknife' – surfaced in public and media discourse. Allegedly head of internal security in the IRA – the so-called 'nutting squad' – the Belfastman is also claimed to have been a much-prized agent of the British, something he has always very firmly denied. The implication is that he was executing alleged British agents, while also being one himself but Scappaticci has rejected this out of hand. Shauna Moreland said on the programme that she wanted to meet Martin McGuinness to ask him: 'Were you on the Army Council? Did you give the order for my Mum's death?' McGuinness said in a statement that he was not on the Army Council, and that he had no knowledge of Caroline Moreland's death. A Sinn Féin spokesman said that the Deputy First Minister would be happy to meet Shauna Moreland.[25]

At least as disturbing from the Provo viewpoint as the claims about Scappaticci, was the admission by a very senior Sinn Féin figure, Denis Donaldson, that he had been a paid British agent for more than twenty years. There were few with a more impeccable background in the 'struggle' than this member of a republican family from the Short Strand, a small Catholic community in loyalist East Belfast. Born in 1950, he joined the movement at an early age and, when his community came under siege in June 1970, was one of the IRA members who defended the area from the enclave of St Matthew's parish church. In later years, he was arrested and imprisoned with the iconic hunger striker Bobby Sands. A photograph depicts a smiling Donaldson with his arm around his fellow-republican. Donaldson was later released and subsequently recruited as a British agent, in or around 1983. In his 'confession', issued when his spy role was revealed, Donaldson said: 'I was recruited in the 1980s after compromising myself during a vulnerable time in my life. Since then I have worked for British intelligence and the RUC/PSNI Special Branch. Over that period I was paid money.' The origins of his vulnerability and the manner in which he compromised himself have not been revealed.[26] He was in charge of the international dimension of the movement, keeping in contact with the Palestinians and the Basques. He tried to secure the release of fellow-Irishman Brian Keenan (not to be confused with the IRA leader of the same name) who was held hostage in Beirut. He was dispatched to the US in the late 1980s to promote the leadership's perspective among the Irish-American community. In his 2009 book on Sinn Féin's strategy from the Bobby Sands hunger strike onwards, Martyn Frampton says that, prior to his exposure, Donaldson 'was known only for his unswerving loyalty to the Adams-McGuinness leadership', and that he was an internal 'ambassador', policing dissent whether it arose in the North or in the US.[27]

Covering the negotiations for the Good Friday Agreement (GFA), I used to notice Donaldson talking to people outside Stormont's Castle Buildings. Unlike some of the other Sinn Féin officials, he kept his distance from journalists, but I recall overhearing him half-jokingly reply to someone who had asked how he was getting on: 'Not bad for someone living under British occupation.' When the GFA was concluded in 1998, Donaldson became the chief administrator of the Sinn Féin team at the Northern Ireland Assembly. In a bizarre series of events, the Police Service of Northern

Ireland raided Sinn Féin's offices at Stormont in 2002. Donaldson and two others were arrested, and charged with running an IRA spy-ring. This episode, which quickly became known as 'Stormontgate', precipitated the collapse of the power-sharing executive, and brought an end to the political career of the unionist First Minister, David, now Lord, Trimble. Charges against Donaldson and the other two were later dropped 'in the public interest'. But three years later, in December 2005, Gerry Adams said, in a statement, that Donaldson was a British agent. A few hours later, this was confirmed by Donaldson himself. This would have resulted in his rapid execution by the Provisional IRA in the past, but there was no such retribution at that stage. Instead of leaving the country for his own safety, he moved to an isolated cottage outside Glenties, County Donegal. His new life in the northwest was the subject of a report in a tabloid newspaper. On 4 April 2006, he was killed with a shotgun, at the age of fifty-six. The Real IRA, a dissident breakaway from the Provisionals, later claimed responsibility. It has been variously suggested that it was republicans from West Tyrone or Derry who carried out the shooting.

Brian Rowan, a leading journalist covering security issues in the North, quoted a senior intelligence source, who said that Donaldson's main value was as a provider of information to the Special Branch on the thinking at the highest level of Sinn Féin for about twenty years, but that he hadn't revealed details of IRA activities.[28] A well-placed source of my own, who did not go into specifics, said that Donaldson did considerable damage to the republican cause. It has been suggested that he passed on information about the planned IRA attack on British soldiers in Gibraltar, but there is no concrete evidence that he was responsible for the deaths of the three Provisional activists on that occasion. His role in the US can be assessed from articles in the *Irish Voice* newspaper, based in New York. In November 1995, the *Irish Voice* newspaper described how a debate was held in a fashionable restaurant on Manhattan's East Side, prior to President Bill Clinton's visit to Ireland a few weeks later.

At the time, eleven men from Northern Ireland were facing deportation from the US because they did not have the proper immigrant documentation. Their American-born wives and other backers were contemplating a picket on Clinton while he was in Ireland. On the other side of the argument were Irish-Americans who would normally be sympathetic to the men's plight, but did not want to see Clinton embarrassed on his lap of honour – this was the President, after all, who defied the British to give Gerry Adams a visa the year before. The article continues:

> Representing the latter at J's Grill was Denis Donaldson, a Belfast man close to the Sinn Féin leadership. Donaldson has become ubiquitous at republican events in the New York area since moving here from Belfast six months ago, and he is seen as being very close to Sinn Féin HQ in Belfast... Donaldson got up before the crowd and issued a statement: the republican movement does not want the protests against Clinton to proceed... After the meeting, Donaldson was seen in heated discussion with some of the deportee supporters at the bar. There was no deal struck or any other resolution, and as it stands now, the protests will likely happen.[29]

In the event, there was little in the way of protest on this issue. Publisher of the *Irish Voice* and leading US campaigner on issues related to Ireland, Niall O'Dowd wrote later of the shock felt in Irish-America at Donaldson's admission that he was a paid British agent. Recalling how the Belfastman had first come to the US as a Sinn Féin representative in 1988, he pointed out that it wasn't long after the split in the movement over abstentionism and Ruairí Ó Brádaigh's Republican Sinn Féin had set up a support group, the Friends of Irish Freedom. In previous contests of this nature in the US, the hardliners usually won. Donaldson was sent over to ensure that the majority of Irish-American sympathisers stayed with Irish Northern Aid

(Noraid), which supported Provisional Sinn Féin. O'Dowd writes: 'He arrived from Belfast with impeccable credentials. The diminutive, heavy-smoking Donaldson also had a quick wit and a disarming manner, which ensured that tensions rarely boiled over... Oftentimes business was done in bar settings, the affable Donaldson winning someone over to his situation over a pint or two, though no one ever remembers him being drunk.' He travelled widely, holding meetings in different cities. His efforts proved successful and O'Dowd recalls: 'By the time he returned to Belfast, Donaldson had smoothed out the personal rivalries, made clear Irish Northern Aid were the chosen group, and helped dispatch the Friends of Irish Freedom to history's dustbin. It was a job well done.'

Donaldson came back again after the 1994 IRA ceasefire, when there was grave suspicion in some circles of Irish-American republicanism about the move towards exclusively peaceful means. He calmed the situation, steadied the ship and cleared the way for setting-up a US branch of Friends of Sinn Féin (FoSF), which raises very substantial sums of money each year. Presumably, the benefit for the British in all this was that it ensured most Irish-Americans involved with the republican cause were supporting democratic, non-violent activities, rather than supplying weapons of war or the funds to buy them. This does not square with the British Government's fury over the granting of a US visa to Adams by President Clinton. O'Dowd quotes a party source in Ireland as saying: 'No Sinn Féin representative would have done anything different than Donaldson did.'[30]

Well-placed sources have suggested that at least one more, so-far-unnamed senior republican was working for 'the other side'. As one observer put it: 'The British security services are very good at what they do.'[31] The Irish Government is not behind the door either. Michael McDowell was Tánaiste (*deputy prime minister*) and Minister for Justice when the St Andrews Agreement on Northern Ireland devolution was being agreed in October 2006. In an interview for this book, he said the Fianna Fail-Progressive

Democrats Government of the day had a source that was privy to the thinking inside the republican camp, who advised them that Sinn Féin would accept the Agreement even though it involved recognition of the new Police Service of Northern Ireland: 'I knew that we had somebody there, but I don't know who it was or where that person was …I got absolutely reliable information and, when the whole peace process was going towards the St Andrews Agreement, [British Prime Minister Tony] Blair and [Downing Street Chief of Staff Jonathan] Powell were always asking us to make concessions… I was getting a briefing that none of those were necessary, that the decision had been made, and just to ignore the Brits. My information turned out to be right.'[32]

In an in-depth investigation for the *Irish Times*, Pamela Duncan and Simon Carswell examined the quantity and sources of funding to Friends of Sinn Féin in the US. They reported that FoSF had raised US$12 million (€10.6 million or Stg 7.57 million at time of writing) over a twenty-year period. Between 1995 and 2014, there were 15,000 contributions by sources ranging from major US construction firms to trade unions, Hollywood stars and small donors. The leading benefactor was philanthropist Chuck Feeney, who donated US $780,000 personally and through two of his companies, to fund the setting-up of an office by FoSF in Washington DC and the running of it for three years.All donations are reported to the US Department of Justice, under a law which requires full compliance by agents of a foreign political party. From an analysis of these figures, it emerged that union donations exceeded €1 million, with the biggest contributor being the Laborers' International Union of North America, which gave more than $220,000. There were donations made by a wide range of companies that included, among others, plumbing contractors, restaurants, IT service providers, funeral homes, air conditioning firms and fish suppliers. Big names in the movie world, such as Martin Sheen, *Lord of the Rings* star Viggo Mortensen, Fionnula Flanagan, Oscar-winner Anjelica Huston and the late Dennis Hopper also donated money. Judges, lawyers and doctors also contributed.

James Cullen, president of Friends of Sinn Féin, told the *Irish Times* that, in compliance with electoral rules in the Republic, he ensured all money raised was sent only to Northern Ireland where it went towards the cost of running the party's offices and items such as mobile phones, computers and used cars to transport party workers. Using hypothetical examples, he said: 'I actually pay the bill, so I make the cheque to Joe's Used Auto Lot or to Fred's Printing Company in Derry.' In an interview with Simon Carswell, Cullen said that his interest in the North was sparked by a visit there in 1969, when the Troubles were just starting. He saw parallels between the treatment of nationalists by the RUC and the position of African-Americans in the Deep South. Born in New York to a Sligo father and Offaly mother, he was drafted into the US Army as a private after he completed law school. He went on to become a brigadier general, a one-star general and, eventually, chief judge of the US Army court of criminal appeals. When he retired from the army, he took up a position as a commercial property lawyer with a New York firm. He became president of FoSF in 2012, succeeding another New York-based lawyer, Larry Downes.

In the period from February to June 1995, FoSF raised almost $900,000. That was in the heady atmosphere that prevailed after the first IRA ceasefire but, even in the twelve months up to the end of October 2014, the figure was $361,242. Out of the $12 million raised since FoSF was founded, slightly more than half – or almost $6.3 million – was raised in the state of New York, with New Jersey second at $1 million and California third with $613,804. No other Irish party has come close to this: Friends of Fianna Fáil Inc (now defunct) collected $1.32 million in a twenty-year period to 2003. Friends of Fine Gael raised $140,000 in 1995 and Supporters of Fine Gael Inc, set up in 2007, brought in $28,350 the following year.[33] It was also reported in the *Irish Times* that a group of American business people, some of them with Wall Street backgrounds and including donors to the party, flew into Dublin for a meeting in

January 2015, in which concerns were raised with Sinn Féin leaders over what were seen as 'anti-business policies'. The two-hour meeting with Adams, Mary Lou McDonald, finance spokesman Pearse Doherty and enterprise spokesman Peadar Tóibín took place in a conference room at Leinster House. The paper quoted a Sinn Féin source as saying: 'I suppose some of them might have had a classic American approach to economics in that they would prefer lower taxes and lower spending on public services. We explained we had a more European approach and believed in funding public services.' James Cullen, who was at the meeting, said afterwards: 'It was very well received because I stayed after they left and the consensus [among the party's elected representatives] was, "Look, these guys make a good point; we need to listen, we certainly need to address any perception that Sinn Féin would be hostile in any way with business."'[34]

Whereas Cullen looks after the finances, the task of representing Sinn Féin politically in the US is undertaken by Rita O'Hare. In an interview for this book, she said: 'I work very much through the Irish-American organisations, all of them – well, all of the pro-peace process ones of course.' She also keeps in contact with Irish-American politicians on Capitol Hill.' But our support and the interest is not confined solely to the Irish-American constituency and Irish-American representatives,' she says. 'There is a lot of interest in the whole peace process story and in what Sinn Féin is trying to do, in the political system in the States.'

During the presidency of Bill Clinton, policy on the Irish peace process was run from the White House. It has since reverted to the State Department. During the annual St Patrick's week of Irish-related events in the US in March 2015, the department cancelled a meeting between Gerry Adams and deputy secretary of state Tony Blinken. The Sinn Féin leader called the decision 'bizarre'. A meeting later took place with a lower-ranking official. The department said that meetings between Mr Blinken and 'Northern Ireland officials' were being postponed until the negotiations on welfare reform and implementation of the Stormont House Agreement were concluded.[35] Asked about the role of the department, O'Hare comments: 'I have to say that I have found them, by and large... the personnel there interested, supportive, helpful, in the main.' She says there is no difficulty with Irish-America over left-wing policies espoused by Sinn Féin. 'What Irish-Americans are interested in is seeing an Ireland that is based on equality and justice and fairness,' she says. 'The common ground Sinn Féin has with Irish-America is wanting to see Irish unity.' It would make a 'huge' impact in the US if Sinn Féin were in government on both sides of the Border in Ireland. O'Hare says there is great interest in the Irish political scene:

> You would be amazed at the amount of people that literally follow what's happening in Ireland every single day, through the internet, and they're still interested, hugely interested. And it's not just, 'Is Stormont working?' People are interested in the South. They're hugely interested in how partition continues to affect any sort of normal relations or the economy.

Media coverage in the US has never been a major problem for Sinn Féin, especially since the IRA ceasefire, but this has changed in the recent past. A lengthy article in the *New Yorker* magazine during the all-important St Patrick's week in 2015 reflected this. 'Letter from Belfast: Where the bodies are buried' by Patrick Radden Keefe, repeated the claims by former IRA activists that Adams gave the order to 'disappear' Jean McConville and that he chaired a meeting in Belfast to plan the IRA's London bombings of 1973. Adams declined to be interviewed for the article.[36]

However, the Sinn Féin leader did agree to an interview on the CBS flagship television programme *60 Minutes*, which was broadcast on 5 April 2015. He denied any role in the McConville episode, but the exchange that got the most attention was one where interviewer Scott Pelley, referring to the fact that the IRA killing left the

McConville children without a living parent, said to Adams: 'How do you orphan ten children? What kind of depravity is that?'

'That's what happens in wars, Scott,' Mr Adams replied. 'That's not [to] minimise it – that's what American soldiers do, British soldiers do, Irish republican soldiers do – that's what happens in every single conflict.'[37]

Responding on RTE's *Morning Ireland*, Mrs McConville's son Michael said: 'If this was a war then the execution and death and burial, the kidnapping of our mother, is a war crime... Gerry Adams is a hypocrite. If this had happened to an IRA family and ten children were left orphaned would he say the same thing? I don't think so.'[38]

On the same programme, Adams repeated his long-standing denial of IRA membership but Michael McConville said: 'Everybody knows he was in the IRA. The only person who didn't know was Gerry Adams.'[39]

Nobody outside the Sinn Féin sphere of influence corroborates the Adams denial, as far as I am aware. Michael McDowell, who has some experience in the security area as a former justice minister and attorney general, said:

> I know it's untrue. It's some kind of technicality, that there is no such thing as a member of the IRA, there are only volunteers or whatever. It's something semantic in his head... a Jesuitical distinction of some kind. Or maybe he never swore himself in or something... But he was the Commanding Officer of the Belfast Brigade... for a long, long time. It's well-known to be so. He was always, at all material times, from the mid-1970s, on the Army Council. I think he possibly still is. I don't know what has happened to the Army Council, I don't think it's ever dissolved itself... Adams was at all stages in command of the IRA and the head of Sinn Féin.

McDowell said this was the de facto situation even where someone else held the title of Chief of Staff: 'He was... the head honcho on the Army Council'.[40]

Whatever he may or may not have done in the North, Adams gets favourable mention for his role in the anti-apartheid struggle from one of the leading figures in that campaign. Kader Asmal (1934-2011) was a founder of the Irish Anti-Apartheid Movement who went on to become a cabinet minister under Nelson Mandela and Thabo Mbeki in liberated South Africa. In a memoir published the year he died, Asmal recalls how a 'daring and audacious' bomb attack on the apartheid regime's main oil refinery at Sasolburg was 'the result of reconnaissance carried out by members of the IRA'. The actual bombing was the work of the MK, armed wing of the African National Congress, but Asmal writes that the advance feasibility report by IRA volunteers was arranged with 'Gerry Adams of Sinn Féin' through the general secretary of the Communist Party of Ireland, Michael O'Riordan (1917-2006). Asmal writes that it was 'a huge morale-booster' for the anti-apartheid struggle.[41] It does appear, at times, that if Adams was a combination of Martin Luther King, Mahatma Gandhi and the Dalai Lama, he would still be subject to a barrage of criticism and denunciation for anything he had ever said or done. At the same time it has to be said that he has a special talent for putting his foot in it. His use of the expression, 'That's what happens in wars', in relation to the tragic fate of Jean McConville was inappropriate, and bound to give offence. Likewise, his attempt at humour during a speech to supporters at an FoSF dinner in the Sheraton Hotel in New York on 6 November 2014 caused him serious damage. Referring to critical coverage of his activities by the *Irish Independent*, the Sinn Féin chief recalled how guerrilla leader Michael Collins dealt with similar treatment by that paper during the War of Independence: 'He went in, sent volunteers in, to the offices, held the editor at gunpoint, and destroyed the entire printing press.' Members of the audience of about 650 at the $500-a-seat occasion laughed when Adams continued: 'I'm obviously not advocating that.'[42] The remarks incurred criticism from the National Union of Journalists as being 'ill-judged and inappropriate'; Justice Minister Frances Fitzgerald of Fine Gael said that Adams's comments were 'abhorrent'; Tánaiste and Labour leader Joan Burton accused him of issuing a 'veiled threat to our free press in Ireland'; the World Association of Newspapers and News Publishers called for the remarks to be withdrawn. But the Sinn Féin leader said in a brief statement: 'I have no intention of withdrawing my remarks. They were simply referencing a historical fact.'[43]

In June 2015, this writer went along to observe the annual Sinn Féin commemoration at the graveside of Wolfe Tone, founder of Irish republicanism, at Bodenstown, County Kildare. I had reported on other commemorations, but this was the first one I attended that was organised by Provisional Sinn Féin. There was a republican band with a drum as loud as any of the Lambeg variety favoured by Orange bands in the North. Actor Jim Roche, dressed in an 18th-century French revolutionary uniform, recited Tone's speech from the dock. Mary Lou McDonald gave the main oration. For the duration of the ceremony, Adams sat facing the crowd and tapped away constantly on his mobile phone, as eagerly as any teenager. It appeared somewhat disrespectful but when I later checked his Twitter account there was a total of nineteen messages to his followers, including twenty-four photographs.

The Sinn Féin leader clearly revels in this branch of social media, but all the time his opponents and critics are closely watching every item. A classic example occurred with a Tweet he sent out to mark his sixty-fifth birthday. Adams attached a screenshot of *Still I Rise* by African-American poet and civil rights activist Maya Angelou (1928-2014).[44] In the words of one critic: 'Clearly addressed to the white oppressors of black persons, the poem presents us with a black woman willing to speak up for herself, for other living blacks, and even for her black ancestors. The poem is both highly political and highly personal. The speaker is implicitly responding to decades and even centuries of oppression and mistreatment.'[45]

It is, in fact, a very moving and powerful anthem of protest against racial oppression. The seventh out of nine verses – it's not the start of the poem as one critic of Adams has claimed – drew adverse reaction towards the Sinn Féin leader. It reads: 'Does my sexiness upset you?/Does it come as a surprise/That I dance like I've got diamonds/At the meeting of my thighs?' It was considered insensitive of Adams to post such material on Twitter in the week that a jail sentence was imposed on his brother Liam for the abuse of Áine, his daughter and niece of the Sinn Féin leader. The controversy over Mairia Cahill's allegations was still raging, and Adams was quizzed by the media about his taste in poetry. He urged the reporters to read the complete poem rather than focusing on a small part of it.[46]

Further questions about his Twitter acount were raised by Eilis O'Hanlon, a niece of Joe Cahill and one of Sinn Féin's most trenchant critics, in the *Sunday Independent*. She pointed out, for example, that Adams had tweeted a link to a page from a book by Michael Harding, which referred to the average man as 'a half-evolved Neanderthal with a fragrant penis'. It's part of a 150-word meditation on male untidiness that is intended to be humorous, but tweeting such an item in the middle of a controversy over sexual abuse was bound to draw unfavourable reaction. O'Hanlon asks: 'Why did Adams think it appropriate that night to take a photo of that page on his phone, then link to it on Twitter? Did it never cross his mind how it might look to others?'[47]

Adams is also known for hugging trees and, perhaps most bizarrely of all, has claimed that he engaged in naked trampolining with his dog – although this comes across as a Monty Python-style fantasy. Writing in the *Belfast Telegraph*, longtime observer of the Northern Ireland scene Henry McDonald suggested that, far from losing the plot, Adams was carrying out a well-calculated political and public relations strategy. In his tweets, he can portray himself as cuddly, mildly eccentric and, that most cliched, over-played, exaggerated virtue of all in Irish life, good craic [fun]. Asserting that

Adams would go to 'extraordinary lengths' to deflect criticism, McDonald wrote: 'Think of how he reacted to the Liam Adams' scandal by revealing that his own father (until then a republican icon given an IRA funeral) had abused members of his family.'[48] (The Sinn Féin leader revealed in 2009 that, when he was 50 years old, he discovered that his father, the late Gerry Adams Sr., had abused some members of the family.[49])

It is almost certainly the case that, if a new leader or leaders from a different generation were to replace Gerry Adams, the party would have to endure a great deal less controversy in the political sphere and the media. But no matter what accusations are levelled against the man, his party colleagues continue to back him. Unless some material emerges which is so damning that even his loyal supporters cannot withstand the pressure, Gerry Adams looks set to continue as Sinn Féin president for as long as he himself sees fit. Born on 6 October 1948, he appears fit and healthy, and shows no sign of retreating to his Donegal holiday home to pursue literary activities. If he stepped down, some argue that it would make the party a good deal more attractive to middle-class voters in the Republic. Others suggest that his history of involvement in the 'struggle' – despite his much-derided denial of IRA membership – is ultimately more of an asset than a liability, and that Irish voters like their leaders to have a 'whiff of cordite' about them, as was the case with Eamon de Valera and Charles Haughey, provided that it arises from a previous period and not the present or, heaven forbid, the future.

9. THE ROCKY PATH TO POWER

SINN FÉIN HAS SHOWN from time to time that it can be out of touch with the mood of the people. This was evident in its decision, following a lively internal debate, to support the abolition of Seanad Éireann– the Irish Senate – in a referendum on that issue. The party had initially opposed the Government move and Gerry Adams told the Dáil on 13 June 2013 that reform, not abolition, was the correct approach. Four months later, a majority of voters opted to retain the Upper House of their parliament in the referendum. Sinn Féin advocates of a No vote could argue that the party still benefited by taking a stance against an institution they regard as outmoded and elitist, but others would say that it's never a great idea to be on the losing side on such issues.

The Irish people's political choices are hard to predict, and popular sentiment can change without warning. At time of writing, it looks as if Sinn Féin will at least double its Dáil representation in the next general election, from the present 14 seats. Fianna Fáil currently has 21 TDs and a key challenge facing that party is to stay ahead of Sinn Féin. Then we get into the issue of government formation. It is generally expected that no party will have an overall majority. Different coalition options are possible. On 4 August 2015, bookmaker Paddy Power was offering odds of 5/4 on a Fine Gael-

Fianna Fáil coalition; Fine Gael-Labour (the current combination) was at 7/2; FiannaFáil-Sinn Féin, at 9/1 and Fine Gael-Sinn Féin at 16/1.[1] While parties tend to forswear alliances of any and all kinds going into an election, these declarations don't always apply when the votes are counted and the make-up of the new Dáil is revealed.

The terms of Motion 52 at the Derry ardfheis (national conference) on 6 March 2015 forbid Sinn Féin to enter a 'Fianna Fáil-led or Fine Gael-led government' after the general election. But, as previously noted, the motion also commits Sinn Féin 'to form broad alliances with like-minded parties and independents... to maximise the potential for an anti-austerity government in the 26 Counties'.[2] Labour's electoral performance after various coalitions with right-of-centre parties over the decades shows that minority participation can come with a heavy price at the subsequent general election. By the same logic, Sinn Féin would lose out at the ballot-box afterwards if it became a minority partner in a government led by Fianna Fáil or Fine Gael. But a coalition where Sinn Féin and 'anti-austerity' TDs held the majority and Sinn Féin was the dominant force in that element of the partnership would arguably be a different matter. Predicting election outcomes is a highly-speculative exercise and one guess may be as good as another, but a very tentative estimate as to the make-up of the next Dáil (which will be reduced in strength from 166 to 158 TDs) goes something like this: Fine Gael: 50; FiannaFáil: 35; Sinn Féin: 30; Labour: 10; Independents and others (i.e., smaller parties): 33. If those were the actual post-election figures, Fine Gael and Fianna Fail would have a majority between them, perhaps with a handful of Independents added on for extra comfort. However, this would be such a major shift away from Fianna Fáil's traditional attitude to 'The Blueshirts' that an internal rift of some kind among 'The Soldiers of Destiny' would seem to be almost inevitable – the question is, how big?

A very well-placed and vastly-experienced Fianna Fáil insider predicted to the author that, in the event of coalition with Fine Gael, a third of the Fianna Fáil membership 'would start looking at Sinn

Féin' and another third would simply drop out of the party. The other main options for Fianna Fáil would appear to be twofold: joining a coalition that includes Sinn Féin, or remaining in opposition and perhaps supporting a minority Fine Gael-led government on a case-by-case basis. If the figures given above were to apply in reality, then the Fianna Fáil-Sinn Féin combination would need the support of Labour and/or sufficient 'Independents and others'. It would not be an easy task putting such an alliance together, and parallels with the inter-party government of 1948 come to mind. In addition, Fianna Fáil leader Micheál Martin has carried out something of a moral crusade against Sinn Féin. Labour has also taken the high moral ground, and there have been bitter exchanges across the floor of the Dáil, especially in the weekly jousts between Tánaiste (Deputy Prime Minister) Joan Burton and Sinn Féin Deputy Leader Mary Lou McDonald. Labour doesn't easily turn down the chance of serving in government but perhaps on this occasion it would stand aloof, especially if another general election was expected in the near future. The Independents by their nature are not amenable to strict discipline, but a deal could more than likely be made with some of them. It might be a 'confidence and supply' arrangement for external support, or else a group of Independents could actually join the new coalition and take up ministerial appointments.

When I asked the Fianna Fáil leader, in an interview conducted in his home city of Cork in March 2014, if there was anyone he wouldn't go into government with, on principle, Micheál Martin replied: 'We have made it very clear we wouldn't go into government with Sinn Féin.'

D de B: Ever?

MM: We're not saying ever, ever. I mean, we wouldn't go into government in terms of their policy platform and in terms of how, in certain aspects of their behaviour, still, they stretch the democratic parameters - I'll put it that way - even still. They're improving. I think they're too rigid a party; they're too dictatorial in how they organise their members and so on like that. We've been on a number of protest marches and so on and they try and commandeer the protest, they try and take over an organisation and they actually turn on others who might be sympathetic to the organisation. Myself and [FF Health Spokesman] Billy Kelleher were on one particular home-help march, only over twelve months ago and the Shinners came along and tried to abuse us for walking the streets, [despite our] having been invited by the home-help organisation and by SIPTU [Ireland's biggest trade union]. And they tend to do that a lot...

Q. And after the next election?

A. After the next election – it's too early to be talking about who's going into power with who.

Q. You're not categorically ruling Sinn Féin out as a government partner after the next election?

A. Right now, we wouldn't go into government with Sinn Féin.

Q. Right now?

A. There would have to be a transformation of some kind.

Q. That could theoretically happen between now and the next election.

A. It's far too early [to be talking about.]

Q. Would you rule out Fine Gael?

A. Well, the problem with Fine Gael is that you would have a massive majority of Fianna Fáil and Fine Gael and I think that's the last thing the country needs.

Fianna Fáil's Environment Spokesman Barry Cowen addressed the issue at his party's selection convention on 16 February 2015 for the upcoming Carlow-Kilkenny by-election, where he was reported as referring to a famous speech by his brother, former taoiseach Brian Cowen, when Fianna Fáil was in coalition with the Progressive Democrats. 'As for Sinn Féin,' Barry Cowen said, 'I am mindful of an Ardfheis comment made by my brother when speaking about the PDs. He said: "If in doubt, leave them out". Now, of Sinn Féin we say: "Let there be no doubt, they must be left out". Any prospect of coalition with Fine Gael was also rejected.[3] And what are the prospects of a governmental liaison between Fine Gael and a Sinn Féin-led alliance? On the face of it, this looks next to impossible, but the post-election Dáil arithmetic can be a powerful force for convergence. Both sides would be holding their noses, but the prospect of spending the next five years or so on the opposition benches is not an enticing one.

Prior to the 2002 general election, Sinn Féin TD Caoimhghín Ó Caoláin said Fianna Fáil's objection to a possible coalition with his party was at odds with its participation alongside Sinn Féin ministers from the North's power-sharing executive on various cross-border bodies. He was speaking after Fianna Fáil's Dermot Ahern, who was then Minister for Social, Community and Family Affairs, had ruled out a coalition with Sinn Féin because of that party's 'adherence to an army'. Ahern added: 'That link is still there, whether they say it publicly or not'.[4]

At the time, Ó Caoláin was Sinn Féin's only TD. That number went up to five in the 2002 general election, but dropped down to four in 2007. When the general election of 24 May 2007 failed to give any party a clear majority and Fianna Fáil were in talks with the Green Party and others – but not Sinn Féin – Ó Caoláin sent out a very strong signal to Fine Gael that his party would be willing to discuss coalition. Speaking on RTÉ Radio 1's *This Week* programme on 10 June he said: 'We are available and willing to speak with all different opinion, including Enda Kenny and Fine Gael; we have ruled out absolutely nothing.'[5] But within days, Fianna Fáil were voted back into office with support from the Greens, Progressive Democrats and four Independents.

Shortly before the 2009 European elections, Frank Flannery, a senior Fine Gael strategist and close adviser to party leader Kenny at the time, said Sinn Féin was now a mainstream political party and that he believed his organisation would, if necessary, be prepared to join forces with it to oust Fianna Fáil. Flannery's views were quoted by John Lee in the *Irish Mail on Sunday*: 'In the past, Fine Gael has been doctrinaire in its opposition to Sinn Féin but I wouldn't say that is the case now. We are willing to work with any party that has the aim that we have – to get the current government out of office,' he said. 'We have been working together in the Dáil and we have put forward many of the same policies,' he added. 'Sinn Féin has moved fully into mainstream politics. It has received a mandate north and south and is willing to work to get the current government out of power. There is still the outstanding issue of their private army and that situation has to be fully articulated. We also must see that they are fully committed to condemning atrocities like the murder of Jerry McCabe, which some of their candidates did not do recently.[6] But we are willing to work with Sinn Féin,' he added. Mr Flannery, regarded as the mastermind of Fine Gael's current lead in the opinion polls, said his personal view was that the party would, if necessary, become coalition partners with Sinn Féin. 'Let's suppose that Fine Gael and Labour were short and Sinn Féin had the numbers. Could I see that, theoretically? I could see that happen,' he said... But Mr Flannery stressed that coalition with Sinn Féin was not yet official Fine Gael policy. 'I'm speaking now in a personal way. Fine Gael hasn't had that particular discussion. It's a discussion I'd say will happen around a general election.'[7]

Almost immediately, Enda Kenny dissociated himself from Flannery's remarks: 'I made it perfectly clear that Fine Gael would not be doing business with Sinn Féin and I have no intention of revisiting that.' But Fianna Fáil's Dermot Ahern pointed out that Flannery wasn't just some low-ranking party official: 'He is the architect and conductor of all Fine Gael strategy under Enda Kenny. He never says anything in public which hasn't been prepared well in advance as part of a clear blueprint.'[8] There was indeed a widely-held view at the time that Flannery's move, coming at the time that it did, was intended to draw Sinn Féin transfers to Fine Gael candidates in the elections to the European Parliament.

As soon as the European vote was over, it was reported that Flannery was losing his position as director of elections but staying on as director of organisation in Fine Gael headquarters. Another dimension was added to the story with a claim by former Green Party leader Trevor Sargent that he had been requested by Enda Kenny after the previous general election in 2007 to ask Sinn Féin if they would help him achieve a majority among the Dáil's 166 members in the vote for taoiseach. Fine Gael could only get 77 votes between themselves, Labour and the Greens. Sargent said he had been telling Kenny that the figures didn't add up, and Fine Gael would have to talk to Sinn Féin: 'I said that if you want to be taoiseach you don't have a choice. It was then that he said, could you give them a nod or ask them a question, would they be prepared to vote for him as taoiseach? I said, that is a very unusual thing. You have a phone and a voice. Why don't you ask your own questions?' It was clear that the Fine Gael leader did not want any direct contact with Sinn Féin, and Sargent commented: 'The only way I can rationalise it is that Enda Kenny had some experience in the Ballrooms of Romance in Mayo when he asked a fellow to ask your sister "Will she go out with me?"'

There are no indications that anything was on offer to Sinn Féin in return for its support in the Dáil vote, which was eventually won by Fianna Fáil under Bertie Ahern. Sargent recalled that when he mentioned the phone-call in passing to Caoimhghín Ó Caoláin the latter's response was 'a hearty laugh'. But when the Sinn Féin TD spoke on radio, as mentioned above, he was clearly taking the issue of possible talks with Fine Gael more seriously. Sargent's successor as Green Party leader, John Gormley, recalled a similar approach from Fine Gael at the time.[9] However, Kenny and his party sharply rejected the claims and the Fine Gael leader said: 'If I had been prepared to do business with Sinn Féin after the last election I would have been taoiseach for the past two years.'[10]

The Sinn Féin motion of 2015 and the debate about it were significantly different from a previous discussion at the March 2010 ardfheis in the Royal Dublin Society (RDS) at Ballsbridge – it's a favoured Sinn Féin venue, and the party has no problem with the title. When the clár (agenda) for that conference was issued on 24 February 2010, it featured a motion from the Charlie McGlade cumann (branch), based in Drimnagh, Dublin, which read as follows: 'This ardfheis calls on Sinn Féin not to go into power with other parties in government such as Fianna Fáil or Fine Gael, as this would be incompatible with our policies and would damage the party.'

The terms of the motion were more sweeping than the 2015 proposal, as the latter excludes only governments where Fianna Fáil or Fine Gael is the leading partner. The present writer covered a news conference to announce the 2010 clár, where Mary Lou McDonald was asked if the party leadership would be supporting the Drimnagh motion. She replied: 'Yes, we will, for the simple reason that we are not in the business of propping-up failed politics and failed policy.' Asked if Sinn Féin would even be prepared to talk to other parties after the general election, Dublin South-Central TD Aengus Ó Snodaigh said: 'We would be willing to talk to any political party, whatever the outcome of an election is. The only basis of any of those talks is if our political agenda, our political platform, are being taken on board and that the policies of any future government which we would support would be compatible with those.' And he added: 'We're not going to, at this stage, rule out sitting down with parties, but only on that basis.'

Ó Snodaigh's position clearly contradicted that of the leadership, as conveyed by McDonald: how could you talk to Fianna Fáil or Fine Gael about coalition if an ardfheis motion rejected any prospect of government with either of those parties? But despite McDonald's assurance that the leadership would support the Drimnagh motion, the ardchomhairle (executive council) put down an amendment which kept Sinn Féin's options open: 'We will only contemplate entering a coalition government on the basis of a programme for government rooted in republican principles, agreed and approved by a special delegate conference'.

I covered the ardfheis debate, in which the chairman of Sinn Féin in Dublin, Eoin Ó Broin said: 'The ardchomhairle amendment sends out an ambiguous signal.' He said participation in government with a 'right-wing' party would entrench partition and damage Sinn Féin, and he cited the experiences of Clann na Poblachta (dissolved), Democratic Left (absorbed into Labour) and the Green Party (major decline in popularity).

However, Kerry North TD Martin Ferris urged the delegates to support the amendment. The former republican prisoner who had been a high-profile figure at the time of the IRA campaign said: 'The sensible thing for us to do after the next election is to come back to a conference. I have faith in you, in the ardchomhairle, and the wider republican family to make the correct decision.' But chairman of the party in Dublin South-Central, Cormac Ó Dálaigh spoke against the amendment, which he interpreted as saying, in effect: 'If the offer is good enough, we might take it.'

In favour of the amendment, Caoimhghín Ó Caoláin, Sinn Féin's leader in the Dáil at the time – before Adams was elected TD for Louth – said: 'Let us not lock ourselves out of the political debate.' This was in line with the Cavan-Monaghan TD's previously-stated position that Sinn Féin ruled out talks with no other party. Pearse Doherty, then a Senator and later a TD, supported the amendment, but assured delegates that Sinn Féin 'would not prop up anybody unless they subscribe to our ideas and ideals'. (Five years later and speaking as a TD from Donegal, he opposed taking part in a coalition led by Fianna Fáil or Fine Gael.)

The amendment was passed by a large majority. A previous motion, which stated that Sinn Féin 'will not, under any circumstances, enter into coalition or any other electoral pact with

Fianna Fáil before, during or after a general election' (it made no mention of Fine Gael), was defeated in a card vote, by 142 votes to 59. Commenting on the debate afterwards, *Phoenix* magazine said the Dubliners who proposed the original motion were winning the day, but that, 'as the ringing rhetoric about Fianna Fáil reactionaries and sell-outs from speakers for the anti-coalition motion (all Dubs) began to swing the hall behind them', rural-based speakers Ferris and Doherty intervened to change the mood. The writer noted that 'in the countryside, disaffected Fianna Fáil voters are needed for either first-preference votes or transfers'.[11] The next day, Martin McGuinness said in a speech to the ardfheis: 'We have absolutely no interest in government with Fine Gael or with their policies. More of the same isn't what is required in the Ireland of 2010. We need new thinking and new ideas.'

In an analysis piece on the ardfheis for the *Irish Times*, I observed that there was 'something of a generation gap' in the debate on coalition: 'The Young Turks – mainly Dublin-based – argued passionately for a go-it-alone policy but they hadn't a chance, particularly when Kerry North TD Martin Ferris weighed in on the other side. It was reminiscent of Labour Party conferences in days of yore. There is the added attraction for Sinn Féin that, should they attain political office on both sides of the Border, then the party's ministers from Belfast and Dublin can meet each other in the context of the North-South Ministerial Council. That, in turn, can be presented as a further step along the road to Irish unity which Sinn Féin sees as one of its "unique selling-points".[12] The Communist Party of Ireland's *Socialist Voice* commented that the motion in its amended form, 'effectually leaves the door open for participation in a future Government' and the piece, bylined 'EMC', continued:

> The experience of the dumping of central policies just before the last general election is still a painful memory for a large number of Southern members. The position of the ardchomhairle was that any decision in relation to joining a government would be taken by a special

party conference. Given that Sinn Féin is in effect a Northern party, controlled from Belfast, its priorities are shaped by political developments and the priorities surrounding the Northern situation. The majority of delegates to the recent ardfheis, as with previous ardfheiseanna, were from the North. If the opportunity arises to enter government in the Republic, the likelihood of their joining a coalition is very high – simply because the political priorities are determined by that relationship... From reading the motions and the speeches of leading figures in Sinn Féin one cannot help seeing that it is a party moving steadily to the centre. It is caught up in electoral politics and is prepared to make whatever compromises are required to secure participation in government. It will surely end up in government but with nothing radical to bring to the table.[13]

Writing in the *Irish Times* a few days after the ardfheis, columnist Vincent Browne was of the view that, 'a gobbledegook amendment was passed with predictable fudges, allowing the leadership more or less absolute discretion to do what they like, subject of course to endorsement by a special ardfheis.'[14] Browne's analysis was rejected by one of the supporters of the original anti-coalition motion. Eoin Ó Broin, who had expressed concern at the ardfheis about ambiguity in the leadership's amendment to the motion, wrote in *An Phoblacht*: 'Unfortunately, his opinion piece misrepresents the content and outcome of the coalition debate... I listened carefully to the contributions in support of the ArdChomhairle amendment from Caoimhghín Ó Caoláin, Pearse Doherty and Martin Ferris. Nothing in their speeches indicated that they believe that entering a Fianna Fáil or Fine Gael coalition would advance our struggle.'[15]

Four years later, Browne was being attacked from another quarter because he was still predicting that Sinn Féin would form a government with Fine Gael after the next election. Independent Senator John Crown wrote in the *Sunday Independent*: 'For Fine Gael to do so, in the absence of an explicit Sinn Féin repudiation of, and apology for, the terrorist campaign which their doppelgangers in the so-called IRA waged against our own Republic and its police force, would be indefensible when a perfectly valid democratic alternative exists.'[16]

The issue of coalition came up again after the local and European elections in May 2014, when the Irish edition of the *Sunday Times* carried a report of an interview with the Sinn Féin vice-president by Stephen O'Brien, who wrote:

> Mary Lou McDonald has admitted Sinn Féin's promises of a 1% wealth tax on assets over €1m and a 48% tax rate for high earners – those paid over €100,000 – could be sacrificed in negotiations to agree a Programme for Government. The deputy leader of Sinn Féin has revealed her party's commitment to abolish the property tax will be the only red line in any talks with other parties about formation of a government after the next general election... McDonald, the favourite to succeed Gerry Adams as party leader, said she would be more comfortable in government with 'the party of Connolly' [Labour] and other left-leaning groups and independents than with either Fianna Fáil or Fine Gael... However, McDonald did not rule out the prospect of coalition with either Fianna Fáil or Fine Gael, though she agreed a Fine Gael/Sinn Féin alliance seemed 'incompatible' and the least likely outcome 'given their background, their past...' McDonald declined to state what number of seats Sinn Féin would need to win in order to consider entering government, but did say having 30 TDs would put it 'in the mix' in terms of considering the options.[17]

Her interview came a week after Adams was quizzed about coalition terms on RTÉ Radio's *Morning Ireland*. When pressed on specific non-negotiable issues for Sinn Féin, he confirmed it would insist on property tax being scrapped. But in response to persistent questioning he refused to say if a 48 per cent rate of tax for those earning €100,000 or more would be a deal-breaker.[18] Shortly afterwards, Eoin Ó Broin, whose position in Sinn Féin is somewhat akin to the relationship Tony Benn had with the British Labour Party leadership, wrote on his blog on 1 July 2014:

> Voters and the media will want to know who we would enter government with and what economic policies will form the core of our campaign. In the 2007 election we fudged the first question and backpedalled on the second. The electorate punished us for both mistakes. In 2011 we set out a real alternative to the austerity consensus and pledged not to enter coalition with Fianna Fáil or Fine Gael. The electorate rewarded us with an extra 10 seats... The electorate are realising that a better, fairer southern Ireland requires an end to the dominance of Fianna Fáil and Fine Gael... Sinn Féin should loudly declare that we will not participate in a Fianna Fáil- or Fine Gael-led government after the next general election... If the post-election numbers don't allow this, people need to know that we won't go back on our word, but will continue to build popular support for a real alternative from the opposition benches. We also need to set out our key political commitments – the red-line issues that must form the basis of Sinn Féin participation in any government.[19]

When Harry McGee raised the coalition issue with the Sinn Féin president in an interview at the start of 2015, Adams replied: 'Here the party is very clear and I am very clear; we do not want to go into government as a minority party. The only point of being in government is if you can improve the conditions for all of the people and if you can advance your overall project. The question of who would form a coalition and who would go in, that is dependent on the mandate you receive and vote you receive.' When asked if that meant Sinn Féin would have to be the dominant partner, Adams responded in terms that evoked historical memories of 1948: 'Not necessarily. I do not want to speculate too much around this. You could have a three- or five-party coalition.'[20] Subsequently, the abolition of water charges was declared to be another red-line issue for Sinn Féin, but otherwise there appeared to be flexibility.[21]

Meanwhile, the news and current affairs website www.journal.ie reported, in the aftermath of the local and European elections of May 2014, that the Taoiseach and Fine Gael leader had declined to rule out coalition with Sinn Féin or Fianna Fáil. Speaking at the Castlebar election count-centre in his home county of Mayo, he said that Sinn Féin had emerged from the latest elections as 'a significant political entity'. Fine Gael had been in 'alliances' with both opposition parties at council level in the past: 'Who knows what the future holds in politics? People here are masters in the democratic situation – they make the decisions. We'll wait and see what result there comes [in the General Election].'[22]

More recently, in the *Sunday Independent*, Jody Corcoran and John Drennan reported: 'On RTE, Mr Kenny twice failed to take an opportunity to explicitly rule out coalition with Sinn Féin ... And in his opening address at party's ArdFheis in Mayo this weekend, he again honed his attack on Fianna Fáil without mentioning Sinn Féin.'[23]

In a separate article headed 'Too early to rule out Fine Gael/Sinn Féin Coalition' in the same issue of the *Sunday Independent*, Drennan wrote: 'One of the most curious features of Irish coalitions is that they generally occur between parties which genuinely detest each other... Now we are being told there is absolutely no possible chance that Enda and Gerry would indulge in the foul coalition deed.

In fairness, few individuals arouse such a visceral sense of loathing in Mr Kenny as Mr Adams. But, what is Mr Kenny to do should we arrive at a scenario after the next election where the only alternatives are a Fianna Fáil/Sinn Féin coalition of incompetence or a patriotic union of Fine Gael and Sinn Féin?... And it would ultimately require a standing aside by Mr Adams (Don't worry Gerry, you can be Minister for Poetry or something) and the apotheosis of Mary Lou, before Fine Gael could swallow the Sinn Féin fly.'[24]

The article in the *Sunday Independent* by Corcoran and Drennan (who later became director of communications and political strategy with the newly-founded centre-right Renua party) also noted that, 'The Davy group, which advises corporations and institutional investors, says Sinn Féin will be "perfectly happy" to "moderate" its economic views in a "middle of the road" coalition. This assessment will come as a shock to a substantial number of voters who have been looking to Sinn Féin as the main anti-austerity party, according to recent polls.' As it happened, Davy arrived at the same general conclusion as a rather different source, namely the Socialist Party, which has always been sceptical about the depth of Sinn Féin's radicalism. Under the heading, 'Are Sinn Féin a genuine left alternative?' Conor Payne wrote:

> Given their 14 TDs and 154 councillors, it would be of huge benefit if Sinn Féin were to use their position to build the kind of active movement against austerity which is needed; for example by supporting a non-payment campaign to defeat the Water Tax ... In an interview on Morning Ireland (RTÉ Radio One, 11 September 2014) Sinn Féin TD Pearse Doherty essentially said that abolition of Water Charges would not be a red-line issue for Sinn Féin in entering a coalition government ... In government in the North, Sinn Féin have implemented cuts and privatisation ... Like the other main parties, Sinn Féin actively seek

support and finance from big business, particularly in the US.[25]

There was a further critique from longtime radical activist and trade unionist Paddy Healy. Under the heading 'Sinn Féin's 32-county organisation would not survive coalition' he wrote on his blog in August 2014: 'In Northern Ireland, Sinn Féin has vetoed Tory welfare cuts. This has led to reductions in the British financial subvention and increased tensions within the Stormont Executive. Supporters of the party will say that this would have happened in any event. However, it is a fact that it would be seriously damaging to Sinn Féin in the Republic if it had supported such cuts.'

Returning to the subject on 12 March 2015, he said: 'Since I wrote the piece, Sinn Féin has done a deal on cuts in the six counties with the Unionists and the two governments through the Stormont House Agreement. But now the party has had to step back from that deal under pressure from southern workers and northern workers ... The right wing of Sinn Féin want to be in coalition administrations in Stormont and Leinster House. The revolutionary republicans, genuine socialists and conscious workers north and south see the lifting of austerity throughout the island as the first priority. This is causing severe tensions in Sinn Féin. Claims by Sinn Féin leaders that they were misled by the DUP [Democratic Unionist Party] and Stormont officials in relation to the Agreement do not bear examination.' [26]

On the same date, 12 March 2015, another seasoned radical, Eamonn McCann wrote in his *Irish Times* column: 'One of the factors behind Sinn Féin's decision on Monday to pull out of the Stormont House Agreement was a series of trade union demonstrations tomorrow calling for rejection of the agreement... The unions' main concern is that the Agreement involves the loss of 20,000 public sector jobs ... The prospect of being at loggerheads with the unions has dismayed many in Sinn Féin.

The 2015 ardfheis motion represented a hardening of Sinn Féin's position on coalition. Ruling out participation in a government led by Fianna Fáil or Fine Gael, albeit with some possible flexibility in a situation where Sinn Féin was the largest element in an anti-austerity wing of such a partnership, was a change from the party's previous stance whereby an arrangement of that kind was not specifically excluded. When Ó Caoláin made his remarks in 2007, urging Enda Kenny 'for God's sake' to make contact about the vote for taoiseach, Sinn Féin had only four TDs, one fewer than in the previous Dáil. Ruling out participation in a government led by Fianna Fáil or Fine Gael might have been open to ridicule. Having suffered a setback in that general election, it could have been regarded as a minor triumph to get into office after all. Certainly the Cavan-Monaghan TD made a strong pitch when he told RTÉ interviewer Róisín Duffy that the identity of Sinn Féin's coalition partner was not the main issue: 'What we are interested in talking to people about is the programme for government and we have a clear, outlined position in relation to what is important in delivering to the electorate...'[27]

At the time of the Derry ardfheis in March 2015, Sinn Féin still had only 14 TDs but there was persuasive evidence in the polls that this number was going to increase substantially. In parallel with the improvement in Sinn Féin's electoral performance and prospects, there was a very significant change in the political climate and the mood of the people, both at home in Ireland and in other parts of the European Union. Along with the arrival of Syriza into power in Greece, the remarkable rise of Podemos ('We Can') in Spain, led by Pablo Iglesias, also evoked parallels with the Sinn Féin story.

Sinn Féin traces its roots back to the party of that name founded in 1905, whereas Podemos was not set up until January 2014. But, like Sinn Féin, it scored highly in the European elections in May of that year, winning eight per cent of the vote and five out of the Spanish allocation of 54 seats in Strasbourg. Sinn Féin won three seats out of eleven in the Republic, with 19.5 per cent of the vote (plus one seat out of three in Northern Ireland where it got 25.5 per cent).

Tobias Buck of the *Financial Times* wrote about the Spanish movement in terms that some observers would apply to Sinn Féin: 'In less than 12 months, Podemos has done what no other political force has achieved over the past three decades – it has ended the duopoly of power held by the two mainstream parties, and plunged Spain's stable political system into a volatile new era... For Spain's Socialist Party, the arrival of Podemos has indeed been disastrous: of the 7 million voters who backed the Socialists at the last election, 1.8 million say they now support Podemos... There is no risk-free option: a pact with one of the established parties will hurt the Podemos claim to stand against Spain's tired elite. A refusal to join forces with the Socialists, however, will probably mean keeping the centre-right in power in key regions – not the outcome that most Podemos voters are seeking.'[28] Substitute 'Sinn Féin' for 'Podemos', 'Ireland' for 'Spain', 'Labour and Fianna Fáil' for 'Socialist Party', then adjust the numbers of voters and you could arguably be talking about Ireland. As with Podemos, if Sinn Féin enters an alliance with Fianna Fáil or Fine Gael, it will hurt the party's claim to stand against Ireland's 'tired elite'. But remaining aloof does not look like a viable option either. Buck's analysis of the Spanish situation could easily be transferred to Ireland: 'Perhaps the most serious challenge faced by Podemos lies in the possibility that economic and political sentiment will start to shift again. The circumstances that have allowed it to flourish over the past year may no longer be so prevalent in 2016 or 2017.'

Both Podemos and Sinn Féin will be facing into a general election in their respective countries in or around the same time: the Spanish one must be held on or before 20 December 2015 and Ireland must go to the polls by 9 April 2016 at the latest. The Spanish party has, of course, a rather different heritage, and looks to Latin American role-models such as Bolivian President Evo Morales and Argentinian political theorist Ernesto Laclau for inspiration. Sinn Féin has its own gallery of heroes, mostly from the Irish republican tradition. Perhaps because of the tightly-knit nature that is part of Sinn Féin's heritage it does not have the same level of popular involvement in its activities that Podemos has achieved, nor has it made use of the internet and social media in the wholesale manner of its Spanish counterpart. And Sinn Féin does not have the use of an English-language equivalent of Iran's state-run Spanish-language television service, HispanTV, which in January 2013 began carrying a programme called *Fort Apache*, presented by Podemos leader Pablo Iglesias. The channel was later banned in Spain but Iglesias had already made his name.

One of the guest-speakers at the March 2015 Sinn Féin ardfheis in Derry was Euclid Tsakalotos, a minister in the newly-elected Greek government. An articulate speaker with a lively sense of humour, the Oxford PhD apologised for his English accent but quipped that, by way of mitigation, he was married to a Celt. The following month, Tsakalotos made international news when he effectively replaced controversial Finance Minister Yanis Varoufakis as head of the Greek Government's team in the negotiations with its European partners that culminated in Syriza's eating humble pie. In his Derry speech, he had said: 'Syriza and Sinn Féin as well as others [such] as Podemos are part of a great realignment in European politics that has become apparent over the last couple of years. That realignment is a necessity exactly because we have such a crisis in the existing arrangements, in which traditional parties are unable to address effectively their social base on an agenda of wages, jobs and welfare. Of course, those arguing against any realignment, those, that is, that have most to lose from any such change, convict us all on the charge of populism, needless to say, without any trial. They have mistaken populism for the popular. They do not want to believe, because it is not in their interests to believe, that the needs of the many, an equality agenda, in an economic crisis, can be part of a solution and not part of the problem.'[29]

Tsakalotos, who has since been given the title of Finance Minister in Greece, got a standing ovation at the beginning and end of his speech and, when he had finished his contribution, Adams came over to the platform to shake his hand and put an arm around his shoulder. There was also loud applause at another stage when Sinn Féin's Northern MEP, Martina Anderson characterised the changing political mood in Europe: 'In Athens it's called Syriza, in Spain it's called Podemos, in Ireland it's called Sinn Féin.'

Speakers from Syriza and Podemos took part in a conference in Dublin on 1 May 2015 organised by the Right2Water campaign, an alliance of trade unions and others to oppose water charges. Brendan Ogle of the Unite trade union said: 'What we want to do is start off with ideas and principles and see if they lead to policies and then see does that lead to candidates or some sort of alliance.' The conference at the Communication Workers Union Headquarters on Dublin's North Circular Road was intended to launch a consultation phase with a follow-up planned later, to agree concrete proposals. Along with union officials and community activists, the attendance of about 200 included ten members of the Dáil: Independents Róisín Shortall, Clare Daly, Mick Wallace, Joan Collins, Thomas Pringle, Seamus Healy and Catherine Murphy; Socialist Party TDS Ruth Coppinger, Joe Higgins and Paul Murphy; and Sinn Féin's Mary Lou McDonald, who headed a ten-member party delegation including Dublin MEP Lynn Boylan and a number of city councillors. Former Labour TD Declan Bree from Sligo also attended.

Deputy McDonald told reporters on the way in: 'We believe that this is a very important meeting. It's a mixture, as you know, of political parties, community groups, trade unions, all with a common purpose: to discuss, to deliberate on, an alternative politics for this state, obviously with an eye on the next general election.' When I asked her if Sinn Féin had much in common with Syriza and Podemos, or were they loose mass movements of a different nature, she replied: 'Well they're different from Sinn Féin, inasmuch as they are amalgams of different strains within Greek and Spanish society respectively, whereas Sinn Féin is a unitary political party... I suppose what we have in common with them is that we reflect and that we wish to deliver an alternative kind of politics.' She pointed out that they were all part of the GUE/NGL group in the European Parliament.

On the relationship between SIPTU and the unions in the Right2Water group, McDonald pointed out that SIPTU was represented at the conference.

Podemos was represented by Eduardo Maura from Bilbao who said: 'There is a new political space in Spain, but this political space is not on the left side of the political board, nor is it on the right side of the political board. It's at the heart of Spanish politics.' There was loud applause for this sentiment. He got further approval from the audience when he said: 'I have been a left-wing person for a long time and I have been an activist for a long time... and it took me some time to accept this, that neither the Left nor the activists change countries, it's the people.' He went on to make other key points, which included: (1) 'Most people, and we are talking about a huge majority, are not left-wing and activists'; (2) 'Most people are not militants of any left-wing or far-left-wing party, most people do other stuff'; (3) 'We try too often to make everyone think like us... It's the worst part of the leftist tradition of the 20th Century'; (4) 'We cannot keep on doing politics like that... That means maybe sticking to more basic demands, what we call citizens' demands'.

His message was that you must start from where the people are, not where you want them to be. Rory Hearne, one of the other speakers on the conference programme, commented afterwards on Facebook: 'The talk by Eduardo Maura... was really ground-breaking for me in trying to think how we can progress a new anti-establishment politics in Ireland... What is clear when we look to Latin America and Podemos and the SNP [Scottish National Party] is that there is an opening for new people's movements that are not defined by the purity of their Left positions... We have to decide are we going to sit on the margins or take power democratically through a process of citizen empowerment.'[30]

The issue of timing was taken up in the conference by Syriza's Konstantina Tzouvala. 'We need at some point to come to terms with the idea that social movements don't last forever. That's their nature,' she said. Seize the moment, was her message. These upheavals were 'anarchic', and did not obey the laws of logic. 'There is no rational reason, to be honest, why in Ireland austerity was implemented and then people freaked-out so much [about] water,' she said. 'I think it's brilliant, but you can't entirely rationalise it. People say, well, the charge is small, but... that's the nature of social movements.'

A close observer of the political scene at the conference gave me his assessment that the Sinn Féin leadership had not been happy with Motion 52 at the Derry ardfheis, which ruled out participation in government unless Sinn Féin were the majority party. He said that Sinn Féin was hoping the Right2Water conference would repair some of that 'damage'.

Adams spoke at his party's May 2015 ceremony in Dublin to mark the execution of socialist leader James Connolly after the 1916 Rising and, talking to reporters afterwards, he said that 'if Sinn Féin gets a mandate for government here we will scrap water charges'. When I asked him if it was a 'red-line' condition for entry to government, he replied: 'It's a commitment we're giving. We will give very few commitments but any that we give we will keep.' He added: 'The first thing we need is a mandate. Once we get a mandate then it's a matter of businesslike negotiations. It's just so blatant a betrayal of ordinary people that this additional charge should be imposed upon them.'

> DdeB: But is it your position: 'We're not going to go into government unless you abolish water charges'?
> GA: Well we're seeking a mandate
> DdeB: But if you get a mandate
> GA: Well of course that would be one of our issues, but I don't want to be negotiating out with yourself, Deaglán, you've been too long around
> DdeB: What about property tax?
> GA: I don't want to go through a shopping-list. I think that's a mistake that some of the parties make on

their way into an election, they promise the sun, the moon and the stars, but we will set out clearly-costed propositions in our manifesto and we will stick by whatever – ifwe get the mandate, now, I mean, it's very presumptuous to talk about forming a government when we haven't got a mandate.

In a speech to the Derry ardfheis, Martin McGuinness had said it was the party's goal to emerge as the biggest party in the Dáil after the next general election. It was also Sinn Féin's aim to become the biggest party in the North at the 2016 Assembly elections. He added: 'Both those goals are achievable and the symbolism of doing so on the 100th anniversary of the Rising would be massive because Sinn Féin is the only party on this island which is serious about building the kind of nation which was declared in 1916.'[31] McGuinness was more specific when taking part in a TV debate on the BBC with representatives of other parties in the forthcoming Westminster elections in the North. He said: 'Last year, the people of Ireland made Sinn Féin, in the local and European elections, the largest-supported party on the island. Next year we will face into the Assembly and Leinster House elections, with the prospect of Sinn Féin being in government, north and south.'[32]

Becoming the largest party in the Assembly would entitle Sinn Féin to the position of First Minister. In the South, as McGuinness put it in his interview for this book, it would mean that 'we can dictate terms in relation to the formation of a new government'. The slight drop of one per cent in the Sinn Féin vote at the Westminster elections and the loss of Michelle Gildernew's seat in Fermanagh-South Tyrone – although the actual number of votes went up by more than 4,000 – suggests that it will not be plain sailing in Northern Ireland. In the South, Sinn Féin is still a very long way indeed from the overall majority that all parties covet, so it may be faced with a Yes or No decision on joining a coalition in Dublin.

That could be crucial in determining the party's future. If Sinn

Féin was in government, north and south, at the centenary of the 1916 Rising, it would be seen from one perspective as a major political and propaganda boost for republican sentiment and the cause of Irish unity. It would be trumpeted as a big step forward for the nationalist community in Northern Ireland and would play well among the Irish-American community. An alternative viewpoint would be that entering a coalition in Dublin as a minority partner, i.e., without a Sinn Féin taoiseach heading it up – even on a job-share basis as Labour has suggested in a different context in the past – would be fatal politically, given that the smaller parties tend to suffer badly as a result of such alliances. Of course, as Cavan-based Senator Kathryn Reilly has pointed out, any such decision would have to be discussed, and a vote taken, at a specially-convened ardfheis.[33] The path to power is indeed a rocky one, and once you get there it doesn't get any smoother.

EPILOGUE: THE STORY SO FAR

There's a man with a gun over there, telling me I got to beware (Stephen Stills, for Buffalo Springfield)

FINISHING A BOOK ON Sinn Féin in current political circumstances is like calling half-time in a hotly-contested football match – except the stakes are a lot higher in Irish politics, north and south. At time of writing a major controversy has erupted over the Provisional IRA – does it still exist and, if so, what is its role?

On 5 May 2015, 47-year-old Gerard 'Jock' Davison was shot dead in the Markets district of Belfast. Widely-reported to have been a leading figure in the IRA in Belfast, he supported the 1998 Good Friday Agreement. After the January 2005 killing of Robert McCartney in a row at a Belfast pub, Davison was questioned by police but later released without charge.

The motivation for the Davison killing was unclear and there was speculation - but no hard evidence - that it might have been the result of a personal grudge or else in revenge for actions the deceased had taken against drugdealers in the past.

In a previous era, the Provisionals would have very swiftly

launched a counter-attack on the person or persons they deemed responsible: assuming, of course, that anyone had the nerve at the time to kill a leading IRA figure. About two months after Davison's death, nothing had happened and a senior security source in Dublin told me this was a clear indication that the Provisional IRA was no longer active.

On 12 August, more than three months after the Davison murder, another Belfast man, 53-year-old Kevin McGuigan, was shot dead outside his home in the Short Strand area of the city, not far from the Markets. It was said to be a ruthless and well-planned attack.

A senior PSNI officer was quoted as saying that Mr McGuigan had been interviewed 'as a potential witness as opposed to a potential suspect' in the Davison case. Subsequently another PSNI officer said: 'One of our major lines of enquiry is that members of the Provisional IRA were involved in this murder. I have no information to say at this stage whether this was sanctioned at a command level or not and I am not prepared to speculate about that.'

It appeared as if PIRA members had come out of retirement to avenge, as they saw it, the Davison killing and perhaps prevent further such actions which might be directed at more high-profile figures in the movement.

One thinks of Winston Churchill's phrase about Belfast's 'murky underworld'. In a statement, PSNI Chief Constable George Hamilton said that 'some of the PIRA structure from the 1990s remains broadly in place, although... a primary focus of the Provisional IRA is now promoting a peaceful, political Republican agenda...'

The minority Ulster Unionist Party withdrew its minister, Danny Kennedy, from the Executive and UUP leader Mike Nesbitt urged the DUP to do the same. In a press release, Gerry Adams said: 'The war is over. The IRA is gone and not coming back... Sinn Féin have and will continue to support the PSNI in bringing those involved in the killings of Jock Davison and Kevin McGuigan to justice'.

The arrest of Sinn Féin's northern chairman Bobby Storey - later released unconditionally – caused convulsions. Peter Robinson stepped aside as First Minister and his colleague Arlene Foster took over while crisis talks took place.

In a different sphere Sinn Féin was subject to what was regarded as a sign of political normalisation: an internal row between party rivals at constituency level. The constituency in question was Cork East where Sinn Féin candidate Sandra McLellan was elected a TD in 2011. The party's only other female TD at the time was Mary Lou McDonald.

Deputy McLellan's profile was rather lower but an interview with the *Irish Mail* on Sunday 10 June 2012 attracted considerable attention.

The paper's Political Editor, John Lee reported on her difficulties with Sinn Féin's policy of limiting its TDs to the average industrial wage of €34,000 while the rest of the €92,672 Dáil salary went to the party.

Becoming a TD meant having to spend more on appearance, e.g. make-up and hairdos, and she expressed concern that the salary rule might deter well-paid professionals from running for the party.

Out of the ten seats on Cork County Council that Sinn Féin won in the 2014 local elections, five came from Cork East. Councillor Kieran McCarthy proposed that Sinn Féin could win two Dáil seats next time if it ran himself and Cllr Melisssa Mullane in the general election. The sitting Deputy wouldn't be on the ticket.

The Sinn Féin press office issued a statement on 23 June that, following a number of complaints, a review of the constituency was carried out which resulted in the expulsion of Cllr McCarthy and the suspension of Cllr Mullane for six months.

A further statement a month later said a request from Cllr Mullane for an appeal against her suspension had been granted and that Cllr McCarthy's expulsion had been lifted to allow him to further assist the party's inquiry into the finances of the cumann (branch) in Cobh. (Cllr Mullane later won her appeal.)

But Cllr McCarthy said he would continue with a legal action against Sinn Féin and had no intention of dealing directly with the party. A former republican prisoner, in April 1991 he was jailed for two years by a Belgian court in connection with planned attacks on British Army personnel on the continent. Two other Irishmen were convicted at the same time and the trio were arrested in Antwerp the previous December, shortly before a visit to Belgium by the late Princess Diana, leading security forces to believe they had foiled a plot to assassinate her. McCarthy was released after a year. Another ex-prisoner and Long Kesh hunger striker, Leo Green went on to become a special adviser to Sinn Féin at Stormont. However, he ended up taking a case against the party on the grounds of discrimination, unfair dismissal and breach of contract. In August 2014, Sinn Féin announced that the issues had been 'resolved amicably on terms which are confidential to both parties'. There was speculation about a disagreement over the party's stance on welfare reform in the North. Sinn Féin's critics said its hardline position was motivated by electoral considerations south of the border where the party's opponents claimed it was opposing austerity in the Republic and implementing it in the North.

The Cork East row didn't augur well for Sinn Féin's prospects in that particular constituency. However, the outlook generally for Sinn Féin appeared fairly positive.

To some extent, the party was overcoming its image as a closed, Stalinist-type sect where dissent was quashed and everyone parroted the leadership's line.

The handling of Meath West TD Peadar Tóibín's breach of discipline on the issue of abortion was in contrast with the more heavy-handed approach of Fine Gael. In July 2013, he was suspended from the party for six months for defying the whip by voting against legislation allowing for abortion where a pregnant woman's life was in danger, including from the risk of suicide.

By January 2014, he was back in the fold and is currently the spokesman on Jobs, Enterprise and Innovation as well as Gaeltacht Affairs. Fine Gael on the other hand expelled five TDs and two Senators, only one of whom has been re-admitted to membership at the time of writing, while some of the others went on to form the new right-of-centre Renua party.

An ex-Fianna Fáiler who joined Sinn Féin told me his new political home was more democratic internally than the previous one. But the shadow of authoritarian paramilitarism hung over the party once again with the Davison and McGuigan killings.

Sinn Féin can dish it out as well as take it, as seen in the combative approach of Mary Lou McDonald in the Dáil when she staged a four-hour sit-in in November 2014 following a dispute with the Ceann Comhairle (Speaker) of the House, Sean Barrett over her insistence that Tánaiste and Labour Party leader Joan Burton should answer questions about the water charges.

There was further controversy a month later when she listed, under Dáil privilege, a number of prominent individuals alleged to have links to Ansbacher offshore bank accounts to evade tax, following claims by a whistleblower. The Oireachtas Committee on Procedure and Privileges ruled that her comments were 'in the nature of being defamatory'.

Four former government ministers named by Ms McDonald in relation to the issue had complained to the committee. Three of them were alleged to have Ansbacher accounts but they categorically denied this was the case.

The Sinn Féin deputy leader was unapologetic and responded that she had exercised her constitutional right 'in good faith and the public interest' to draw attention to 'very serious' allegations about offshore accounts and political obstruction.

Meanwhile, financial issues continue to be raised elsewhere in relation to the republican movement, with former Tánaiste and justice minister Michael McDowell claiming that the Provisional IRA accumulated a multi-million war-chest.

Although the party's MPs do not take their seat at Westminster and therefore don't get paid salaries, they can and do claim expenses which amounted to £647,047 (approximately €885,000) in 2014.

In the North, a BBC Spotlight investigation revealed that 36 Sinn

Féin members of the Stormont Assembly claimed a total of about £700,000 (approximately €957,000) in expenses over a ten-year period to pay a company called Research Services Ireland.

As is the case with TDs in the Republic, Sinn Féin Assembly members are expected to live on the average industrial wage and contribute the remainder of their salaries to the party. And as detailed in Chapter 8, funding from the US is way ahead of anything other Irish parties have been able to raise.

No matter how much unfavourable publicity Sinn Féin attracts, it always seems to recover and that is likely to be the case in the general election, unless some fresh storm breaks over the heads of Adams and Co. as voters get ready to cast their ballot.

Whether we like it or not, Sinn Féin is now part of the mainstream political system: it is already in office in Northern Ireland and looks set to get into government in Dublin, sooner or later, which could have significant but unpredictable implications for the North-South dynamic on the island. The time-honoured republican slogan in the Irish language, 'Tiocfaidh ár lá' (Our day will come)' is gradually coming true but perhaps not in the way that republicans originally expected. The party has raised high expectations among its followers and supporters and the coming years will tell whether it can live up to them.

ENDNOTES

N.B. Online sources can be subject to change: references in this book apply to the time when they were last accessed by the author.

CHAPTER ONE: WE NEED TO TALK ABOUT SINN FÉIN...

1. Link to poll figures since 2011 general election:
   http://en.wikipedia.org/wiki/Next_Irish_general_election
   (Last accessed 8 August 2015).
2. Television interview on '60 Min- utes', CBS, 5 April 2015.
3. 'The Rise of Sinn Féin and the Abuse of the Past'
   Irish Left Review, November 14, 2014, Fergus O'Farrell:
   http://www.irishleftreview.org/2014/11/14/rise-sinn-Féin-abuse/
   (Last accessed 20 April 2015).
4. The international O'Connell: parliamentarian, liberal, reformer – Daniel O'Connell Comm- emorative Lecture by Dan Mulhall, Irish Ambassador to Britain, Glasnevin, 18 May 2014:
   https://www.dfa.ie/irish-embassy/great-britain/news-and-events/2014/oconnell-commemorative-lecture/ (Last accessed 20 April 2015).
5. http://www.siptu.ie/media/media_18793_en.pdf
   (Last accessed 21 April 2015).
6. Issued by Sinn Féin press office, 31 January 2015.
7. *Sunday Times,* 1 February 2015.
8. Northern edition *of The Socialist*, March 2015: http://socialistparty.ie/2015/03/trade-unions-sinn-Féin-dangerous-times/

(Last accessed 22/5/2015).
9. *An Phoblacht,* February 2015.
10. *Sunday Business Post,* 1 February 2015.
11. *Phoenix,* 13 February 2015.
12. *Sunday Times,* 15 February 2015.
13. https://www.facebook.com/Right2WaterIreland/posts/1649206368641770?fref=nf
    (Last accessed 24 April 2015).
14. *Irish Times,* 25 March 2015.
15. www.sinnféin.ie (Last accessed 4 April 2015) http://republican-news.org /current/ news/ 2015/03/taoiseach_or_bust.html#.Vdg-euaFPMw
    (Last accessed 20 August 2015).
16. *Sunday Business Post,* 19 April 2015. http://www. businesspost.ie /#!story /Home/News/Martin+in+the+middle/id/1ac70353-b260-4926-98e7-d054e2d3ec1c
    (Last accessed 22 April 2015).
17. *Irish Times,* 20 April 2015: http://www.fiannafail.ie/news/entry/12392/
    (Last accessed 22 April 2015).
    http://www.thejournal.ie/michael-martin-sinn-féin-1916-2057680-Apr2015/
    (Last accessed 21 August 2015).
18. *Sunday Independent,* 26 April 2015: http://www.independent.ie/opinion/columnists/eoghan-harris/martin-had-adams-on-the-ropes-until-royal-rescue-31171631.html

(Last accessed 21 August 2015).

19. *Irish Times,* 11 June 2007.

CHAPTER TWO: HELLO MARY LOU – GOODBYE GERRY?

1. *Phoenix,* 13 February 2015.
2. *Sunday Business Post,* 29 April 2012.
3. *Irish Independent,* 1 June 2014.
4. *Irish Times,* 2 November 2013.
5. Interview with the author.
6. *Belfast Telegraph,* 2 December 2013: http://www.belfasttelegraph.co.uk/news/politics/sinn-féins-mary-lou-mcdonald-tipped-to-succeed-gerry-adams-as-leader-of-sinn-fein-29797577.html (Last accessed 21 August 2015).
7. Mary Banotti, *There's Something about Mary: Conversations with Irish Women Politicians* (Currach Press, Dublin, 2008) pp. 110-22.
8. Michael Gallagher and Michael Marsh (Eds) *How Ireland Voted 2011: The Full Story of Ireland's Earthquake Election* (Palgrave Macmillan, UK, 2011) p.124.
9. Interview with the author.
10. James Durney, *The Civil War in Kildare* (Mercier Press, Cork, 2011) pp.121-35.
11. Interview with the author.
12. *Ibid.*
13. *Ibid.*
14. *Ibid.*
15. *Irish American News Ohio*: 'Sinn Féin's Rising Star' by Sabina Clarke.
16. Interview with the author.
17. *Irish Independent,* 17 September 2014: http://www.independent.ie/irish-news/education/private-schools-pupil-numbers-and-day-fees-30592044.html (Last accessed 21 August 2015).
18. Interview with the author.
19. Banotti *op.cit.* p. 111.

20. Interview with the author.
21. *Ibid.*
22. *Ibid.*
23. Leaders' Questions in the Dáil, 19 April 2012: http://debates.oireachtas.ie/dáil/2012/04/19/00003.asp (Last accessed 6 April 2015).
24. Interview with the author.
25. *Ibid.*
26. *Ibid.*
27. http://www.inc-cne.com/cne-n-apr00.pdf (Last accessed 6 April 2015).
28. Interview with the author.
29. http://www.inc-cne.com/cne-n-apr00.pdf (Last accessed 6 April 2015).
30. *Irish Times,* 29 May 2000.
31. *Irish Times,* 21 May 1998.
32. Interview with the author.
33. *Irish Times,* 23 November 1998.
34. Interview with the author.
35. Interview with the author.
36. *Belfast Telegraph,* 2 December 2013. (See Note 6.)
37. www.electionsireland.org
38. *An Phoblacht,* 21 August 2003.
39. *Guardian,* 22 May 2008 (obituary by the author): http://www.theguardian.com/uk/2008/may/22/northernireland.northernireland (Last accessed 21 August 2015).
40. *Irish Times,* 5 September 2003.
41. *Irish Times,* 7 June 2004.
42. *Sunday Business Post,* 4 September 2005.
43. *Irish Times,* 5 January 2004.
44. *Ibid.,* 3 April 2004.
45. *Ibid.,* 22 May 2004.
46. *Ibid.,* 31 May 2004.
47. www.electionsireland.org
48. *Irish Times,* 15 June 2004.
49. *Ibid.,* 14 July 2004.

50. *Ibid.*, 17 October 2004.
51. *Ibid.*, 4 March 2005.
52. *Ibid.*, 10 May 2005.
53 *Sunday Business Post,* 25 February 2007.
54. *Irish Times,* 12 May 2007.
55. www.electionsireland.org

CHAPTER THREE: THE ARMALITE AND THE BALLOT-BOX
1. Arthur Griffith, *The Resurrection of Hungary: A Parallel for Ireland* (UCD Press, 2003 reprint).
2. 'It's time Sinn Féin took its seats in Westminster' by Tom McGurk, *Sunday Business Post* 5 April 2015.
3. 'Time Sinn Féin called Westminster's bluff' by Tom Collins, *Irish News,* 16 March 2015
4. 'Irish interests may never have been more relevant' by Tom Kelly, *Irish News,* 30 March 2015.
5. 'The View', BBC Northern Ireland, 29 January 2015.
6. Robert W.White, *Ruairí Ó Brádaigh: The Life and Politics of an Irish Revolutionary* (Indiana University Press, Bloomington and Indianapolis, 2006) p. 283.
7. http://www.rte.ie/archives/2015/0 09/671502-anti-apartheid-protests/ (Last accessed 21 August 2015).
8. Brian Hanley and Scott Millar, *The Lost Revolution: the Story of the Official IRA and the Workers' Party* (Penguin Ireland 2009/Penguin Books 2010) p. 146.
9. Patrick Bishop and Eamonn Mallie, *The Provisional IRA* (Corgi Books, London, 1989) p. 138.
10. *Irish Times,* 29 December 1969.
11.'Irish republican legitimatism' www.wikipedia.org
12.http://www.historyireland.com /20th-century-contemporary-history/no-photos-extant-of-i-ran-away-slogan/ (Last accessed 21 August 2015).
13. Gerry Adams, *op. cit.,* p.129.
14. White, *op.cit.,* pp.153 and 157.
15. Hanley and Millar, *op.cit.,* pp 180-81.
16. Paul Bew and Gordon Gillespie, *Northern Ireland A Chronology of the Troubles 1968-99* (Gill & Macmillan. Second edition, 1999 pp. 99-100.
17. Kieran Conway, *Southside Provisional: From Freedom-Fighter to the Four Courts* (Orpen Press, Dublin, 2014) pp. 180-82.
18. Richard English, *Armed Struggle: The History of the IRA* (Macmillan, London, 2003) p. 179.
19. University of Ulster: CAIN (Conflict Archive on the INternet) Web Service – Conflict and Politics in Northern Ireland: http://cain.ulst.ac.uk/hmso/ gardiner. (Last accessed 4 September 2015).
20. See also 'Michael Collins' unfinished revolution' by Mick Derrig, *An Phoblacht,* 21 October 1999 Edition: http://www.anphoblacht.com/ contents/5476
21. John F. Morrison, *The Origins and Rise of Dissident Irish Republicanism* (Bloomsbury, New York and London, 2013) p. 115.
22. Quoted by Dr Brendan Lynn in 'Republicanism and the Abstentionist Tradition, 1970-1998', a paper presented to the Institute of Irish Studies, Queen's University Belfast, May 2001 http://cain.ulst.ac.uk/issues/politics/ docs/lynn01.htm
23. Gerry Adams, *op. cit.,* p. 264.
24. Bishop and Mallie, *op. cit.,* p. 335.
25. *Ibid.* pp. 310-15.
26. Lynn *op.cit.*
27. 'Sands ruffles the Delhi air', column by Claud Cockburn, *Irish Times,* 22 April 1981.

28. Richard O'Rawe. *Blanketmen: An Untold Story of the H-Block Hunger Strike* (New Island, Dublin, 2005).
29. *Irish Times,* 31 December 2011 http://www.irishtimes.com/news/sands-rejected-pope-s-order-to-come-off-hunger-strike-1.17036 (Last accessed 21 August 2015).
30. Bew and Gillespie, *op. cit.,* p. 160.
31. *Ibid.,* p. 184.
32. *An Phoblacht,* 16 October 1986.
33. White, *op.cit.,* p.301.
34. *Ibid.,* p.304.
35. *Ibid.,* p. 306.
36. University of Ulster: CAIN Web Service: http://cain.ulst.ac.uk/issues/ politics /docs/sf/mmcg021186.htm
37. White, *op. cit.,* pp, 307-10.
38. Martyn Frampton, *The Long March: The Political Strategy of Sinn Féin, 1981-2007, p. 67.*
39. *An Phoblacht,* 14 October 2014: http://www.anphoblacht.com/contents/24477
40. Agnès Maillot, *New Sinn Féin: Irish republicanism in the twenty-first century* (Routledge, London and New York, 2005) p. 7.
41. For an in-depth study of this major episode in Irish history, see Jim Maher, *The Oath is Dead and Gone* (Londubh Books, Dublin, 2011).

CHAPTER FOUR: FROM REBEL TO RULER – MARTIN MCGUINNESS

1. *Irish Times,* 28 October 1969.
2. *Irish Times,* 10 April 1972.
3. *Irish Times,* 19 April 1972.
4. Northern Ireland House of Commons, 24 April 1934 From: 'Quotations on the topic of Discrimination' http://cain.ulst.ac.uk/issues/discrimination/quotes.htm (Last accessed 13 April 2015).
5. *The lilac creature lay silent and unmoving / As the peaty water flowed over the last of the Mohicans. / Stones were the wigwam in a Donegal river / For a decimated breed of free spirits.* (*Guardian,* 10 October 2009).
6. See also *News Letter* 6 May 2008: http://www.newsletter.co.uk/news /regional/mcguinness-pays-tribute-to-paisley-1-1869311 (Last accessed 29 April 2015).
7. A close aide of the SDLP politician described Trimble and Mallon as 'two prickly pears, with a hard, spiky exterior that's always on view but inside they are quite soft, although rarely to each other'. From *Trimble* by Henry McDonald, published by Bloomsbury, London, 2000, p. 270.
8. Tony Blair's Chief of Staff, Jonathan Powell describes a meeting on 23 April 2004 in the Prime Minister's weekend residence at Chequers with Adams and McGuinness where the latter, who had previously been sceptical, said he now believed Paisley wanted to be First Minister. They were in contact with the DUP through an intermediary and Powell writes that the British already knew about this contact 'which passed through a journalist'. From *Great Hatred, Little Room* by Jonathan Powell, published by the Bodley Head, London, 2008 pp. 241-2.
9. http://thebrokenelbow.com/ 2014 /01/21/british-cabinet-account-of-1972-ira-ceasefire-talks/ (Last accessed 18 April 2015).
10. http://webarchive.national archives.gov.uk/20101103103930/htt p:///report.bloody-sunday-inquiry.org/transcripts/Archive/Ts39 1.htm

11. *Irish Times,* 28 June 2012.
12. *Irish Times,* 10 February 2015:
    http://www.irishtimes.com/news/
    ireland/irish-news/martin-
    mcguinness-receives-death-threat-
    from-continuity-ira-1.2098069
    (Last accessed 21 July 2015).
13. *News Letter,* 11 March 2009:
    http://www.newsletter.co.uk/news
    /regional/murderers-are-traitors-to-
    ireland-mcguinness-1-1882222
    (Last accessed 29 April 2015).
14. *Belfast Telegra*ph, 16 March 2009:
    http://www.belfasttelegraph.co.uk
    /opinion/columnists/ed-
    curran/after-37-years-martin-
    mcguinness-at-last-reaches-point-of
    -no-return-28471806.html
    (Last accessed 19 April 2015).

CHAPTER FIVE: NOW GET OUT OF THAT:
DISOWNING FATEFUL ECONOMIC DECISIONS
1. *Irish Times,* 18 September 2007.
2. *Irish Independent,* 7 May 2015:
   http://www.independent.ie/ opinion
   /comment/incoherent-sinn-fin-
   economic-policy-will-penalise-the-
   lowest-paid-workers-31202064.html
   (Last accessed 10 May 2015)
3. http://www.tv3.ie/3player/show
   /41/93519/1/Tonight-with-Vincent-
   Browne
   (Last accessed 19 May 2015).
4. *Irish Times,* 15 February 2011.
5. *Irish Times,* 17 February 2011.
6. http://www.centralbank.ie/
   regulation/industry-sectors/credit-
   institutions/pages/governmentguara
   nteescheme.aspx
   (Last accessed 21 August 2015).
7. *Irish Times,* 1 October 2008.
8. *Irish Times,* 4 October 2008.
9. http://oireachtasdebates.oireach
   tas.ie/debates%20authoring/debates
   webpack. nsf/takes /dáil

2008093000018 (Last accessed 5
September 2015).
10. http://www.labour.ie/download
    /pdf/sf_wrong_then_wrong_now_q
    uotes_ 2.pdf. (Last accessed 5
    September 2015).
11. Link to Oireachtas debates is at
    http://oireachtasdebates.oireachtas.ie
    /debates%20authoring/debateswebp
    ack.nsf/startpage?readform
12. *Irish Times,* 1 October 2008.
13. *Irish Times,* 4 October 2008.
14. *An Phoblacht,* 9 October 2008.
15. *An Phoblacht,* 16 October 2008.
16. http://www.irishtimes.com /news/sf-
    pledges-platform-of-citizenship-
    1.871514
    (Last accessed 24 May 2015).
17. https://www.youtube.com/watch
    ?v=enIyVP1jp0k
    (Last accessed 24 May 2015).
18. Ibid.
19. http://www.irishtimes.com/
    business/adams-says-sinn-fein-has-
    no-plans-to-increase-business-taxes-
    1.1309120
    (Last accessed 24 May 2015).
20. http://www.irishtimes.com/news
    /ahern-rules-out-any-union-with-
    sinn-fein-in-dáil-1.517734
    (Last accessed 21 August 2015).
21. http://www.irishtimes.com/news
    /sinn-fein-targets-14-seats-for-next-
    election-1.512615
    (Last accessed 21 August 2015).
22. http://www.irishtimes.com/news
    /corporation-tax-should-rise-to-17-
    sinn-fein-1.1000969
    (Last accessed 21 August 2015).
23. http://www.taxnews.com/news
    /Sinn_Fein_Calls_For_Increase_In_
    Irelands_125_Corporate_Tax____22
    392.html (Last accessed 21 August
    2015).
24. *An Phoblacht,* 19 January 2006.

25. http://www.irishexaminer.com /archives/2006/0120/opinion/sfapos s-corporation-tax-policy-a-threat-to-economy-921845007.html (Last accessed 21 August 2015).

26. http://www.sinnfein.ie/contents /15206 (Last accessed 21 August 2015).

27. http://www.sinnfein.ie/contents /6439 (Last accessed 21 August 2015).

28. *Irish Times,* 29 December 2006.

29. http://www.anphoblacht.com/ contents/16573 (Last accessed 21 August 2015)

30. *Irish Times,* 19 April 2007.

31. http://www.irishtimes.com/news /sf-drops-plan-to-increase-corporate-tax-rate-to-17-5-1.1295630 (Last accessed 21 May 2015).

32. http://www.labour.ie/download /pdf/thefairsociety_manifesto2007.p dfhttp://www.irishtimes.com /news/greens-vow-to-tackle-rising-inequalities-1.806407 (Last accessed 24 May 2015).

33. http://www.businesspost.ie/ #!story/Markets/Insider/EU +battle+on+ corporate +tax+looms/id/e9196f17-d641-4c95-9b08-eae316058083 (Last accessed 21 August 2015).

34. *Fortnight,* June-July 2007.

35. http://www.businesspost.ie/#!story /Home/News/Where+it+all+went+ wrong+for+Sinn+Fein/id/3488f81b-933a-44bb-8ab7-ff17df427eff (Last accessed 21 August 2015).

36. http://www.businesspost.ie/ #!story/Home/News+Focus/Sinn+Fe in+seeks+to+rebuild+after+election +setback/id/296ea3ba-dcd0-4c9b-a7fc 5e49ae4dcddc (Last accessed 21 August 2015)

37. http://www.irishtimes.com/news/lead ership-wins-heated-debate-on-party-s-tax-policies-1.899285 (Last accessed 24 May 2015).

38. *Irish Examiner,* April 01, 2009 http://www.irishexaminer.com /ireland/sf-does-u-turn-on-raising-corporation-tax-88207.html (Last accessed 24 May 2015).

39. http://www.sinnfein.ie/files/ 2012/Budget_2013.pdf. (Last accessed 5 September 2015).

CHAPTER SIX: TURNING SWORDS INTO PLOUGHSHARES: GOOD FRIDAY AND ITS AFTERMATH

1. Deaglán de Bréadún, *The Far Side of Revenge: Making Peace in Northern Ireland* (Collins Press, Cork, 2001 and 2008) p. 19.

2. Gerry Adams, *op. cit.,* p. 319.

3. *Hot Press,* 17 December 1987, quoted in Thomas Hennessey's *The Northern Ireland Peace Process: Ending the Troubles?* (Gill & Macmillan Ltd., Dublin, 2000) p. 39.

4. *Irish Times,* 17 February 1992.

5. *Ibid.*

6. *Irish Times,* 20 February 1992.

7. *Assassination, Ambush and Impunity: The Killings of Kevin Barry O'Donnell, Patrick Vincent, Peter Clancy and Sean O'Farrell* (Published by Relatives for Justice, Belfast and Dungannon, February 2012). http://relativesforjustice.com/pdfs /clonoe.pdf. (Last accessed 5 September 2015).

8. Kevin Rafter, *Martin Mansergh: A Biography* (New Island, Dublin, 2002) p. 183.

9. Department of Foreign Affairs and Trade website: http://web.archive.org/web/2013040 4221626/http://dfa.ie/home/index.as

px?id=8734
(Last accessed 22 August 2015)

10. John Major: *The Autobiography* (HarperCollins UK, 2013).

11. *Irish Times*, 17 August 2013.

12. Conor O'Clery, *The Greening of the White House: The Inside Story of How America Tried to Bring Peace to Ireland* (Gill & Macmillan, Dublin, 1996) p. 109.

13. *Irish Times*, 2 February 1994.

14. *Irish Times*, 3 February 1994.

15. *Irish Times*, 25 July 1994.

16. *Irish Times*, 25 August 1994.

17. *Ibid.*

18. CAIN Web Service: http://cain.ulst.ac.uk/events/peace/docs/ira31894.htm (Last accessed 22 August 2015).

19. *Irish Times*, 11 May 1998.

20. Bew and Gillespie, op. cit., p. 365.

21. https://en.wikipedia.org/wiki/Irish_general_election,_1992 (Last accessed 11 September 2015).

22. *Evening Herald*, 20 September 2000.

23. *Irish Times*, 1 April 2002.

24. http://en.wikipedia.org/wiki/Irish_general_election,_2002

25. *Irish Times*, 6 January 2011.

26. *Irish Times*, 4 February 2011.

27. *Irish Times*, 11 February 2011.

28. Michael Gallagher and Michael Marsh (Eds.), *How Ireland Voted 2011: The Full Story of Ireland's Earthquake Election.* (Palgrave Macmillan, Basingstoke and New York, 2011).
Derek S. Hutcheson, *The February 2011 Parliamentay Election in Ireland.* Institute for British-Irish Studies working paper 109: http://www.ucd.ie/ibis/filestore/wp2011/109_hutcheson.pdf (Last accessed 5 September 2015).

29. *Irish Times*, 28 February 2011.

30. https://electionsireland.org/result.cfm?election=2011&cons=167 (Last accessed 22 August 2015).

31. *Irish Times*, 4 March 2011.

32. *Irish Times*, 23 March 2011.

33. *Irish Times*, 10 September 2011.

34. *Irish Times*, 14 September 2011.

35. *Irish Times*, 17 September 2011.

36. *Irish Times*, 21 September 2011.

37. *Irish Times*, 29 September 2011.

38. *Irish Times*, 30 September 2011.

39. Irish Times, 4 October 2011.

40. Reddy, op. cit. pp. 147-8.

41. Ibid., p. 173.

42. *Irish Times*, 11 October 2011.

43. *Irish Times*, 14 October 2011.

44. *Belfast Telegraph*, 18 October 2011: http://www.highbeam.com/doc/1P2-29886818.html (Last accessed on 16 June 2015).

45. https://www.youtube.com/watch?v=uUhFdi7iRL0 (Last accessed 15 June 2015).

46. *Irish Times*, 8 March 2012.

47. www.electionsireland.org

48. http://www.ark.ac.uk/elections/fa98.htm (Last accessed 22 August 2015)

49. http://www.ark.ac.uk/elections/fa03.htm

50. http://www.ark.ac.uk/elections/fa07.htm

51. http://www.ark.ac.uk/elections/fa11.htm

52. www.electionsireland.org

53. *Irish Times*, 19 May 2014: http://www.irishtimes.com/news/politics/labour-faces-wipeout-in-euro-elections-as-poll-gives-ff-chance-of-three-seats-1.1800628 (Last accessed 5 September 2015).

CHAPTER SEVEN: MEMBERS, CRITICS AND OBSERVERS

1. Interview with the author, 23 June 2015.

2. J.J. Barrett, *Martin Ferris: Man of*

Kerry (Published by Brandon, an imprint of Mount Eagle Publicationts, Dingle, Co Kerry, 2005).

3. In an interview with Ursula Halligan for TV3 documentary series *Sinn Féin: Who Are They?* https://www.tv3.ie/pr_sub.php?type=1&view_pr=367 (Last accessed 22 August 2015).

4. Interview with the author, 3 June 2015.

5. http://www.thejournal.ie/sinead-oconnor-sinn-Féin-2-1906705-Jan 2015/ (Last accessed 12 July 2015).

6. Eoin Ó Broin, *Sinn Féin and the Politics of Left Republicanism* (Pluto Press, London and New York, 2009).

7. *Irish Times*, 14 March 2009.

8. http://www.historyireland.com/20th-century-contemporary-history/sinn-Féin-and-the-politics-of-left-republicanism/ (Last accessed 12 July 2015)

9. Eoin Ó Broin, *Matxinada: Basque Nationalism and Radical Basque Youth Movements* (Left Republican Books, 2003).

10. Interview with the author, 4 June 2015.

11. Interview with the author, 16 June 2015.

12. http://www.thejournal.ie/sinn-Féins-doherty-forced-to-clarify-job-qualifications-78067-Feb2011/ (Last accessed 12 July 2015).

13. www.electionsireland.org

14. *Irish Times*, 4 November 2010

15. http://www.irishtimes.com/search/search-7.1213540?q=finance%20rockstar%20AND%20pearse%20doherty&sortOrder=newest (Last accessed 12 July 2015).

16. http://www.anphoblacht.com/contents/24832 (Last accessed 12 July 2015).

17. http://www.belfasttelegraph.co.uk/news/teenager-who-stabbed-greengrocer-harry-holland-in-head-jailed-for-12-years-28485472.html (Last accessed 5 July 2015).

18. Interview with the author, 11 June 2015.

19. Interview with the author, 19 June 2015.

20. Interview with the author, 13 June 2015

21. Interview with the author, 23 June 2015.

22. Interview with the author, 14 July 2015.

23. Interview with the author, 15 June 2015.

24. http://www.anphoblacht.com/contents/21249 (Last accessed 14 July 2015).

25. http://www.irishtimes.com/news/policing-policy-to-be-decided-at-special-conference-1.1017782 (Last accessed 14 July 2015).

26. Interview with the author, 16 July 2015

27. http://www.irishtimes.com/news/key-republican-player-linked-to-us-supernotes-1.957920 (Last accessed 17 July 2015).

28. Interview with the author, 22 July 2015.

29. Jonathan Powell, *Great Hatred, Little Room: Making Peace in Northern Ireland* (The Bodley Head, London, 2008).

30. Interview with Gerry Moriarty, *Irish Times*, 2 April 1997.

31. Interview with the author, 24 July 2015.

CHAPTER EIGHT: IN THE EYE OF THE STORM

1. 'Timeline: How events unfolded', *Irish Times*, 22 October 2014.
2. *Irish Times*, 17 October 2014.
3. *An Phoblacht*, 19 October 2014.
4. Interview with the author, 13 June 2015.
5. *Irish Times*, 23 October 2014.
6. *Irish Times*, 15 November 2014.
7. RNU website http://www.republicanunity.org/about-us-2/who-we-are/ (Last accessed 26 June 2015).
8. http://sluggerotoole.com/2014/10/26/mairia-cahill-a-statement/ (Last accessed 28 June 2015).
9. Sir Keir Starmer was later elected as a Labour MP for Holborn and St Pancras in the UK general election, 7 May 2015.
10. 'Independent Review of the Prosecution of Related Sexual Abuse and Terrorism Cases'. Report, 6 May 2015, by Sir Keir Starmer KCB QC and Katherine O'Byrne: http://www.ppsni.gov.uk/Branches/PPSNI/PPSNI/Files/Documents/PPS%20Press%20Office/StarmerReview.pdf (Last accessed 5 September 2015).
11. *Irish Times*, 11 March 2015.
12. *An Phoblacht*, 10 March 2015.
13. *Irish Times*, 6 May 2015.
14. http://thebrokenelbow.com/2013/10/09/eilis-mcdermotts-cross-examination-of-gerry-adams-the-full-text/ (Last accessed 19 June 2015).
15. *Irish Times*, 29 November 2015.
16. *Irish Times*, 10 June 2015.
17. http://www.irishtimes.com/news/crime-and-law/analysis-clarification-issue-behind-adams-non-prosecution-1.2243291 (Last accessed 20 June 2015).
18. *Irish Times*, 8 July 2015.
19. https://docs.google.com/spreadsheets/d/1hRidYe3-avd7gvlZWVi1YZB7QY6dKhekPS1I1kbFTnY/edit?pli=1 (Last accessed 22 August 2015).
20. CAIN Web Service http://cain.ulst.ac.uk/othelem/organ/ira/ira080706.htm (Last accessed 22 August 2015).
21. http://www.rte.ie/news/2006/0707/78095-mcconvillej/ (Last accessed 22 August 2015).
22. *Irish Times*, 31 October 2014.
23. http://www.irishtimes.com/news/politics/full-text-of-adams-speech-following-his-release-1.1784146 (Last accessed 21 June 2015).
24. On 4 June 2015, the North's PPS announced that it was going ahead with the prosecution of another long-time republican in the McConville case. There was no outcome to the prosecution at time of writing.
25. *Irish Times*, 11 June 2015.
26. *Belfast Telegraph*, 17 December 2005 : http://www.highbeam.com/doc/1P2-10725928.html (Last accessed 22 June 2015)
27. Martyn Frampton, *op. cit.* pp. 116-7.
28. *Belfast Telegraph*, 5 April 2006: http://www.highbeam.com/doc/1P2-10730454.html (Last accessed 22 June 2015)
29. *Irish Voice*, 14 November 1995: http://www.highbeam.com/doc/1P1-2372944.html (Last accessed 22 June 2015).
30. *Irish Voice*, 3 January 2006: http://www.highbeam.com/doc/1P1-118146199.html (Last accessed 22 June 2015).
31. Deaglán de Bréadún, op. cit., second

edition, p. 395.

32. Interview with the author, 13 June 2015.

33. *Irish Times*, 5 and 6 March 2015.

34. *Irish Times*, 6 March 2015.

35. http://www.irishtimes.com/search/se arch 7.1213540? q=blinken%20AND%20carswell%20 AND%20adams (Last accessed 25 June 2015).

36. *New Yorker*, 16 March 2015.

37. *Irish Times*, 6 April 2015.

38. http://www.irishexaminer.com /ireland/mcconville-my-mothers-murder-is-a-war-crime-322535.html (Last accessed 26 June 2015).

39. Ibid.

40. Interview with the author, 13 June 2015.

41. Kader Asmal and Adrian Hadland with Moira Levy, *Politics in My Blood: A Memoir* (Jacana Media [Pty] Ltd, South Africa, 2011) pp-65-69.

42. http://www.irishtimes.com/news /politics/adams-rounds-on-critics-at-500-a-head-ny-fundraiser-1.1992058 (Last accessed 22 August 2015).

43. http://www.thejournal.ie/gerry-adams-michael-collins-1775345-Nov2014/ (Last accessed 27 June 2015)

44. http://www.poets.org/poetsorg/ poem/still-i-rise (Last accessed 5 September 2015).

45. http://www.enotes.com/topics/ still-i-rise (Last accessed 27 June 2015).

46. http://www.independent.ie/irish-news/politics/i-dance-like-i-have-diamonds-at-the-meeting-of-my-thi ghs-gerry-adams-defends-tweeting-poem-on-womans-sexiness-30717616.html (Last accessed 27 June 2015).

47. *Sunday Independent*, 2 November 2014: http://www.independent.ie/opinion/ hey-bby-gurl-how-gerry-adams-is-serially-insensitive-to-abuse-victims-30710539.html (Last accessed 28 June 2015).

48. http://www.belfasttelegraph.co.uk /opinion/debateni/cold-and-calculating-gerry-adams-is-never-a-twit-31000282.html (Last accessed 28 June 2015).

49. http://www.theguardian.com/ politics/2009/dec/20/gerry-adams-sexual-abuse (Last accessed 28 June 2015).

CHAPTER NINE: THE ROCKY PATH TO POWER

1. http://www.paddypower.com/bet/ politics/other-politics/irish politics?ev_oc_ grp_ids=591647 (Last accessed 8 August 2015).

2. Sinn Féin Ardfheis Clár 2015, p. 16

3. *Irish Independent* 'Light Edition', 19 February 2015.

4. http://www.irishtimes.com/news /sinn-Féin-criticises-ff-over-coalition-stance-1.411486 (Last accessed 3 May 2015).

5. *Irish Times*, 11 June 2007.

6. Detective Garda Jerry McCabe (52) was shot dead during an attempted robbery of a post office van by a Provisional IRA unit at Adare, Co Limerick, on 7 June 1996. The killing aroused widespread revulsion and 50,000 people lined the streets of Limerick for his funeral.

7. *Irish Mail on Sunday*, 31 May 2009: http://www.highbeam.com/doc/ 1G1-200883585.html (Last accessed 2 May 2015).

8. http://www.irishtimes.com/news /kenny-dismisses-talk-of-agreement-with-sinn-Féin-1.841311 (Last accessed 4 May 2015).

9. http://www.irishtimes.com/news/
   sargent-stands-over-kenny-claim-
   1.841425
   (Last accessed 4 May 2015).
10. http://www.irishexaminer.com/
    ireland/politics/denials-and-
    accusations-as-parties-do-battle-on-
    alleged-overture-to-sinn-Féin-93373
    .html
    (Last accessed 22 August 2015)
11. *Phoenix*, 12 March 2010.
12. http://www.irishtimes.com/
    opinion/party-still-has-to-learn-
    rules-of-game-in-south-1.634606
    ((Last accessed 10 May 2015).
13. http://www.communistpartyof
    ireland.ie/sv2010-03/01-
    sinnFéin.html (Last accessed 3 May
    2015).
14. http://www.irishtimes.com/
    opinion/no-political-home-for-
    advocates-of-a-just-society-1.635709
    (Last accessed 9 May 2015).
15. http://www.anphoblacht.com/
    contents/21342
    (Last accessed 3 May 2015).
16. http://www.independent.ie/
    opinion/comment/for-fine-gael-to-
    get-in-bed-with-sinn-Féin-would-
    be-indefensible-30729203.html (Last
    accessed 3 May 2015.
17. *Sunday Times,* 29 June 2014.
18. http://www.irishtimes.com/news
    /politics/property-tax-removal-a-
    condition-for-coalition-says-adams-
    1.1842252
    (Last accessed 8 May 2015).
19. https://eoinobroin.wordpress.
    com/2014/07/01/after-the-
    election/#more-340
    (Last accessed 8 May 2015).
20. http://www.irishtimes.com/news/
    politics/gerry-adams-stresses-sinn-
    f%C3%A9in-s-durability-1.2070502
    (Last accessed 8 May 2015).
21. http://republicannews.org/
    current/news/2015/01/adams_sees_l
    eft-
    wing_coalition.html#.VU9RvPlViko
    (Last accessed 10 May 2015).
22. http://www.thejournal.ie/enda-
    kenny-fine-gael-coalition-sinn-Féin-
    1483956-May2014/
    (Last accessed 3 May 2015).
23. http://www.independent.ie/irish-
    news/politics/taoiseach-fails-to-
    rule-out-fg-and-sf-in-coalition-3101
    1565.html
    (Last accessed 4 May 2015).
24. Supplement to the *Sunday
    Independent* of 22 February 2015,
    entitled 'John Drennan's Guide to
    Politics'.
25. http://socialistparty.ie/2014/09/ are-
    sinn-Féin-a-genuine-left-alternative/
    (Last accessed 5 May 2015).
26. https://paddyhealy.wordpress.
    com/?s=sinn+féin
    (Last accessed 5 May 2015)
27. http://www.irishtimes.com/
    opinion/eamonn-mccann-union-
    protests-pushed-sinn-f%C3%A9in-
    to-pull-out-of-agreement-1.2135367
    (Last accessed 5 May 2015).
28. RTÉ Sound Library.
29. *Financial Times,* 20 February 2015
30. https://www.youtube.com/watch?
    v=WOfKCeMBRGE
    (Last accessed 6 May 2015)
31. https://www.facebook.com/rory.
    hearne?fref=ts
    (Last accessed 6 May 2015).
32. http://www.sinnfein.ie/contents/
    33971
    (Last accessed 10 May 2015).
33. BBC Northern Ireland 5 May 2015
34. http://www.thejournal.ie/sinn- fein-
    off-message-coalition-fine-gael-
    fianna-fail-2276624-Aug2015/
    (Last accessed 18 August 2015).

INDEX